This book provides a complete history of the US Fleet Ballistic Missile programme from its inception in the 1950s and the development of Polaris to the deployment of Trident II in 1990. Writing in an accessible yet scholarly manner, Graham Spinardi bases his historical documentation of FBM development on interviews with many of the key participants. His study confronts a central issue: is technology simply a tool used to achieve the goals of society, or is it an autonomous force in shaping that society? FBM accuracy evolved from the city-busting retaliatory capability of Polaris to the silo-busting 'first strike' potential of Trident. Is this a case of technology 'driving' the arms race, or simply the intended product of political decisions? The book provides a comprehensive survey of the literature on the role of technology in the arms race, and seeks to explain technological development using a 'sociology of technology' approach.

FROM POLARIS TO TRIDENT: THE DEVELOPMENT OF US FLEET BALLISTIC MISSILE TECHNOLOGY

Cambridge Studies in International Relations is a joint initiative of Cambridge University Press and the British International Studies Association (BISA). The series will include a wide range of material, from undergraduate textbooks and surveys to research-based monographs and collaborative volumes. The aim of the series is to publish the best new scholarship in International Studies from Europe, North America and the rest of the world.

CAMBRIDGE STUDIES IN INTERNATIONAL RELATIONS

Series list continues after index

FROM POLARIS TO TRIDENT: THE DEVELOPMENT OF US FLEET BALLISTIC MISSILE TECHNOLOGY

GRAHAM SPINARDI

CAMBRIDGE
UNIVERSITY PRESS

Published by the Press Syndicate of the University of Cambridge
The Pitt Building, Trumpington Street, Cambridge CB2 1RP
40 West 20th Street, New York, NY 10011–4211, USA
10 Stamford Road, Oakleigh, Victoria 3166, Australia

© Cambridge University Press 1994

First published 1994

Printed in Great Britain at the University Press, Cambridge

A catalogue record for this book is available from the British Library

Library of Congress cataloguing in publication data

Spinardi, Graham.
  From Polaris to Trident: The development of US Fleet Ballistic
  Missile technology / Graham Spinardi.
      p.   cm. – (Cambridge studies in international relations: 30)
  Revision of author's thesis (Ph.D.) – University of Edinburgh.
  ISBN 0 521 41357 5
  1. Fleet ballistic missile systems.
  2. United States. Navy – Submarine forces.
I. Title.   II. Title: Development of US Fleet ballistic missile
technology.   III. Series.
V993.S65   1994
623.4'5197 – dc20   93–9267   CIP

ISBN 0 521 41357 5 hardback

CONTENTS

ACKNOWLEDGEMENTS

This book is a revision of a PhD thesis undertaken in the Science Studies Unit at the University of Edinburgh and supported by the UK Science and Engineering Research Council. I would like to thank Carole Tansley, Moyra Forrest and Pauline Walker of the Science Studies Unit for their friendly help, especially in dealing with interminable requests for inter-library loans. Likewise I am grateful to everyone in the Space Science and Exploration Department of the National Air and Space Museum in Washington for the help provided during my five-month visit to the United States in early 1987 and to everyone at the Center for International Security and Arms Control, Stanford University where I was a research fellow during 1988–89. I am also very grateful to those who agreed to be interviewed for this study, or who otherwise helped, and to those who provided me with hospitality during my visits to the United States. Bob Dietz deserves special thanks for his many readings of drafts, and subsequent helpful comments. I would like to thank Scott Sagan and Lynn Eden for their helpful comments on various drafts of this work.

Donald MacKenzie, who supervised my PhD research, deserves more specific acknowledgement. His work on missile guidance systems eased my path in many ways. Where his work on guidance systems coincided with mine on the FBM programme we freely exchanged material and ideas. Without his help it is doubtful if I could ever have started this study, let alone completed it.

Some parts of this book include material which has already been published in D. MacKenzie and G. Spinardi, 'The Shaping of Nuclear Weapon System Technology: US Fleet Ballistic Missile Guidance and Navigation', in two parts, *Social Studies of Science*, vol. 18 (1988), and in G. Spinardi, 'Why the U.S. Navy Went for Hard-Target Counterforce in Trident II (and why it didn't get there sooner)', *International Security*, vol. 15, No. 2 (Fall 1990), 147–90.

1 THE US FLEET BALLISTIC MISSILE SYSTEM: TECHNOLOGY AND NUCLEAR WAR

An American Trident submarine is 560 feet long, or almost twice the length of a football pitch. Each can carry twenty-four missiles capable of delivering nuclear warheads to targets thousands of miles away.[1] Each of these warheads can deliver an explosive yield many times as powerful as the bomb dropped on Hiroshima to within about a hundred yards of its target.[2] This formidable destructive capability is the culmination of over thirty years of technological development, and six generations of missile: Polaris A1, Polaris A2, Polaris A3, Poseidon, Trident I, and Trident II.

Trident submarines on patrol in the Atlantic and Pacific oceans have just one mission, as have had all fleet ballistic missile (FBM) submarines since the first Polaris submarine went on patrol in 1960; that is to be able to launch some or all of their complement of missiles at any time they are required to. To this end, the submarines must remain undetected by potential enemies, forever awaiting a message that they hope will never come.

Various technologies have been brought together to make this possible. The missile itself principally consists of nuclear warheads inside protective reentry bodies,[3] a guidance system, and steerable propulsion. Once fired, it becomes independent and cannot be recalled or destroyed (except for test missiles).

The pattern for FBM patrols was set by Polaris which initially was restricted to the Norwegian Sea because of the missile's short range. Standard practice was for three submarines to form what is called a chain. Each chain would be allocated two target sets that would be 'passed' from one submarine to another halfway through its patrol. The third submarine would be at the support tender ship and would take up the first target set as the first submarine returned from patrol. Thus between them the three submarines provided continuous coverage to two sets of targets.[4] All subsequent FBM patrols, including those with longer range missiles and operating in both the Atlantic and Pacific, have followed the same operational procedure. The chain system, and the possible need occasionally to replace a submarine in a chain, provides a strong rationale for standardisation of the missiles carried by the submarines. All submarines in a chain must be equipped the same as regards warhead numbers, types, and any penetration aids.

During its patrol the submarine's navigation system must be constantly updating its position and heading and providing this information to a fire control system. Over a typical three-month patrol the self-contained inertial navigation system also requires periodic updating from external sources to maintain accuracy.

Communications systems must be continuously listening, waiting for an emergency action message (EAM). This is the command from the National Command Authority (which comprises in the first instance the President and the Secretary of Defense) to fire some or all of the missiles.[5] Unlike most other nuclear weapons in the US arsenal, the warheads carried by the FBM force (and most other naval weapons) are not fitted with permissive action links (PALs) that require a code to activate them.[6] Instead, unauthorised use is prevented by the need to follow a rigid routine involving several people, none of whom individually could sustain the necessary process. However, so long as the original EAM matches the correct format this process should proceed smoothly.[7]

This would then set in motion the preparation of the missiles for launch. Unlike US Air Force land-based ICBMs, the FBM force does not keep its missile guidance systems continuously running. They are maintained at a suitable temperature, but must be 'spun up' from this dormant state when required. The fire control system prepares the guidance system for launch by telling it which way it is pointing and which way is up (the local vertical), and then by feeding it the information needed to fly the correct trajectory to take it from the launch point – provided by the navigation system – to the target. Much of this information depends on land-based computations done at the Naval Surface Weapons Center at Dahlgren, and in the Trident missiles, on extensive mapping of the earth's gravity fields and of the position of stars. Given an assigned target set and the information it is continuously receiving from the navigation system, the fire control system also continuously updates its computations.

Finally, just prior to launch, the missile is switched over to internal power, the final instructions for the guidance system and for warhead detonation are read in, and the guidance system 'goes inertial'. Then,

2

when commanded, the launcher system expels it from the tube in which it has been cocooned during the patrol. After clearing the surface of the water – typically from an almost stationary submarine at a depth of around a hundred feet, though it can be done from the surface – the first stage rocket motor fires and powered flight begins. After a few minutes flight the rocket stages have imparted enough velocity to the warhead-carrying reentry bodies to take them to the target area. Whereas each Polaris could hit only one target, the later FBMs, Poseidon and Trident, use a manoeuvring platform to dispense the reentry bodies onto trajectories that can hit different targets.

At one level, then, the smooth operation of FBM technology has the end result of nuclear warheads detonating at their designated targets; at another, paradoxically, it is exactly the opposite outcome, the absence of nuclear warheads detonating in conflict, which is seen as the successful working of the technology. All this, however, requires a technological system that encompasses far more than just the submarines and missiles. The final few minutes of independent missile flight are the culmination of a technological system, the development of which has required many disparate parts to be put, and kept, in place. Before describing how this technological system was built, and then maintained over the years (in chapters 3 to 8), some basic ideas about the nature of technology and nuclear war need to be introduced.

WEAPONS TECHNOLOGY AND THE NUCLEAR ARMS RACE

Despite the thaw in the Cold War, and associated arms control agreements, nuclear weapons systems like Trident continue to pose an unprecedented threat to human civilization and the ecological health of our planet. The use of even a fraction of current arsenals could cause massive devastation and millions of deaths.[8] As the inscription on an exhibit of a Polaris A3 missile in Washington's National Air and Space Museum chillingly put it: 'Each Polaris submarine contains as much firepower as was used during World War II.' Each Trident submarine armed with Trident II missiles will carry a lot more.

Also, although by no means the most expensive item in most military budgets, nuclear weapons systems have large opportunity costs, especially in terms of their drain on a nation's industrial and scientific resources. Yet nuclear weapons have come to be considered integral to the defence policies of some of the nations that possess them.[9]

Indeed post World War II 'superpower' relations were characterized by rivalry in nuclear weapons. The central Cold War antagonism

3

between the USA and USSR involved their acquisition of a combined total of some 50,000 nuclear weapons by the 1980s. However, quantitative additions to arsenals were not the most worrisome feature of this 'arms race'.[10] Quantitative limits and reductions are relatively easy to negotiate and verify, and small numerical imbalances are not of much 'military' significance at the high levels in question.[11] More disturbing are qualitative 'improvements' in nuclear weapons technology, which are more difficult to curb with arms control and perhaps more threatening to strategic stability.

The main concern is that new technological developments may increase the risk of nuclear war breaking out during a crisis. That is, they may reduce *crisis stability*.[12] In particular, technologies which make a preemptive attack appear more feasible technically, such as improvements in missile accuracy, may increase the temptation to strike first during a serious crisis.[13]

Nuclear-armed ballistic missiles are central technologies in the nuclear confrontation. Their relatively short flight time for 'strategic' use allows only the briefest possible tactical early warning of imminent attack. With flight times of the order of 30 minutes or less ballistic missiles heightened the concern of preemptive nuclear attack by one superpower on the other.

Central to the concern with stability are two different approaches to the targeting of nuclear weapons. The popular conception of nuclear deterrence is that aggression is prevented by the threat of devastating retaliation. Accordingly, nuclear forces sufficient to assure a certain level of destruction should deter. This 'assured destruction' clearly only requires a level of technological sophistication capable of first surviving an attack and then destroying the aggressor's major cities in return. Assured destruction or 'counter-city' deterrence received its clearest *public* articulation in the 1960s by US Secretary of Defence Robert McNamara (and the distinction drawn here by McNamara should be understood as one of public rationalization rather than of changes in the actual warplan). The primary purpose of US nuclear forces were, he argued, 'to deter a deliberate nuclear attack upon the United States and its allies by maintaining a clear and convincing capability to inflict unacceptable damage on an attacker, even were that attacker to strike first'.[14] The assured destruction level to deter the Soviet Union was set at 'the destruction of, say, one-quarter to one-third of its population and about two-thirds of its industrial capacity'.[15]

However, McNamara had earlier emphasised an entirely different view of the way nuclear weapons should be used. In a reaction against the indiscriminate destruction threatened by the nuclear warplans he

4

inherited from the Eisenhower administration's 'massive retaliation' policy, McNamara first shifted US nuclear warplans away from counter-city targeting. Discriminate use of nuclear weapons against military targets was to replace the all-out 'Sunday punch', with cities to be avoided, at least in the early phases of the exchange. McNamara argued that 'basic military strategy in general nuclear war should be approached in much the same way that more conventional military operations have been regarded in the past. That is to say, our principal military objectives in the event of nuclear war ... should be the destruction of the enemy's military forces while attempting to preserve the fabric as well as the integrity of allied society'.[16] Counterforce targeting was not new to the actual warplans, but this rationalization of it as preferable to targeting cities was a novel step.

However, counterforce targeting raises the fear of a disarming, pre-emptive strike in which one side could eliminate the nuclear forces of the other. Should this be possible, or appear possible, it would in principle seem to increase the incentive to use those forces before they are destroyed. Thus vulnerable forces are considered destabilizing because they increase the potential benefits of striking first, as well as the costs of failing to do so.

That this concern is well recognized is clear from the fact that nations have devoted considerable effort to ways of reducing the vulnerability of their own nuclear forces. At the same time, however, they have been equally vigorous in the pursuit of ways to *increase* the vulnerability of enemy forces. This pursuit of counterforce capability, the ability to destroy enemy nuclear forces, has threatened to undermine the stability which nuclear deterrence seemed to offer.

Central to advances in perceived counterforce capability have been the development of multiple warhead technology and improvements in ballistic missile accuracy. The ability to carry several independently targetable warheads on one missile allows a greater 'exchange ratio', thus considerably adding to the potential effectiveness of a pre-emptive attack.[17] Coupled with increasingly better accuracy – itself a much greater contributor to effectiveness against hardened targets than extra explosive yield[18] – this marked a general trend in the ballistic missile forces of both the USA and USSR towards greater 'hard target kill capability'.[19] These changes in technology have paralleled changes in nuclear strategy which have increasingly emphasized counterforce targeting, and in particular the destruction of hardened targets such as missile silos and command posts.

A number have seen this as a distinctive shift from a policy of deterrence based on the threat of retaliation against cities to a more

5

unstable situation where the apparent ability to implement an 'effective' first strike (against fixed, land-based targets) may be technically available.[20] Some see the shift as actively desired, indeed the result of a 'secret agenda',[21] whereas others, more typically, attribute it simply to the inevitable, on-going advance of technology.

Thus Fred Halliday states that 'the possibility of greater accuracy in targeting missiles *led to* the shift from the "countervalue" approach, aiming at cities and economic targets, to one aimed at specific military targets, i.e. "counterforce"'.[22] But can technology be held responsible for this change in nuclear strategy? Or, to put it more generally, does technology determine the nature of society or vice versa? The theoretical issues surrounding this question will be set out in the next chapter.

US FLEET BALLISTIC MISSILES

This study deliberately focuses not on a single generation of a weapon system, but on the evolution of US fleet ballistic missile technology over a period of over thirty years. (Some of the main features of US FBMs are summarized in Table 1.1.) By tracing the parallel development of technology and nuclear strategy during this time it is hoped that a more sophisticated understanding of their interaction can be obtained.

The shift in missile technology and targeting rationale towards counterforce is particularly evident in the US Navy's Fleet Ballistic Missiles. The original Polaris, first deployed in 1960, seemingly provided the ideal deterrent, able to remain submerged and invulnerable at sea and capable of little other than deadly retaliation against Soviet cities as a last resort. Deployed some thirty years later, the latest FBM, Trident II, is claimed to have a combination of accuracy and explosive yield which makes it comparable to the Air Force MX in its high likelihood of destroying hardened targets.

This shift provides the central focus of this study, which will describe the evolution of those parts of FBM technology that most generally relate to the system's perceived strategic capability. It is not possible to cover every aspect of the development of FBM technology here. Instead some technologies – such as navigation and guidance – will play a much greater part in the story than others because of their greater strategic significance.

Table 1.1. *US Fleet Ballistic Missiles*

	Polaris A1	Polaris A2	Polaris A3	Poseidon C3	Trident C4	Trident D5
Length (feet)	28.5	31.0	32.3	34.0	34.0	45.8
Nominal Range (nautical miles)	1200	1500	2500	2500–3200	4000	4000+
Weight at launch (1000s of lbs)	28.8	32.5	35.7	65.0	73.0	c130.0
Year first deployed	1960	1962	1964	1971	1979	1990
No. of warheads	1	1	3 (MRV)	average of 10 (MIRV)	8 (MIRV)	8 (MIRV)
Yield per warhead (kilotons)	600	800	200	40	100	475 or 100
Warhead type	(W47)	(W47)	(W58)	(W68)	(W76)	(W88 or W76)
Guidance system	Mk. 1	Mk. 1	Mk. 2	Mk. 3	Mk. 5	Mk. 6
Approximate circular error probable (nautical miles)	2	2	0.5	0.25	0.12–0.25	0.06

Sources: General data from *FBM facts/chronology – Polaris, Poseidon, Trident* (Washington, DC: Strategic Systems Program Office, 1986) and earlier editions.
Accuracy and warhead yield figures are officially classified and have been deduced from a number of other sources: T. B. Cochran, W. M. Arkin and Milton M. Hoenig, *Nuclear Weapons Databook*, vol. 1, *US Nuclear Forces and Capabilities* (Cambridge, MA: Ballinger, 1984); W. M. Arkin, 'Sleight of Hand with Trident II', *Bulletin of the Atomic Scientists*, vol. 40 (December 1984), 5–6; R. S. Norris, 'Counterforce at Sea', *Arms Control Today* (September 1985), 5–12.

A NOTE ON SOURCES

As well as the open literature, which is extensive, and some archival material, this study draws heavily on interviews with present and former participants in the FBM programme. A full list of those interviewed is given in the Appendix, and where permission was obtained the interviewees are cited by name in the footnotes. No source material, whether it be an interview, archival document or published article has simply been accepted uncritically at face value. In attempting an explanation of technology which takes care to understand the role of social factors, it would be naive to ignore their role in the way people write or speak about technology!

In addition to over fifty interviews carried out directly for this study it has also been possible to draw on some other related interviews carried out by Donald MacKenzie in his work on inertial guidance and navigation technologies. These are also listed in the Appendix.

7

Interviews were arranged simply by writing to or telephoning the relevant individuals. Once a few key people and organizations had been identified, others 'snowballed' quickly. Simple lack of time meant that it was not possible to interview everyone. However, those interviewed include most of the 'core-set' of major participants in the FBM programme. I am particularly grateful to the Strategic Systems Program Office of the US Navy for their cooperation in arranging interviews (and to Andrew DePrete who was my contact there), as well as to the other organizations and individuals who were helpful.

In these interviews no attempt was made to gain access to classified information, and the study as a whole is based solely on unclassified (and declassified) sources. Perhaps surprisingly this is not an insurmountable obstacle to writing a detailed history of a nuclear weapons system programme. Much technical information is not classified, and where quantitative details are so, it still remains possible to gain adequate qualitative descriptions.

Considerable technical detail can also be found in the open literature, especially in journals such as *Aviation Week & Space Technology*, and for the early period of FBM development, *Missiles & Rockets*. These and other historical accounts have an unfortunate tendency, however, to construct a dichotomy between the 'technical' on one hand and the 'political' or 'social' on the other. Technical accounts are overwhelmingly of the 'B followed A because it was better' variety, in which the social world enters only rarely. Accounts by political scientists, on the other hand, tend to treat the technology largely as a black box, the content of which is not considered especially important.

Nevertheless, although in this vein, Harvey Sapolsky's book remains an excellent source of information on Polaris.[23] Ted Greenwood's account of the development of MIRV technology not only provides one of the best interminglings of the technical and political, but also the best description of the origins of Poseidon.[24] The third book-length account by political scientists of the FBM programme, Dalgleish and Schweikart's discussion of Trident, is less helpful.[25] Numerous other pieces of academic and indeed journalistic writing also provided useful sources of information. Finally, a rich source of information lies in the various Congressional hearings. Most useful for this study have been hearings from the Senate Armed Services Committee Subcommittee on Research and Development, particularly during the 1970s.[26]

2 THEORETICAL MODELS OF WEAPONS DEVELOPMENT

Popular thinking about nuclear weaponry is bounded by two extreme views of technology. One is the fatalistic view that 'the bomb' was an inevitable development, about which nothing much could or can be done. The other is that nuclear weapons are simply tools which we build to achieve a certain end, such as deterring a potential enemy. These two extreme positions, which we can call 'technology-out-of-control' and 'politics-in-command', enclose a spectrum of theoretical possibilities. Within these extremes it is possible to identify three basic models with which we could characterize the nature of developments in weapons technology.

At the technology-out-of-control end of the spectrum there are many authors who argue that there is a 'technological imperative' which drives the arms race. This is a specific case of the more general theory of technological determinism, according to which technological change possesses a dynamic of its own and causes social change.

The politics-in-command viewpoint, on the other hand, sees developments in weapons technology as the product of political decision-making, and is typically characterized as based on a rational assessment of national security 'requirements' in relation to other states. This 'rational actor' model coincides to some extent with another strand of thinking in international relations theory, that of 'realism'. In this it is the competition of states within an anarchic international system which is seen as the main determinant.

Finally, there is a third approach which views developments in weapons technology as the product of the internal social structure of the state. Some such 'domestic' models are based on Marxist interpretations of the nature of capitalist society, whereas others focus simply on the interaction between various competing factions or interest groups within a state.

TECHNOLOGICAL DETERMINISM

In the various technological imperative models technological developments are seen as the driving force in the formulation of policy. Technology is considered to have its own autonomous logic which makes it the dominant, determining factor in the nuclear arms race. Framed broadly, this view holds that technology develops autonomously and then has social effects. Such technological determinism not only reflects popular fatalism about 'the bomb', but also has gained significant credence in the academic literature.[1]

Technological determinism appears in many forms. In some cases it has been put forward explicitly as an explanation of the role of nuclear weapons in the arms race, but more often it is simply an implicit assumption which underpins (and arguably undermines) discussion. Three main varieties of technological determinism can be distinguished within a spectrum of theoretical viewpoints. First, there is 'strong' determinism in which autonomous technical change causes social change. Second, a 'weak' determinism can be envisaged in which technical possibilities play an important, but not absolute, role in shaping the social world. Third, technological determinism can be viewed in terms of the behaviour of the individuals and organizations which foster technical change; not 'technology-out-of-control' but 'technologists-out-of-control'.

To take the first of these, the most extreme form of technological determinism is the notion that technology is simply applied science, and that science is simply the physical world revealed. Technical change is seen as inevitable and monolithic in nature. Thus some appear to argue that technology possesses innate characteristics based on the 'laws of physics' that determine the pathways it will follow – that there are natural 'technological trajectories'.[2] For example, Dietrich Schroeer argues that progress in computer capabilities 'may be a driving force producing a technological imperative towards improved missile accuracy'.[3] Technological imperatives, Schroeer claims, are the result of technologies 'so technically sweet and beautiful that they are difficult to resist'.[4]

This brings us to the more usual, less rigid, formulation of technological determinism. In it, technology is seen as too persuasive and inevitable to resist. Human choice exists, but it is reckoned to be severely constrained by the on-going lure of technical possibilities. These are seen as being constantly generated (at least in the US) 'from the bottom up' and so reach the point of no-return before any effective high-level decision-making can be brought to bear. An important proponent of this kind of technological determinism is Herbert York. For example, in his account of the development of the US hydrogen bomb, he writes:

> This particular episode . . . can be seen as an illustration of just how what Secretary of Defense McNamara called technological momentum can determine the course of the arms race. The possibilities that welled up out of the technological program and the ideas and proposals put forth by the technologists eventually created a set of options that was so narrow in the scope of its alternatives and so strong in its thrust that the political decision-makers had no real independent choice in the matter.[5]

Whereas York attributes this momentum primarily to weapons technologists, Deborah Shapley has suggested that it may be caused by the general technological inventiveness of a society. She argues that the general onward advance of technology – 'technology creep', as she calls it – feeds back into military developments even when not specifically sponsored by them: 'What has happened is that the creep of technology – of the different technologies that bear on ICBM accuracy – has been advancing incrementally, cheaply, and with little public awareness . . .'[6]

In this version of the technological imperative, although often not explictly stated, the emphasis is not on the technology itself, but on the people and organizations that foster it. Rather than technology-out-of-control, one could view 'technologists-out-of-control' as responsible for the on-going pursuit of advances in military technology. For example, Lord Zuckerman, former Chief Scientific Adviser to the UK government, has argued that:

> military chiefs . . . merely serve as a channel through which the men in the laboratories transmit their views. For it is the man in the laboratory – not the soldier or sailor or airman – who at the start proposes that for this or that arcane reason it would be useful to improve an old or devise a new nuclear warhead; and if a new warhead, then a new missile; and given a new missile, a new system within which it has to fit. It is he, the technician, not the commander in the field, who starts the process of formulating the so-called military need.[7]

POLITICS-IN-COMMAND: RATIONAL ACTORS AND REALISM

Directly opposite to the technology-out-of-control viewpoint is the notion that technology is the intended product of political choice. Most discussion of nuclear weapons is at least implicitly framed within

11

the realist paradigm in which nuclear weapons are seen as tools of the state, developed because they are considered useful for deterrence or coercion. This view of nuclear weapons can be analysed from two different perspectives. One focuses on the international system of states, while the other considers the role played by political elites as 'rational actors' in this system.

First, the nature of the international system of states could be seen to be the main determinant of weapons technology. 'Balance of power' or realist theories can be taken as suggesting that it is the pursuit of power by states in an anarchic international system that should dominate their weapons procurement policies. Three basic assumptions underpin classical realism.[8] First, the realist view sees states as the most important actors in international politics. Second, it assumes that the behaviour of these states can be analysed as if they were unitary rational actors, calculating the costs and benefits of various courses of action, and choosing those which offer the greatest benefit. Third, it is assumed that states seek power, and that increasing or maintaining power is what shapes their calculations. The most important recent realist theorist, Kenneth Waltz, also lays great stress on a systemic explanation of international behaviour in what has become known as structural realism. In Waltz's view it is the structure of the international system, the anarchic relations of states to each other, that most determines the behaviour of a particular state.[9]

According to the realist view, military technology is developed by a state with the explicit intention of enhancing its position relative to other states. Much effort has been expended in attempting to model this state military behaviour by the simple mathematical formula suggested by Richardson, though with little success to date.[10] Attempting to improve explanatory power by increasing the complexity of the formula has not helped.

Realism can also be seen from the viewpoint of the 'rational actors' that bring about the balancing, or maximization, of power. According to the realist view these rational actor elites should be able to assess national security requirements and then consciously shape the technology they desire to satisfy them. During the Cold War, US developments in nuclear weapons technology would normally have been argued to be necessary tools to achieve the desired deterrence of the Soviet Union. A classic expression of the balancing of armaments in the nuclear age has been termed the action-reaction effect. Thus, in 1967 US Secretary of Defense Robert McNamara put forward a realist explanation for the decision he had made to go ahead with an ABM system:

12

what is essential to understand here is that the Soviet Union and the United States mutually influence one another's strategic plans. Whatever be their intentions, whatever be our intentions, actions – or even realistically potential actions – on either side relating to the build-up of nuclear forces, be they either offensive or defensive weapons, necessarily trigger reactions on the other side. It is precisely this action-reaction phenomenon that fuels our arms race.[11]

However, national leaders might make decisions on weapons programmes for reasons other than the stated rationale of national security. Domestic politics could instead be the major factor in such decisions, as Desmond Ball argues was the case in the Kennedy administration's decisions on sizing US missile forces.[12] Politicians could still be seen to be deliberately shaping technology to meet their needs, even if these needs are not those that the technology is ostensibly intended for.[13] Indeed McNamara's ABM speech in which he cited the action-reaction phenomenon was aimed not at the ears of Soviet leaders, but at domestic opinion in Washington.[14]

DOMESTIC EXPLANATIONS OF WEAPONS TECHNOLOGY

This view of weapons developments as the product of 'politics' brings us to the central reason for dissatisfaction with the realist analysis of international relations: that it views states as though they were unitary actors able to respond rationally to, say, the Soviet 'threat'. At least in the case of the US, the nature of the political system would not seem to allow for such a unitary actor to hold sway. Such criticism has led to another approach which also assigns primacy to politics in the formulation of policy, as well as in the development of technology. But rather than the products of rational decision-making these are seen as the contested outcome of organizational and bureaucratic conflict and accommodation.[15] In this 'bureaucratic politics' model, technology is seen as an outcome of the many turf battles, compromises and wrangles which particularly predominate in the pluralistic US political system.[16] According to two of the main proponents of this model, 'the "maker" of government policy is not one calculating decision-maker, but rather a conglomerate of large organizations and political actors who differ substantially about what their government should do on any particular issue and who compete in attempting to affect both governmental decisions and the actions of their government'.[17]

A variant on this approach sees some particular organizations and actors as so dominant that they can be termed a 'military-industrial complex'. Weapons technologists, along with military, corporate and political actors are said to be caught up in a massive conspiracy to promote their own interests (and perhaps subvert the democratic political system) by ensuring the continuing development of weapons technology far beyond national 'requirements'.

The role of the military-industrial complex can also be viewed from an explicitly Marxist perspective. In this, 'big business' not only seeks to keep itself in work through 'follow-on' weapons developments, but also takes an active role in foreign policy in order to maintain access to raw materials, markets, and, especially, opportunities for profitable investment throughout the world. Some, also, have depicted unfettered weapons development as a capitalist sickness required to soak up excess production.[18]

Finally, some analysts have focused more narrowly on the way in which the development of military technology is organized within society. Thus, Mary Kaldor considers that, at least in the United States, military 'R&D has played an autonomous role in promoting the arms race'.[19] In particular, she claims, 'the organization of R&D institutions is the main factor which explains the impact of military R&D on the arms race'.[20] Similarly, Kosta Tsipis argues, that starting in the late 1950s and early 1960s 'military research and development has been institutionalized as a continuing, broad-gauge effort that has, as a result, acquired a momentum and dynamic all of its own'.[21] He concludes 'that military R&D plays an important and often independent role in determining the overall US force structure'.[22]

COMPETING THEORIES: SUCCESS AND FAILURE

The general conclusion that can be drawn from this literature is, as Greenwood amongst others has pointed out, that single factor explanations are not very successful in accounting for the complexity of weapons development.[23] What is clear from previous studies is that both international and domestic determinants can be important, while rarely is either completely irrelevant. Nor can the importance of scientific and technical breakthroughs, or the limitations of physical possibilities, be discounted.

Clearly, the three general types of explanatory model all retain some plausibility as playing a part in the development of military technology. Attempting to write yet another case study adopting the theoretically parsimonious approach of using only one model would yield the unsurprising conclusion that the model was inadequate. Such an approach also runs the risk that theoretical suitability will

14

overrule empirical findings when the case study is written. Fitting the historical narrative into a chosen theory may thus end up obviating any insights gained by using the theory in the first place.

One possible solution to this dilemma would be to write, say, three different versions of the same story, each adhering rigorously to a different theoretical perspective. Again, however, the likely result would still be that no single version was wholly satisfactory. Another approach is essentially that followed by Greenwood. All contending explanatory models are kept in mind while the historical narrative is written as if it were unproblematic. However, this still begs the question of what implicit framework has been used to construct the historical account. Simply not stating an explicit theoretical framework does not mean that one is not used.

Broadly speaking, most previous weapons case studies have been framed within a bureaucratic politics perspective. Even Greenwood, who eschews any particular theoretical explanatory framework, still writes his history very much from the point of view of inter-organizational struggle. This is not surprising, because any thorough study which focuses on the day-to-day development of a technology cannot fail to emphasize the organizational conflict and compromise involved. Yet, as Evangelista interestingly points out, many adherents of bureaucratic politics also slip into using realist language when it suits them. In essence, they argued that if only the bureaucratic shaping of US military developments was understood, then it could be changed for the better, and observing this, opponents – the Soviet Union, historically – would react in kind, thus reducing tension all round.[24]

The FBM story presented here has been constructed within a different theoretical framework from those most commonly used by political scientists. This draws on recent work in the sociology and history of technology.[25] This does not purport to be an explanatory theory in quite the same way as the models described above, in that it does not identify a factor (say, 'technology' or 'the military-industrial complex') as being the key determinant. Rather it suggests the overall way in which 'technology' and 'society' interact and so provides a methodology for constructing the history.

TECHNOLOGY AS SOCIAL NETWORKS

The main methodological bulwark of the sociological approach is its empirical relativism.[26] In an oft-cited article, Pinch and Bijker propose that the 'social construction of technology' can be analysed in the same relativist manner adopted in the 'strong programme' of the sociology of scientific knowledge.[27] Technology, they argue, is under-determined by the physical world, and needs to be explained by reference to social factors. Success and failure must be analysed in an impartial and symmetrical manner, without any reference to 'truth': 'The success of an artefact is precisely what needs to be explained. For a sociological theory of technology it should be the *explanandum*, not the *explanans*'.[28]

Pinch and Bijker seek to explain technological outcomes in the same way that the sociology of scientific knowledge explains the 'closure' of scientific disagreements.[29] Firstly, the technological or scientific issue in question is shown to display 'interpretative flexibility' – for example, that there is more than one way to design an artefact, or that more than one conclusion can be drawn from a particular set of experiments. Such conditions are usually apparent only during scientific controversy or in the early stages of the development of a technology, but are always there in principle. A consensus will usually form around one design or one interpretation. This 'closure' is effected by social mechanisms, not simply compelled by some 'natural' logic.

A primary task in constructing an historical case study of a technological development is thus to reopen controversies or disagreements which have long since been resolved, and to set out the factors which led to their resolution. Since 'success breeds success' a particular line of technological development can often appear inevitable unless the reasons why it was originally seen as superior are unravelled.

Another central strand in recent sociological thinking about technology is that successful technological developments are seen as systems held together through the building of social networks. For example, in the work of Hughes, human system builders, such as Edison, are seen to be skilful manipulators, not only of technical and scientific detail, but also of the economic, political and legislative processes, including those apparently external to their system.[30]

Law has coined the phrase 'heterogeneous engineer' to describe what effective system builders need to be when 'attempting to build a world where bits and pieces, social, natural, physical or economic, are interrelated and *keep each other in place* in a hostile and dissociating world'.[31] Like Hughes, Law does not see social factors as necessarily dominant: 'Other factors – natural, economic, or technical – may be more obdurate than the social and may resist the best efforts of the system builder to shape them.'[32] According to Latour, the task facing the heterogeneous engineer is to 'make your environment such that whatever other human or non-human actors think or do, they are either kept at bay or else they help strengthen your position, making the world safer, more predictable and more enjoyable for you'.[33] To do this, the heterogeneous engineer must 'translate' the interests of disparate actors in order to build the desired technological network.[34] This requires other actors' support without, ideally, at the same time surrendering control over the nature of the technology produced.

In other words, technology comprises not only artefacts but also a network of social interests (some of which are, of course, 'embedded' in the design of the artefact).[35] For a technology to succeed this network must be put in place and for it to remain successful the network must be sustained. Technology does not passively 'diffuse' once developed, but is constantly subject to the shifting efforts at translation that necessarily accompany it through its use and modification.[36]

In the context of nuclear weaponry, it is worth noting that what it means for a technology to 'work' is of particular interest precisely because of the difference between war and peace. The purported rationale of a weapons system – let's say, in the jargon, to hit hardened military targets with a nuclear warhead in a time-urgent manner – is something that can only be tested indirectly. Whether it would actually perform to specification in a war situation is a moot point and not actually crucial to the success of the technology. In the absence of actual nuclear war what matters is that the technology succeeds as a network of interests. Of course, many of the people involved with the FBM programme were strongly motivated by the deterrent mission they felt it performed. But even amongst the most patriotic there could be honest argument about how deterrence would best be achieved. Should one, for example, compromise performance in order to achieve earlier deployment? Other actors in the network of such a technological system will be concerned about the plausibility of technical claims over things like accuracy and reliability, but only in so far as it affects matters such as their chances of promotion or the profitability of their company. Others still will not be at all concerned with such issues so long as the technology works in supporting their interests (such as creating jobs in their political jurisdiction).

The FBM programme has clearly been a success. Just how well it would have performed its purported role in a nuclear conflict, had one occurred at any time in the last thirty years, is irrelevant. It has been a programmatic success in terms of developing and deploying a weapons system whose credibility was never effectively challenged. It has also, in the view of many, been a success in its deterrence role, by

17

virtue of not performing its ultimate mission, though this, of course, is not a conclusion that is universally accepted.

This technological success can be explained by reference to social factors rather than to 'natural' logic, and can be seen as requiring networks of interests which need to be actively forged and maintained. These sociological concepts have been used in writing the history of US FBM technology which is presented in roughly chronological order (in chapters 3 to 8). The discussion which follows, in chapter 9, assesses the strengths and weaknesses of the three main approaches to understanding technological change that were introduced earlier in this chapter.

Clearly the sociological approach appears most likely to coincide with and endorse domestic models such as bureaucratic politics. Both see technological outcomes as the result of social interactions. However, the sociological approach does not in principle discriminate against the possibility that parts of a technological network will comprise either inanimate objects or other nations, although of course these may be less susceptible to manipulation than the domestic actors who are the normal realm of bureaucratic politics.

3 HETEROGENEOUS ENGINEERING AND THE ORIGINS OF THE FLEET BALLISTIC MISSILE

> I don't care how big and ornery it is, we're going to take the bastard
> to sea.   Admiral Raborn.[1]

Polaris was not simply the coming together of several ripe technologies, the inevitable outcome of technical progress. Nor did it just appear ready-made in response to a national call to arms. In retrospect, a submarine-launched ballistic missile seems an obvious enough technology, providing as it does a method of basing nuclear-armed missiles that is relatively invulnerable, both to enemy attack and to domestic protest. However, in the early 1950s it was far from obvious that ballistic missiles capable of carrying nuclear warheads over the desired range could be deployed in submarines.

THE WRONG STUFF

Indeed if any missile was going to carry nuclear warheads from submarines, or anywhere else for that matter, to the Soviet Union, it was the conventional wisdom in the decade following World War II that it would be a cruise missile not a ballistic one. In the United States dominant opinion considered ballistic missiles to be the more difficult technology, something to be considered in, say, twenty years time, when the technology had matured.[2] For the time being, cruise missiles, analogues of the German V1 rather than the V2, were thought most promising. Both types of missile had, of course, been brought to fruition as weapons by the Germans. The V1 'doodlebug' was essentially a pilotless aircraft powered by a jet engine capable of carrying a 1 ton warhead a distance of about 150 miles. Some 8000 were used during the war, mainly against southern England. The V2 was a liquid-fuel rocket with sufficient thrust to lift it to an altitude of about 50 miles from which it plummeted ballistically on a parabolic flight path to impact.

As Germany was overrun, the Allies scrambled to capture the V weapon technology – both the hardware and the know-how of the German engineers. Most of this went to the United States, where the Armed Services each had their different approach. The Army Ordnance Corps was already sponsoring work which had led to the invention in 1943 of the Corporal E at Caltech's Jet Propulsion Laboratory.[3] After the war, in project Hermes, the Army used the captured V2s and the German missile engineers and scientists to carry out high-altitude research.[4]

Whereas Ordnance favoured a short-term approach to a military missile, making the best of the available technology, the Army Air Forces wanted one of intercontinental range. In 1946 the Air Forces sponsored a 5000 mile range ballistic missile, extrapolated from V2 technology. However, soon it was agreed that such a missile was at least a decade away and the Air Forces dropped the development, deciding instead to concentrate on long-range cruise missiles. Towards the end of the war a semi-formal division of responsibility was agreed between Ordnance and the Air Forces, with Ordnance given jurisdiction over ballistic missiles and Air Forces over aerodynamic designs.[5]

The Navy too initially investigated the V2 technology, and on 6 September 1947 launched one from the aircraft carrier *Midway*.[6] In addition, enthusiasts within the Bureau of Aeronautics (BuAer) secured Navy support for the development of a satellite launch system, a liquid-fuel rocket called Viking. This also demonstrated the feasibility of launching a missile from a ship, and in 1952 spawned a proposal for a 500 mile range military version.[7] This, however, was vetoed by the director of the Navy's guided missile programme, Captain Sides, and by the Chief of Naval Operations.

Cutbacks in Navy funding ensured strong resistance to spending money on new, unproven technology. Moreover, in Operation Pushover in 1949 the Navy had investigated the effects of an accident to a V2 on a mock-up ship. The damage caused by the liquid fuel explosion left a long impression: 'One look at that mess, and a shudder ran through every ship in the Navy.'[8] Instead the only long-range missiles developed by the Navy were again of the aerodynamic cruise missile type. Post-war tests of improved V1s, known as Loons, had been successful enough to lead the Navy to begin developing its own cruise missile, the 575 mile range Regulus, in 1948.[9] A follow-on cruise missile, Triton, was the responsibility of the Navy's Bureau of Ordnance, which, so committed, gave little support to BuAer's pressure for ballistic missile development.[10]

Thus, up until 1954, research and development on long-range ballistic missile technology languished in the United States.[11] Cruise missiles, which then really were just pilotless aircraft, seemed a natural evolution of current technology, compared to which ballistic missiles looked radical and distant. But far from being a 'natural technological trajectory', the preference for cruise over ballistic missiles stemmed more from the nature and expectations of the organizations involved. What seemed technically easier was also organizationally easier for the Navy and the Air Force (in 1947 the army air forces became a separate service), where ballistic missiles implied a radical change in roles.

For one thing, pilotless aircraft required less getting used to; they could simply replace their manned analogues. Also, for the Navy, ballistic missiles seemed at this time to necessarily require the feared liquid fuel, but to offer much poorer accuracy than cruise missiles.[12] The expected low accuracy meant that ballistic missiles were considered to be of little use against 'targets of naval interest'. They could only be used for 'strategic' bombardment against cities, a role which was unpalatable to many in the Navy (who had recently criticized the Air Force's adherence to such a policy) and which would have led to unwanted rivalry over the strategic mission.[13]

DEFINING THE FLEET BALLISTIC MISSILE

But throughout the early 1950s the advocates of a sea-launched ballistic missile became increasingly convinced of 'technical' feasibility. To those working in the area, advances in solid propellant technology showed promising potential. There was a sense that 'even though solid rocketry was in ... its very early phases, we felt that by extrapolation we could see the feasibility of building a solid system that could do the job'.[14] Indeed the recollection of Admiral Levering Smith – a central figure in the development of Navy ballistic missiles – was that 'it was our conclusion at that time that the technology would reasonably support all the elements of such a system except for knowing where the launch platform was with sufficient accuracy'.[15]

But, of course, 'technical' potential alone neither brings new technology into being, nor defines its workability. What did lead to the creation of fleet ballistic missile technology had to do with the many wider concerns which are important to all technology, but which are rarely considered strictly technical. Most important was 'selling' the technological projections, which was all the Fleet Ballistic Missile – as the Navy would dub their sea-based IRBM to highlight its differences from the land-based Jupiter and Thor[16] – constituted at the time.

The nature of ballistic missile technology (in common with many

21

other large-scale technologies) makes this particularly striking. FBM advocates had to convince both the Navy and then the administration to provide funding for a very expensive hypothetical technology based on extrapolations of what had been achieved so far. The only way to really 'know' if it 'worked' was to build it and see; by which time it would be too late to ask for the money back if it was considered a failure. FBM advocates were thus not selling hardware, but rather concepts and a 'paper' system.

Lacking whole-hearted support within the Navy, FBM proponents might have been frustrated for many more years had it not been for the establishment of a special committee by President Eisenhower in the spring of 1954. Officially known as the 'Technological Capabilities Panel', the Killian Committee (after its chairman James Killian) looked at the prospects for and significance of long-range missile developments. Navy FBM advocates in BuAer – Captain Robert F. Freitag and Abraham Hyatt – channelled papers supportive of a Navy missile through the Killian Committee's Navy Department liaison representative, Commander Peter Aurand.[17]

The Killian Committee's report, entitled 'Meeting the Threat of Surprise Attack', was presented to the National Security Council on 14 February 1955. Amongst many other recommendations it gave acceleration of ballistic missiles a high priority, as had the Strategic Missiles Evaluation Committee, headed by John von Neumann, the previous year. What was different, however, was the emphasis which the Killian Committee placed on the urgent development of intermediate range ballistic missiles (IRBMs). In their view, developing 1500 mile range IRBMs would be 'much easier and have much greater assurance of success' than relying entirely on building a 5000 mile ICBM.[18] Their specific recommendation was that: 'There be developed a ballistic missile (with about 1500 nautical miles range and megaton warhead) for strategic bombardment; both land-basing and ship-basing should be considered.'[19] Endorsement by the Killian Committee of the fleet ballistic missile concept, as noted in high-level papers circulated in early 1955, was then used to bolster support for it within the Armed Services. Significantly, Freitag and Hyatt could now count on the backing of senior officers within BuAer, including the most senior of all, their chief, Rear Admiral James S. Russell.

Nevertheless, substantial resistance to a FBM still remained in the Navy.[20] Doubts about feasibility strengthened the position of those concerned about the opportunity costs. As Chief of Naval Operations, Admiral Carney, and the director of guided missile developments on his staff, Rear Admiral Sides, saw it, the technical requirements of a viable FBM system were some way from being satisfied. In short, they felt that there was no proven small warhead of adequate yield, no sufficiently accurate guidance system, no suitable fire control or navi-gation system, and no sufficiently powerful solid propellant. 'There wasn't even a concept as to a launching system', as Admiral Arleigh Burke later recalled.[21] Consequently when Admiral Russell sent a memorandum to the Chief of Naval Operations in July stating that the Bureau of Aeronautics was proceeding with the development of a ballistic missile, Admiral Carney's response was negative. He decided that no research and development should proceed on the FBM concept, and sent a letter directing BuAer to discontinue all efforts in this area, and to enter into no formal budget commitments or contract-ual arrangements.[22]

This arrived too late. By then Freitag and Hyatt had already mailed out a letter to twenty-two aerospace contractors and defence research laboratories. The letter stated Freitag and Hyatt's FBM vision and asked for advice and suggestions. On the whole the responses were encouraging, and helped generate further support for the concept. At about the same time, Admiral Russell exercised his privilege as a bureau chief in by-passing the Chief of Naval Operations and appeal-ing directly to the civilian Secretariat of the Navy. The Assistant Secretary of the Navy for Air, James H. Smith, was converted to the cause, and he, in turn, converted other influential figures. The import-ance of Smith's support was such, according to one observer, that without it 'the Navy would have probably missed forever the oppor-tunity to develop and acquire fleet ballistic missiles'.[23]

Even so, considerable opposition to a Navy IRBM remained. In the summer of 1955 Deputy Secretary of Defense Ruben Robertson pre-pared a memorandum for Secretary of Defense Charles E. Wilson which recommended giving the Air Force a monopoly over IRBM development. Only the strong protests of the Navy Secretariat pre-vented the memorandum from being sent.[24] Robertson had sought to exploit the Navy's internal divisions to limit the cost of missile devel-opment by excluding the Navy (as well as the Army) from long-range missile work. It was only with the appointment of Admiral Arleigh Burke as Chief of Naval Operations (CNO) on 17 August 1955 that the Navy would at last present a unified front on the FBM question.

Whilst preparing to take over as CNO during July, Admiral Burke had visited the Heavy Electronics Division of the General Electric Company in Syracuse, where he was briefed on work done for the Air Force on ICBM guidance. He was told that the guidance systems could be adapted for a sea-launched ballistic missile if the Navy was prepared to sponsor such work.[25] Within twenty-four hours of taking office he called for a briefing on the FBM concept. In less than a week he had made up his mind. The restrictions which Carney had placed on the Bureau of Aeronautics were lifted, and they were urged to make efforts to increase backing for the FBM within the Navy.[26]

Thus, when the Killian report was endorsed by the National Security Council in September 1955, with both land and sea-based IRBMs to be considered, the Navy was at last in a position to put forward a positive proposal. Although still receiving advice from some of his staff recommending that the Navy should not give priority to an IRBM, Burke decided on 19 October to press ahead. At his instigation a widespread campaign was organized to ensure support for a Navy FBM.[27] Written assurance which seemed to say that IRBM costs would be allocated separately from the normal Navy and Army budgets helped quell internal Navy opposition to the project.[28]

However, by this time the President and Department of Defense officials had decided that, although getting the highest priority, ballistic missile programmes should be limited to four. Already the Air Force had three programmes approved – the Atlas ICBM, the back-up Titan ICBM, and the Thor IRBM – and because of their German engineers' experience it was felt that the Army Jupiter IRBM should be the fourth. Only if the Navy could find a partner would they be able to become involved in ballistic missile development at this critical stage. At first the Air Force was approached to see if it would be willing to allow a sea-based version of the Thor to be developed. Unhappy about the technical changes required to make the Thor adaptable to sea launching, and in no need of an ally, the Air Force rejected the offer. The Navy then went to the Army with a proposal for a joint IRBM. Such a collaboration was technically no more appealing to the Army than to the Air Force, but it made more sense organizationally as it seemed to offer better prospects of preventing Air Force hegemony over ballistic missile forces. In early November, Admiral Burke and the Army's Chief of Staff, General Maxwell D. Taylor, agreed to the collaboration.

On 8 November 1955 memoranda were sent from Secretary of Defense Wilson to the service secretaries authorizing the development of an IRBM at the 'maximum speed permitted by technology'. The whole IRBM programme was to consist of 'a land-based development by the Air Force (IRBM No. 1) and a joint Army–Navy program (IRBM No. 2) having the dual objective of achieving an early shipboard capability and also providing a land-based alternative to the Air Force program'.[29]

Thus defined, the FBM was an organizational compromise. Its nature was determined not by any clearly defined strategic role, nor by the technical preferences of FBM advocates, but simply by the need to get a share of the ballistic missile 'pie'. Many in the Navy doubted that this was the correct course to take, either because they preferred to stick with the more evolutionary, 'easier' Regulus technology, or more generally because they feared the effect the financial drain of ballistic missiles would have on the Navy's traditional surface fleet roles: 'most of the senior officers in Washington, with the exception of Admiral Burke, were not deliriously happy to embark on such a risky and costly venture as this'.[30] Burke, however, believed that the Navy needed to take advantage of the new technology, and to compete with the Air Force for a share in the resources allocated to it.[31]

THE SPECIAL PROJECTS OFFICE

Burke moved quickly to consolidate the Navy's ballistic missile role. A new programme office was established on 17 November 1955. Simply named the Special Projects Office (SPO) this broke with Navy tradition whereby procurement was the responsibility of various technical bureaus. Thus Burke avoided the difficult and divisive choice between the Bureau of Aeronautics and the Bureau of Ordnance, both of which now sought control of the FBM programme.[32] With a single programme office bureaucratic intrigues would be minimized, and the rest of the Navy was assured that SPO would only be a temporary deviation, to be disbanded on completion of the FBM's development.[33] Burke's shrewdness also guided the choice of SPO's first director, Rear Admiral William F. Raborn, a naval aviator: 'I did not want a technical expert because a technical expert would be too narrow-minded. I wanted an aviator because if this missile were successful it would jeopardize the aviation branch.'[34]

Burke then gave Raborn the power necessary to assure the FBM of the highest priority in the Navy. The 2 December memorandum with which Burke appointed Raborn soon became known as Raborn's 'hunting license' as he used it to obtain the Navy's best technical officers and civilians:

> If Admiral Raborn runs into any difficulty with which I can help, I will want to know about it at once along with his recommended course of action for me to take. If more money is needed, we will get it. If he needs more people, those people will be ordered in. If there is anything that slows this project up beyond the capacity of the Navy Department we will immediately take it to the highest level . . .[35]

The memorandum also highlights Burke's concern over the urgency of consolidating the idea of an FBM, built and run by the Navy. Believing that 'the first service that demonstrates a capability for this is very likely to continue the project and that others may very well drop out', he called for an early demonstration firing 'even though the equipment in the ships is not as desirable as can be conceived'.[36] In the very first instance, 'technical' feasibility mattered only in so much as it affected the ability of the Navy to retain control of the programme.

Raborn proved to be a felicitous choice for Director of SPO. His personal enthusiasm helped create an atmosphere approaching religious fervour in SPO. A feeling of eliteness was encouraged (unusually for Washington, uniforms were required for Naval personnel), and overtime was the norm, as Raborn 'put himself and everyone around him on a wartime footing'.[37] Raborn made it the standard practice in SPO to work Saturday mornings, reportedly joking that: 'We may not get much done here on Saturdays, but by gosh, people are going to know that we're dedicated.'[38]

Raborn was also adept at working the bureaucracy towards two interlinked objectives: getting the resources needed quickly to meet an urgent schedule, whilst preventing outside interference in the programme. Taking full advantage of the general urgency over missile developments, especially following Sputnik, Raborn and Burke were able to provide SPO with powerful manifestations of its elite status. For all but five months (between February and July 1957) the FBM programme was assigned top priority 'DX' rating which in theory entitled it to priority over 'DO' rated programmes in the allocation of resources.[39] In January 1958 this was supplemented by the creation of a special 'management fund', which, if not in itself greatly adding to SPO's accounting flexibility, provided another powerful symbol of SPO's status.[40]

In any case, it was prior to Sputnik, especially during 1957, that SPO's direct budget allocation most required supplementing. With Burke's support, however, SPO was able to borrow funds originally allocated to other Navy programmes so as to avoid delays whilst Congress made the necessary appropriations.[41] In addition, funds from the cancelled Regulus II, Triton and Seamaster (strategic seaplane) were reprogrammed to pay for early Polaris development.[42]

Raborn, with the help of Burke, 'sold' the FBM as a concept and ensured SPO's programmatic independence and access to almost unlimited resources. To do this required skilful manipulation of the social world (the Administration, Congress, the rest of the Navy, and so on) on the basis of hypothetical technical projections and assumptions. But for SPO to maintain its preeminent position, for the social network they had engineered to remain in place, these promises of technical success would have to be kept. Raborn and Burke gave the programme an ideal start bureaucratically, but the technical people picked by Raborn needed simultaneously to engineer the physical world to produce FBM technology that 'worked'.

JUPITER

At first the newly assembled SPO team had the problem of making the large, liquid-fuel Jupiter IRBM 'work'. Its sheer size and the volatility of its fuel made it seem quite unsuited to submarine launching, and only marginally more attractive for deployment on ships. Whereas the Army's only size limitation was apparently the Berne International Railway Tunnel – to allow 'rapid' transportation around Europe – SPO hoped to carry several on board submarines.[43] In an attempt to make the missile's shape more suitable for basing on ship or submarine, SPO proposed that Jupiter's size envelope be changed from about 90 feet in length and 95 inches in diameter to a 50-foot length, 120-inch diameter missile. This led to a compromise worked out by Secretary of Defense Wilson for a missile of about 58 feet in length and 105 inches in diameter.[44]

This missile would continue to be developed by the Army's German team in conjunction with their main contractor, Chrysler Corporation. SPO's responsibility was to develop a sea-launching platform, with the necessary fire control and stabilization systems for that purpose. The original schedule was to have a ship-based IRBM system ready for operational evaluation by 1 January 1960, and a submarine-based one by 1 January 1965.[45]

However, right from the start the Navy was deeply dissatisfied with the liquid fuel IRBM. Post-war tests of captured German V2s had instilled a deep fear of putting liquid-fuel missiles on Naval vessels. Two other operational problems were also noted, as SPO sought to investigate solid propellant options. Firstly, the cryogenic liquid fuel was not only very dangerous to handle, but also very time-consuming. The time between the firing command and actual launch could be hours, and the missiles could not be kept permanently fuelled. Second, an argument was made that liquid-fuelled rockets provided relatively low initial acceleration, which could be disadvantageous in launching a missile from a moving platform in certain sea states.[46]

Whatever the merit of these particular arguments, SPO also had a strong organizational incentive to move to solids and thus away from

27

dependance on Army collaboration.[47] Admiral Raborn raised the issue of SPO investigating solid propellants at the first meeting of the Joint Army Navy Ballistic Missile Committee in December 1955. This was blocked at the next level of management, the Office of the Secretary of Defense Ballistic Missile Committee (OSDBMC), which saw the Navy request as an attempt to initiate the fifth ballistic missile programme barred only a few months previously.[48] However, the Navy had already taken the initiative by approaching the Aerojet-General Corporation and the Lockheed Missile and Space Division for technical assistance in developing a solid-fuel ballistic missile.[49]

This led to a solid-fuel design based on the largest solid propellant motors that could be developed at the time, using one for the second stage and a cluster of six for the first. Designed to carry the proposed Jupiter payload of 3000 pounds to the designated 1500 mile range, this solid design, though shorter than the Jupiter, was both heavier and larger in diameter. To de-emphasize the radical change in technology the new missile was shrewdly called the Jupiter S. As before, the schedule envisaged was for a ship-launched missile by 1 January 1960 and a submarine-launched one five years later.[50]

Jupiter S soon received the backing of the Navy Secretariat, and in March – after the Navy had persuaded the Air Force to say that the Navy's solid-fuel research was complementary to their own – the OSDBMC approved the solid-fuel missile as a 'back-up program' for the IRBM no. 2.[51] The Navy was now officially in the business of developing a solid-fuel ballistic missile. An experienced missile engineer, Captain Levering Smith, who had previously developed the two-stage solid-propellant Big Stoop missile at the Naval Ordnance Test Station, joined SPO in April to direct this work.[52]

However, the Jupiter S was considered only marginally more practical a weapon system than the liquid-fuel Jupiter. Just as the original joint missile concept was the Navy's way of 'buying' into ballistic missile work, so the Jupiter S was a way of 'buying' into solid propellant missiles. Both served their purpose, but neither was to come near to fleet deployment. Without even being built they proved to be important links in the development of FBM technology. Whilst work continued both on the joint project and on the Jupiter S, other approaches were intensively pursued.

In particular, Captain Smith requested his former staff at the Naval Ordnance Test Station at China Lake in California to do some system improvement studies. These suggested that a radical redesign of all the missile's components could make a 30,000 pound missile feasible within the same time schedule as the 160,000 pound Jupiter S.[53]

SPO, however, did not push for the acceptance of this new approach straightaway. Having just won the right to pursue the Jupiter S it was considered too risky to ask to move to another design apparently requiring even more technological breakthroughs. Instead SPO consolidated its position and the right of the Navy to an FBM. Plans were made to test a liquid-fuel Jupiter on a surface ship in 1958 and to deploy a submarine-based Jupiter S in 1965.[54]

POLARIS CONCEIVED

During 1956 technical advances, both actual and predicted, paved the way for the acceptance of a smaller, solid-fuel design. Solid propellant work sponsored by BuOrd at Atlantic Research demonstrated that the addition of a high proportion of aluminium – much more than the 5 per cent previously thought to be the useful limit – could result in a large increase in specific impulse.[55] Meanwhile MIT's Instrumentation Laboratory kept SPO well informed of its inertial guidance work for the Air Force, which suggested that a lighter guidance system was possible. Then in the summer of 1956 a vital contribution to the FBM programme came from a somewhat unexpected source – a Navy sponsored National Academy of Sciences summer study on anti-submarine warfare. Known as Project NOBSKA (it was held at Nobska Point, Woods Hole, Massachusetts), the study brought Frank E. Bothwell of the Naval Ordnance Test Station together with Edward Teller and others from the recently formed second nuclear weapons laboratory at Livermore.

Bothwell had been working on the studies for SPO which suggested the feasibility of a 30,000 pound solid-fuel FBM, and he relayed the concept to the study group. The problem was that this required too many technological advances for SPO to take the risk of endorsing, and then possibly failing and losing the right to any ballistic missile. Warhead technology seemed particularly crucial because small changes in the weight of the warhead had a multiplier effect on the amount of total propellant impulse required to reach any given range. Yet at the time there remained a strong adherence in the Armed Services to the notion that a militarily useful weapon required at least a 1 megaton warhead.[56]

At the NOBSKA summer study Edward Teller made his famous contribution to the FBM programme. Ever the nuclear salesman and intent on promoting the Livermore laboratory, he suggested that nuclear-armed torpedoes could be substituted for conventional ones to provide a new anti-submarine weapon. This seemed inconceivable

29

with the current size of nuclear warheads, and Teller was challenged to support his assertion. In doing so he pointed to the *trend* in warhead technology, which indicated reduced weight to yield ratios in each succeeding generation. When questioned about the applicability of this to the FBM programme, he asked, 'Why use a 1958 warhead in a 1965 weapon system?'[57]

Teller predicted that the desired 1 megaton warhead could be made to fit the missile envelope within the timescale envisaged.[58] According to Teller, J. Carson Mark, representing the Los Alamos nuclear weapons laboratory, disagreed. When questioned as to what Los Alamos could deliver in the timescale, Mark suggested half a megaton was more realistic.[59] This, of course, simply confirmed the validity of Teller's prediction in the Navy's eyes. Whether the warhead was a half or 1 megaton mattered little so long as it fitted the missile and would be ready on time.

Teller's prediction provided just the technical basis on which SPO could push for their preferred option of a small, solid-fuel missile. Already, by mid-July 1956 the Secretary of Defense's Scientific Advisory Committee had recommended that a solid-propellant missile programme be fully instigated, but not using the unsuitable Jupiter payload and guidance system.[60] Official confirmation of Teller's prediction was sought from the Atomic Energy Commission, whilst Captain Levering Smith was given a couple of weeks to prepare technical specifications for the small missile he had long supported. When the AEC backed up Teller's estimate in early September, Admiral Burke and the Navy Secretariat decided to support SPO in vigorously pushing for the new missile, now named Polaris by Admiral Raborn.

In October 1956 a study group comprising key figures from Navy, industry, and academic organizations was set up. This considered the various design parameters of the Polaris system, and the trade-offs between different sub-sections.[61] The earlier estimate that a 30,000 pound missile could deliver a suitable warhead over 1500 nautical miles was endorsed. Armed with this optimistic assessment, and with the AEC's official warhead prediction, the Navy now decided to quit the Jupiter programme altogether, and to seek Department of Defense backing for a separate Navy missile.

Raborn briefed Secretary of Defense Wilson on the advantages of the smaller missile, completing his slide show with an estimation of how much it would 'save' by comparison with Jupiter, because fewer, smaller ships would be required for deployment. This 'saving' seemed crucial in convincing Wilson, who told Raborn, 'You've shown me a lot of sexy slides, young man. But that's the sexiest, that half-billion-dollar saving.'[62] On 8 December 1956 Wilson issued the directive that officially started the Polaris programme.

THE NAVY, NUCLEAR STRATEGY AND THE FBM PROGRAMME

The Navy's changing attitude to the FBM system – from indifference to advocacy – also meant a shift in thinking about its role in nuclear strategy. Following World War II the Navy had not as a whole been greatly interested in a major nuclear role. Some Navy officers were trained to operate nuclear bombs, and aircraft were adapted to carry these from aircraft carriers, but this was simply considered an extension of the power projection role of the carrier fleet developed during the war.

Despite the important role played by submarines in the war, the surface fleet, and especially aircraft carriers, remained central to the Navy, and were the principal avenue by which officers gained promotion. During the late 1940s cutbacks in the defence budget by the Truman administration were the Navy's main concern. Attempts to prevent reductions in the Navy budget allocation led to what was dubbed the 'Admirals' Revolt' in 1949.[63]

What was at issue was the general shift in funding towards the newly formed Air Force, and in particular to the Strategic Air Command which had responsibility for long-range nuclear bombardment. The specific focus of the debate was a proposed new Air Force bomber, the B-36, which was to be capable of delivering nuclear bombs to any part of the Soviet Union. However, the Navy's attack on the B-36 did not restrict itself to criticism of the utility of that particular system, but instead went right to the core of the Air Force's nuclear strategy.

The objectives of the early nuclear targeting plans drew heavily on the strategic bombing experience of the war, during which German and Japanese cities suffered immense destruction from Allied bombing. American targeting policy concentrated mainly on damaging Soviet war-supporting capabilities such as production of petroleum, steel, and rubber. However, there was little accurate intelligence concerning targets in the Soviet Union, and so up until the end of the 1940s the practical result was that cities were the main targets. After all, Air Force planners noted, 'what was a city besides a collection of industry?'[64]

This trend towards waging war against enemy cities threatened the

31

Navy's traditional military role and looked likely to leave the Air Force as the main beneficiary. Truman's $14.4 billion ceiling on defence spending, announced on 13 May 1948, had fallen far short of the amount desired by the Joint Chiefs of Staff to provide a balanced military capability.[65] Instead, the United States would have to rely more and more on the ultimate threat of nuclear attack on enemy populations. In an attempt to deflect the budgetary cuts, Navy officers argued against the counter-city strategy, on both strategic and moral grounds. In one summary of Navy doubts Rear Admiral Daniel V. Gallery, assistant Chief of Naval Operations for guided missiles, noted, with some understatement, that 'leveling large cities has a tendency to alienate the affections of the inhabitants and does not create an atmosphere of international good will after the war'.[66]

Navy concerns about the efficacy of the counter-city targeting policy were echoed by analysis of the TROJAN war plan. Approved in December 1948 this required an attack on 70 Soviet cities with 133 atomic bombs to be carried out over the duration of 30 days.[67] Such an attack was expected to create 2.7 million mortalities and an additional 4 million casualties.[68] The following year a study of the TROJAN plan, known as the Harmon Report, predicted that even this level of destruction would not by itself 'bring about capitulation, destroy the roots of Communism, or critically weaken the power of Soviet leadership to dominate the people'.[69]

A small group of Navy officers including Gallery and Arleigh Burke proposed an alternative to the Air Force policy of city bombardment:

> They proposed ... that atomic weapons be used primarily against tactical military targets, such as armies, airfields, oil supplies, and submarine pens, which would have to be destroyed to prevent the Soviet Union from taking Western Europe. They argued that scarce budget funds should be spent on conventional tactical air forces and the rebuilding of Western European armies, rather than on expanding capability for an atomic air offensive.[70]

As a corollary to this, they opposed the B-36 bomber, arguing that instead the Navy should build super-carriers to carry aircraft capable of precision bombing of military targets. In October 1949, top Navy officers, including Chief of Naval Operations Denfield, even went so far as to testify to the House Armed Services Committee with their criticisms of counter-city nuclear targeting. The outcome was that several senior Navy officers were relieved of their positions and the Navy suffered a demoralizing defeat over the B-36 issue. The Air Force, in the form of the Strategic Air Command (SAC), became the primary agent of strategic nuclear warfare, with dominance over bombers to add to its ICBM monopoly.

After the B-36 defeat there were few left in the Navy who wanted further confrontation. Instead, during the early 1950s, the Navy stuck to the more central concern of protecting its budget share without publicly questioning nuclear strategy. Navy nuclear forces expanded in line with the Navy's perception of its wartime role, as bombs carried by aircraft were deployed on the surface fleet. Aircraft carriers first achieved a 'rudimentary nuclear capability in 1950–1951', and were considered by the Eisenhower administration to be part of the nation's 'offensive striking power'.[71] These carrier-based nuclear weapons were assigned to 'targets directly or indirectly of naval interest, such as ports, shipbuilding facilities, submarine pens, and naval airfields'.[72] So too was the Regulus I cruise missile, which became operational in May 1954.[73]

It was only with the advent of the FBM programme under Admiral Burke that Navy thinking on nuclear strategy underwent a reorientation, and led to another major attack on Air Force strategic orthodoxy. The issue now was not that the Air Force was targeting cities, but that it was targeting so much else besides, including many speculative military targets, and thus justifying huge force levels. In 1956 Admiral Burke argued that money would be better spent on more conventional forces, especially naval ones, than on more nuclear forces which were already adequate 'to destroy the USSR several times over'.[74]

Air Force policy was for an all-out attack against the whole range of Soviet targets, civil and military – the so-called 'Sunday punch'.[75] If launched preemptively, on warning of imminent hostilities, the Air Force felt that it could thus achieve a decisive blow. Burke and other Navy and Army sceptics argued that SAC's bomber force would soon be vulnerable to the expected Soviet ICBM force and that they therefore could not be sure that they would be able to strike first. Instead they argued that an 'alternative undertaking' should be planned for, providing for the possibility of 'general war initiated under disadvantageous conditions'.[76]

Initially Polaris was spoken of as though it was simply an extension of the Navy's tactical role, intended to cover the same types of targets as Regulus and the carrier-based aircraft, but at a longer range. The Navy tried to avoid direct competition with the Air Force by *differentiating* the role of the FBM from the strategic mission of the Air Force. Thus, up until mid–1957, it was typical to refer to Polaris 'striking targets of naval opportunity', such as submarine pens and port facilities.[77] Indeed, in its early days SPO was particularly careful to reassure

33

not only the Air Force, but also the dominant group within the Navy, those officers committed to aircraft carriers. In a 1957 article, Admiral Raborn described the role of Polaris, stressing subservience to the carrier force: 'Its tactical mission would be to beat down fixed base air and missile defenses to pave the way for carrier strikes aimed at destroying mobile or concealed primary targets.'[78]

However, some Navy planners were keen to 'stake out a claim' to a strategic role.[79] The Naval Warfare Analysis Group's first study of the FBM, distributed in January 1957, recommended that 'population or industrial targets should be specified by CNO as the target for the initial FBM capability'.[80] Polaris was thus acknowledged as a strategic weapon, but was still carefully differentiated from Air Force systems. Skilfully combining national concern over SAC vulnerability with the Navy's dislike of Air Force 'overkill', Burke outlined a strategic concept, now known as 'finite deterrence', whereby retaliation would be threatened by a relatively small, invulnerable force with, as he put it, its size determined by 'an objective of generous *adequacy for deterrence alone* (i.e., for an ability to destroy major urban areas), not by the false goal of adequacy for "winning"'.[81]

Such an invulnerable counter-city weapon was, of course, exactly what Polaris was expected to provide.[82] It was to be a strategic weapon, but not (at least not primarily) a counterforce one – its mission was to destroy cities in retaliation for a Soviet strike. This rationale made sense both *vis-à-vis* the Soviet Union and *vis-à-vis* the Air Force. Both the pressure for early availability and the evolution of the 'assured destruction' rationale tended to de-emphasize the pursuit of accuracy. Polaris had to be accurate enough reliably to destroy cities – but that did not mean very accurate. If it was less accurate than the Air Force ICBMs, this did not matter much – indeed it could even be taken as an advantage, as a clear technical manifestation of the bureaucratic strategy of 'differentiation'. What mattered most of all though, both in the 'Cold War' with the Soviet Union, and in the interservice war with the Air Force, was to get Polaris built as soon as possible, and to show that it 'worked'.

4 BUILDING POLARIS

Our religion was to build Polaris.   Admiral Raborn.[1]

By the beginning of 1957 a combination of technological advances (or predictions of advances) and astute political manoeuvring had created the Polaris programme. Navy opinion remained sceptical, however. At a briefing of senior flag officers following the approval of Polaris, not one was enthusiastic about the Navy taking on Polaris: 'Most of them felt that it would be a waste of money, a tremendous drain on the Navy's budget, and that it would not be successful.'[2]

As director of SPO, Admiral Raborn continued to see his role as managing 'the outside world'. The choice of Washington for SPO's headquarters reflected his judgement of where the success of the programme would be decided.[3] It was the politics, both of the government and of the Navy, which had to be engineered first and foremost. 'Get the money, and keep other people off our program managers' backs', was how Raborn saw his job.[4] In his classic study, Harvey Sapolsky notes four strategies which contributed to SPO's bureaucratic success in doing this: *differentiation* of a special role, which was represented as of crucial national importance; *co-optation* of potential critics and disruptive elements; *moderation* of short-term goals in order to maximize long-term support; and *managerial innovation* in order to create an aura of efficiency.[5]

Differentiation meant not only encouraging a feeling of eliteness amongst those who worked on Polaris, but also creating a distinct mission for the FBM force to justify its existence alongside the missile programmes of the other services.[6] No effort or expense was spared in public relations aimed at enrolling support for Polaris, whereas technical difficulties were downplayed.[7] Co-optation involved drawing potential critics into being involved with, and so committed to, the programme while not at the same time conceding any actual power. Thus money was always available to fund someone who had ideas relevant to Polaris, and good relations with scientists were particularly

35

encouraged.[8] Likewise, in an attempt to placate the concern of the surface Navy, SPO frequently raised the possibility of basing Polaris on surface ships during the late 1950s, though only one such proposal was ever given the go-ahead. This plan to deploy Polaris on the nuclear-powered cruiser *Long Beach* was instituted in January 1961 by the Eisenhower administration, but cancelled two months later under Kennedy.[9]

Moreover, whilst SPO sought autonomy over anything affecting the development of Polaris, it was careful to show restraint on issues that were not vital to this concern and that might foster long-term resentment. Such moderation meant, for example, that SPO avoided publicly returning the Air Force's vocal criticism of Polaris. Finally, SPO developed a range of new management techniques, the best known of which was the programme evaluation review technique or PERT.[10] This was initially very unpopular with SPO's technical staff and with the contractors, but it soon came to be valued for the image it created: 'It had lots of pizzazz and that's valuable in selling a program'.[11] The image of managerial efficiency thus created greatly aided SPO in their job, as Sapolsky has noted:

> An alchemous combination of whirling computers, brightly colored charts, and fast-talking public relations officers gave the Special Projects Office a truly effective management system. It mattered not whether parts of the system functioned or even existed. It mattered only that certain people for a period of time believed that they did.[12]

Thus SPO engineered the 'politics' of the programme so as to provide resources without interference. This skilful heterogeneous engineering extended to issues of technical definition too. Just what exactly the FBM system should comprise was an important matter of social relations. Although given high priority, and the considerable support of CNO Admiral Burke, SPO lacked absolute jurisdiction over other Navy technical organizations (which were not then under the formal command of the CNO). Partly to avoid familiar Navy problems with transferring technology from a procurement branch to an operational branch and partly to maximize its control, SPO defined the FBM system very broadly. It was not simply going to produce some equipment and then hand it over, but instead, in so far as was possible, SPO was going to put in place and maintain a complete system.[13]

TECHNICAL DECISIONS

A Polaris Steering Task Group (STG), headed by Captain Levering Smith, was set up to oversee the technical development of the programme. This convened for the first time on 7 January 1957. The next few months were then spent defining the technical specifications of the Polaris system, even though 'the exact characteristics of the reentry vehicle and payload were still an educated guess'.[14] An initial, fundamental issue was to decide on the performance goal of the system. Delivery of a 1 megaton warhead to a range of 1500 miles was the original goal set for the IRBMs by the Killian Report. This remained SPO's eventual goal, but was relegated to a later development. In the meantime an interim Polaris missile was to be rapidly built, providing the nation with deterrent capability at the earliest possible time, and consolidating the Navy's claim to a ballistic missile. William Whitmore, SPO's first chief scientist, recalls the flexible way they viewed the performance goal of the first Polaris:

> So it was clear that we were not confronted with a standard request to design an optimum system meeting a fixed operational requirement. The task was rather to set minimum acceptable initial operational performance, expecting the total system capability to improve with time ... In very crude terms, we felt that the Polaris missile had to be able to reach Moscow from a position at sea and cause a reasonable amount of damage when it got there. Based on our knowledge of geography and weapon effects in 1957, this implied about 900 miles range and a half-megaton yield.[15]

The FBM system operational requirement specified in February 1957 was: 'provide an all-weather capability to deliver from ships to strategic land targets at intermediate ranges, with minimum susceptibility to countermeasures, a weapon which will provide the required damage probability'.[16] In May 1957 SPO redefined their schedule, calling for an interim Polaris A missile, with a nominal range of 1200 nautical miles, to provide a surface launch submarine capability by 1 January 1963. Full submerged launch and a 1500 mile range were to be provided with the Polaris B by 1 January 1965.[17]

The programme was then accelerated further following the Soviet launch of the Sputnik satellite on 4 October 1957 and the recommendations of the Gaither Report in early November.[18] Deployment of the interim missile, now known as Polaris A1, was rescheduled first to 1961, and then to November 1960. Deployment of A1X test missiles to provide an even more 'interim' capability – of about 1000 mile range – somewhat earlier was also considered, if emergency measures were invoked.[19]

To meet this schedule SPO decided to use the hull of an existing nuclear-powered submarine currently under construction at Electric Boat's shipyard in Groton, Connecticut. This was literally to be cut in half and a missile section inserted. The length of this section was determined by the number of missiles each submarine was to carry and the method of stowage. The preferred stowage configuration was vertical, two abreast. There was less consensus about the optimum number of missiles per submarine. Economic considerations pushed towards large numbers, up to thirty-two per vessel, whereas operational flexibility, survivability, and the preferences of submarine commanders pushed the other way. The question defied exact analysis and in the end was put to 'a sort of opinion poll of ship designers, analysts, and submarine operators'.[20] This looked likely to result in a twenty-four tube design, but sixteen was chosen by the intervention of Admiral Raborn – as always, sensitive to the need to enrol support – once he learnt that this was the maximum that the submariners felt desirable.[21]

Submarine conversion was estimated to take about four years and thus needed to begin without delay. Missile development was not expected to take as long, perhaps only two years, but obviously the roughly simultaneous development of the various elements of the system had to be compatible when brought together. It was thus critical right at the start to define the subsystem 'envelopes' and their interfaces, something which the STG did during the first few months of 1957.

Each subsystem was assigned to a separate technical branch of SPO, most of which had already been formed for the sea-basing of the Jupiter. The Jupiter experience also influenced the unusual decision not to have a contractor as overall 'prime contractor'. Chrysler had been the Army's prime contractor for Jupiter and so naturally, had also been chosen by SPO for the same job on the sea-based version. However, Chrysler were committed to the Army's Jupiter whereas SPO was intent on moving to solid fuel if at all possible. The relationship with Chrysler thus proved unproductive and in practice SPO's technical branches were soon dealing directly with the various subcontractors. When the switch to Polaris was made it was decided not to impose a prime contractor on to these relationships, especially as the obvious candidate, Lockheed, was relatively new to the programme.[22]

Thus the division of work amongst the SPO technical branches was based on the Jupiter experience. SP-22 remained responsible for the launcher subsystem, which needed to be able to store the missile for long periods of time, and ideally allow submerged launch. SP-23 had handled fire control for the Jupiter and now took on missile guidance as well. Guidance was initially intended to be assigned to the missile branch, but the chosen guidance team at MIT's Instrumentation Laboratory doubted Lockheed's expertise in that area and in any case were institutionally prohibited from entering into a subcontractual relationship.[23] In fact grouping guidance together with fire control also made sense because of the difficulty of clearly defining their interface at this early stage.[24] SP-24 was navigation, critical to the overall accuracy of the system because of the importance of knowledge of the initial launch position, azimuth and speed over the ground. SP-26 was ship installation, devoted to the building of the submarines and installing the other subsystems. SP-27, which had been formed recently to develop a solid-propellant propulsion system for Jupiter – the Jupiter S – became responsible for the missile subsystem, including warhead and reentry vehicle but not guidance.

Each branch chief would have responsibility for their own subsystem, reporting regularly to Levering Smith, who became Technical Director of SPO in June 1957, and to the steering task group which met every few months.

LAUNCHER SUBSYSTEM

By the time Polaris was approved, SPO's launcher branch, SP-22, had already spent a lot of time thinking about the problem of launching the Jupiter missile from a surface ship. A major concern with the liquid-fuel Jupiter, of course, was safety, and launching from the rolling, pitching, windswept deck of a ship exacerbated this concern. It was decided that the dangers involved in fuelling the missile would be minimized if done below decks, with the missile then raised immediately prior to launch. This would require an elevator system, but that was a technology much used by the Navy for moving planes around in aircraft carriers.[25]

This scheme was approved and Westinghouse Electric Corporation's Sunnyvale division – just winding down from Navy work on a gun mount – were contracted to build it. The plan was to install three missiles per ship, starting initially by converting a Mariner-class merchant vessel, the *Observation Island*.[26] Submarine launching for Jupiter seemed a much longer term prospect because no current nuclear-powered submarine design was anywhere near large enough to accommodate the missile. Although large by the standards of the day, the world's first nuclear powered submarine, the *Nautilus*, had a displacement less than half that considered necessary to carry four Jupiter missiles.[27] Although slightly shorter the solid-fuelled Jupiter S was both fatter and heavier.

With the arrival of the concept of Polaris, size was no longer a

Length (feet)	28.5
Nominal range (nautical miles)	1200
Weight at launch (1000s of lbs)	28.8
Year first deployed	1960
No. of warheads	1
Yield per warhead (kilotons)	600
	[W-47]
Guidance system	Mk. 1
Approximate accuracy (circular error probable, nautical miles)	2

Figure 4.1 Polaris A-1

problem, and the sixteen-tube submarine was decided upon. Surface launch also seemed relatively simple to achieve, at least in calm sea conditions, but the militarily preferable submerged launch did not: 'The means to do this were simply not identified and the capability to do it was completely unknown.'[28] Westinghouse were retained as the launcher contractor, and they established a systems group to tackle the problem. Two main options were identified. The more conservative option involved releasing the missiles from the submarine in capsules which would then float to the surface and open up to allow launch. The other was bare missile launch, where the missile would be launched unprotected through the water.

The two approaches were pursued simultaneously for some time on the basis of a missile size, shape, and weight 'envelope' defined by the Steering Task Group. However, although size and shape were defined quite precisely by now, weight and structural load were not. The launcher branch was thus in the difficult position of having to meet an urgent schedule whilst retaining some flexibility:

> The missile was the least well defined of all these things in this timescale and so the people who were designing the launcher were caught between the ship-builder who was actually making things and the missile people who were still trying to define what this missile was like in terms of its structural load, and so on . . . So the job of designing the launcher got to be to figure out how you could build something that was sufficiently flexible in its design that you could define the interfaces it had with the ship under circumstances when the interfaces it had with the missile were only vaguely defined. . . . You didn't know what the shock resistance of the missile was going

to be. You simply had to have enough rattle space that whatever it turned out to be you could accommodate that. And because of that you ended up considerably overdesigning things.[29]

Sufficient 'rattle space' to protect the missile during a depth charge attack along with the need to keep the backup option of encapsulated launch thus sized the submarine mount tube. This 'over-designing' of the launcher system would later prove highly significant, allowing larger missiles to be developed for use within the same submarines.

In June 1957, Captain Ela of SP-22 established a deadline for the first underwater launch of a dummy missile – by January 1958.[30] Scale model testing done at the Naval Ordnance Test Station suggested that the bare missile could be launched at a depth of the order of a hundred feet and still arrive at the surface sufficiently vertical to recover its trajectory when ignited.[31] The launcher subsystem was required to provide 'a protective cocoon that would cradle the missile against both lateral and vertical shock', eject it with sufficient velocity when required, and withstand the effect of the backflooding seawater.[32]

It was decided to hold the missile snug within the launch tube with three rings of flexible pads, known as stowage launch adaptors, which would fall off when the missile was ejected. The nature of these pads was considered to require a very rigid, smooth launch tube for which heavy-walled, machined steel was chosen. This launch tube was to be suspended within the submarine mount tube, with a requirement that it be able to withstand the shock of an under-water depth charge explosion. Oil-filled double-acting shock absorbers were chosen to provide this suspension as they could be made with a 'null' position from which they deviated only after experiencing a significant force. The advantage this had over competing spring technologies was that it facilitated the precise positioning of the missile for the optical alignment required by fire control to 'ready' the missile guidance system.[33]

Missile ejection was achieved by compressed air pressure controlled by a programmed air valve adapted from the type used in catapult equipment for assisting plane take-off from aircraft carriers. Prior to launch the heavy outside hatches covering the launch tubes would be opened leaving the tube sealed only by a thin diaphragm, and the tube would be pressurized to the hydrostatic pressure at this diaphragm. The diaphragm would then be explosively removed at the instant of launch.

Thus the main elements of the launch system were developed.[34] At each stage testing was carried out, with the scale models replaced first by redwood logs launched from the 'Peashooter' test facility at the San Francisco Naval Shipyard, and then by inert test vehicles supplied by

41

the missile contractor, Lockheed. Underwater testing was performed at the 'Pop-Up' test site of the Naval Ordnance Test Station's underwater test range near San Clemente Island.[35] The first underwater test was carried out there in March 1958 after a delay due to bad weather, when a dummy missile was successfully 'launched'.

GUIDANCE AND FIRE CONTROL

SP-23 was initially set up to develop a fire control system to coordinate the Jupiter guidance system, designed by the Army's German team, with the ship or submarine navigation system, and to perform all the functions necessary for launching at the desired target. When the switch was made to Polaris the Navy became free to choose its own guidance team rather than relying on the Army's team, whose approach, although feasible, 'was not well suited to solid propellant propulsion systems'.[36] The German team had worked with Bendix on a smaller guidance system which might have been suitable for Polaris, but their enthusiasm was not matched by that of the head of the Army's Ballistic Missile Office, General Medaris. One SPO officer recalls that Medaris 'was not very fond of the Navy from the beginning and he and Raborn didn't get along worth a dime'.[37]

In any case SPO's urgent schedule, as well as their service pride, made relying on the Army's expertise an uninviting option, if it could be avoided. It could be avoided, as indeed SPO had become increasingly aware, prior to the break with the Army. An alternative was to be found at the MIT Instrumentation Laboratory with which SPO had contracted to investigate ship stabilization for the Jupiter missile, and whose pioneering work on inertial navigation was also to feed back into the Polaris submarine navigation system.

Under the directorship of Charles Stark Draper the Instrumentation Laboratory had been at the forefront of developing inertial technology for navigation and guidance since 1945. Refining a gyroscope design developed during the war for gun control systems, Draper became an influential proponent of inertial technology.[38] Whilst working with SPO on ship stabilization for the Jupiter, the Instrumentation Laboratory was also developing a guidance system for the Air Force's Thor IRBM. One member of the team working on the Air Force contract, Ralph Ragan, suggested to Instrumentation Laboratory alumnus Commander Sam Forter, then in SP-23, that the laboratory could design a guidance system for a smaller missile. A meeting was then arranged with Captain Levering Smith.[39] In addition, SP-23's branch engineer Dave Gold had worked with the Instrumentation Laboratory as the

Bureau of Ordnance's project engineer on Project MAST, an early application of inertial technology to weapon system stabilization.[40] SPO arranged a contract with the Instrumentation Laboratory using Bureau of Ordnance funds ('the Navy didn't care too much as long as we didn't embezzle it').[41] So the Instrumentation Laboratory 'had six months' head start on a design for a ballistic missile for submarines before the Polaris program was signed and given a name'.[42]

As well as their general inertial expertise and their familiarity to many in the Navy, the Instrumentation Laboratory also could offer another crucial 'technical detail': a mathematical guidance formulation which seemed particularly well suited to Polaris. Moving to a smaller missile placed a high premium on miniaturization, which was clearly a constraint on the onboard computer that had to perform the computations necessary to guide the missile. Digital computation seemed to be taking over from analogue, but by modern standards was slow and bulky. Two mathematicians at the Laboratory, Richard H. Battin and J. Halcombe Laning Jr, through work they were doing for the Air Force Atlas ICBM, had developed a mathematical scheme that became known as 'Q-guidance'. The enormous advantage of this method was that, though a lot of computation was involved, much of it could be done well in advance of firing the missile (the calculation of the elements of the Q matrix), leaving only fairly simple tasks for the onboard computer.[43]

Whilst still working on the liquid-fuel Jupiter, SPO was discussing Q-guidance with people at the Instrumentation Laboratory. On one occasion Ralph Ragan and David Hoag of the Instrumentation Laboratory and Sam Forter of SP-23 tried to explain the principle of Q-guidance to SPO technical director, Levering Smith. When they became confused over how it really worked, it was left to Levering Smith to clarify the principle.[44] He became convinced that it was particularly suitable for guiding solid-fuelled missiles 'because Q-guidance did not need to adjust the thrust program in flight as others did. Unlike liquid-fuelled missiles there was no practical means for adjusting the thrust program of solid-fuelled missiles.'[45] Admiral Levering Smith recalls that MIT was chosen over the Redstone Arsenal at Huntsville 'primarily because of the Q-guidance. It did appear that we could work more closely with Draper than with Huntsville, partly because I thought the [Draper] fluid floated gyro would adapt easier to the solid motor accelerations, but to my way of thinking the choice was driven more by Q-guidance than anything else.'[46]

The official culmination of all this was that on 10 October 1956 Raborn and some of his staff 'visited Draper to elicit his interest in developing the Polaris inertial guidance. The result was a direct contract for its development. . . . The General Electric Company was selected to provide industrial support and to build the resulting guidance system.'[47] Air Force opposition, stemming from concern over interference with MIT's work on their missile guidance systems, also had to be placated.[48]

Thus was set the organizational pattern that has persisted to this day for the development of fleet ballistic missile guidance systems: a direct contract awarded to the Draper Laboratory (the Instrumentation Laboratory was renamed the Charles Stark Draper Laboratory after its dissociation from MIT), with the systems designed by the laboratory being produced by major industrial firms. The Instrumentation Laboratory's policy of not taking subcontracts from industry meant that the guidance system was the only part of the missile not subcontracted through Lockheed. For the first few years this led to 'considerable tension and friction in carrying out the interface tasks and arguments between Lockheed and the Lab'.[49]

Working on a very tight schedule, which became even tighter in December 1957 following the launch of Sputnik, the Instrumentation Laboratory designed and developed the Mk. 1 guidance system for Polaris. The gyroscope was a paradigmatic Draper 'floated gyro' design: the 25-size (i.e. 2.5 inch diameter) inertial rate-integrating gyroscope (IRIG), which had been developed for the Air Force.[50] The accelerometer was a pendulous integrating gyro accelerometer (PIGA) based on the same 25-size gyroscope. 'Each PIGA contained a [gyroscope] which was the same design as the 25-size IRIG with an additional unbalanced mass.'[51] Three 25-IRIGs mutually at right angles held a stable platform carrying three similarly positioned 25-PIGAs in a known orientation. This platform was supported by three gimbals made of beryllium allowing relatively free, but not unlimited, movement. The onboard computer was the first digital fully transistorized guidance computer, but it was not a full general-purpose digital computer. Of the type known as a digital differential analyzer, it was customized to perform the few repetitive calculations required to solve the differential equations used in Q-guidance. Using germanium components – discrete diodes and transistors – the Mk. 1 electronics had a total gate count of about 400, comparable to a modern digital wristwatch.[52]

The Mk. 1 guidance system combined inertial components and electronics into one module weighing 225 pounds.[53] Relatively simple in concept, the Mk. 1 was a nightmare to make, with difficulties in 'every aspect of production'.[54] The computer – said to be the first digital computer used in a missile – had 'a lot of trouble with the memory cores ... trouble in the wiring and testing ... and there was trouble with the transistors ... they had a terrible time getting any degree of reliability out of it'.[55] There was also the problem of the 'purple plague': 'At the junction of the lead to the transistor they would start to rot, mould, or whatever you call it, and under the right light, or maybe by bare eye, it turned purple, and you lost connection ... it was like a disease that went through all the early transistors.' Gyroscopes also were very difficult to produce to the standard required: 'You'd make a batch of bearings that would work phenomenally ... and had life times of 100,000 hours. And then a year later all the production people ... were getting poor gyros. All the bearings would go bad in all the production lines.'[56]

Nevertheless, the Mk. 1 guidance system was ready in time to meet Polaris schedules. Although its mean time between failures was not ideal, with careful attention it was adequate for the short duration of guided flight – of the order of two minutes. During first stage flight the missile carried out a preprogrammed turn. Q-guidance control then took over and controlled second stage flight up to thrust termination and separation of the reentry vehicle.[57]

Meanwhile SP-23 was also working on a fire-control system – called the Mk. 80 – to prepare the missile guidance systems for launch. In essence, fire control had to tell the guidance system what trajectory the missile needed to fly to take it from the patrol position to the target. The targets were fixed and of a finite number, but the continuously changing patrol position presented a serious problem with computer capabilities of the day. Using precomputed punched card inputs for a sufficiently fine grid of all conceivable patrol positions would have required a card library too large to fit the submarine. However, calculating initial conditions in real time using data from the navigation system would have required too large a computer with the current state-of-the-art. Fortunately it was possible to combine these two extremes to achieve a workable compromise. A punched card library of a coarse grid of patrol area launch squares provided the basis for real time 'computer interpolation for the exact submarine position and heading within the square'.[58]

Other data, such as the components of the Q-matrix, were calculated onshore, at the Naval Ordnance Station in Dahlgren, Virginia, and the data for a particular target read into the fire control system on cards. After the first ten submarines, and for the UK Polaris fleet, the Mk. 80 was replaced by the Mk. 84 system. This did have a digital computer integral to the system – 'a "militarized" version of Control Data Corp's

45

"1604" commercial computer' – which provided a more rapid onboard retargeting capability.[59]

Fire control not only provides the missile guidance systems with navigation information and targeting data, but it also plays a role in preparing them physically for launching: the processes known as 'alignment' (determining azimuth or orientation in the horizontal plane) and 'erection' (determining the direction of the vertical). Particularly critical was a system to physically determine the relationship between the missile guidance pitch axis and the submarine navigation system so that the guidance system could be aligned during launch preparations. This was achieved optically (in what is called the optical alignment group) with rail-mounted carts that could 'look' through windows in the launch tubes and missiles to observe a porro prism on the guidance system's outer gimbal.

> The guidance interface was quite complex in that all the loops ... were closed through fire control, so that alignment and erection was done through fire control ... All of that interface ... connected through resolvers, was extraordinarily complex, very touchy. Everything had to be done just right for both alignment and erection. Quite honestly I look back on it and it's a miracle it ever worked, but it did, and does.[60]

NAVIGATION

Whereas many of the FBM technologies were relatively new, at least to the Navy, navigation had, of course, been a long-standing concern. SPO's navigation branch could thus draw on much existing Navy expertise, and SP-24 personnel – such as branch director Captain Lew Schock and his civilian chief engineer Joe Cestone – were largely drawn from BuShips.[61]

Navigation was seen as a critical aspect of the FBM's feasibility because of the effect that it had on overall system accuracy, and because this issue was repeatedly raised by the Air Force in an attempt to undermine the Navy's claim to a missile role. An error in knowledge of the submarine's position at launch would lead to missing the target by that same error. A small error in azimuth, erection, or ship's velocity at launch would lead to a very large miss. State-of-the-art submerged submarine navigation was approximate at best, and the capacity of the nuclear submarine to remain submerged for long periods would be of no value if frequent surfacing was required to work out position and azimuth.

A possible solution existed, but in 1956 had not been proven for submarine use. Self-contained inertial navigation had been developed at the MIT Instrumentation Laboratory, under Draper, and at the Autonetics Division of North American Aviation, for use in bomber aircraft and long-range cruise missiles. The Instrumentation Laboratory had also worked for the Navy on applying this technology to submarines, even before the FBM was conceived. In 1951 the Laboratory was awarded a Navy Bureau of Ships contract to develop a prototype Ships Inertial Navigation System (SINS), which they delivered in 1954. For the Polaris programme, the laboratory's work was taken up by the Sperry Corporation, pioneers of gyroscope technology, and a firm with especially strong links to the US Navy.[62]

Problems with the MIT/Sperry design led to almost as much anxiety for the developers of Polaris as any other issue. Charles Stark Draper of MIT believed in the elegant virtues of letting gyroscopes remain in fixed orientation in inertial space (i.e. with respect to the stars). In practice, however, this led to a system that rapidly lost accuracy. As the earth rotated and the submarine's position changed the gyroscopes were subjected to a varying gravity field. The slightest mass imbalance of their rotors would lead to significant errors. But achieving perfect or near perfect mass balance was an exceedingly difficult task, especially as one moved outside the laboratory to the 'real world' of production. Also the gyroscope whose sensitive axis was parallel to the earth's axis had to rotate a full turn every day, making it more sensitive to air currents moving over the thermally stabilized gyro case.[63]

Fortunately for Polaris's tight schedule an alternative was available.[64] As interest in ballistic missiles grew during the 1950s, air-breathing cruise missiles fell out of favour. In July 1957 the 5000-mile US Air Force Navaho was abruptly cancelled and the Autonetics Division of North American Aviation were left with a guidance system known as the Autonavigator. As Captain Schock recalled, this 'left them with half a dozen of these, roughly half a dozen of them surplus. They had to fire ten thousand people in forty-eight hours when Navaho was cancelled. And so they assigned a physicist PhD as the Washington pedlar to sell the Navy.'[65]

The XN6 guidance system developed for Navaho incorporated a novel feature – each of the three axes had two gyroscopes which could be reversed, averaging out 'drift' of the gyros. Unlike the MIT/Sperry design, it was a 'local level' system, kept horizontal at all times, so the gyros were not subject to change in the direction of gravity. By 1958, the XN6 system, modified as the N6A Inertial Navigator, was mature and reliable enough to be taken on a submarine mission that ensured its fame and rescued it from the status of a component in a cancelled system. It navigated the USS *Nautilus* on its widely publicized voyage from the Pacific to the Atlantic under the ice surrounding the North Pole.

SPO ran sea trials on their test platform, the USS *Compass Island*, to compare the performance of the Sperry/MIT SINS, known as the Mk. 1, and the N6A. The Autonetics SINS performed much better, but both companies were awarded contracts to develop a SINS for Polaris. With navigation requirements so stringent by the standards of the day, Sperry supporters found it easy to argue for duplication; Admiral Raborn himself particularly favoured maintaining competition in the navigation system.[66]

At this point a programme initiated in 1954 by the Underseas Warfare Branch of the Office of Naval Research came to fruition.[67] This led to the development of gyroscopes in which the the ball-bearings of the early designs were replaced with gas spin bearings with a substantial improvement in performance. A new SINS using the gas spin gyro was developed by Autonetics.

Meanwhile, it seemed the modified Sperry system, the Mk. 3 Gyronavigator, would be installed in the first five submarines, the 598-class. The new Autonetics design, the Mk. 2 Autonavigator, was to go in the next five 608-class. However, when it came to the decision the Autonetics SINS was 'much nearer to being ready than the Sperry' and this deployment pattern was reversed.[68] After a few years these Sperry systems were replaced and the Autonetics Mk. 2 (in various modifications) became standard on FBM submarines. Sperry, however, retained a major role in the FBM programme when it became the navigation system manager in 1958.

The Mk. 2 SINS was based on a stable platform carrying three orthogonal G7A self-activating gas spin gyroscopes which sense rotation and maintain the known orientation of the platform via servo motors. Two accelerometers sense horizontal linear acceleration, one in the north–south direction and the other in the east–west direction. Integrating their output once yields velocity; a second integration yields distance. Thus the submarine's position can continuously be updated.[69] To achieve this, the SINS, like any inertial system, needs knowledge of the gravitational field through which it is passing so that accelerations due to the submarine's movement can be distinguished from those due to gravity.

Moreover, even the best SINS cannot operate autonomously for an indefinite time. Periodic 'resets' – updates from external sources of navigational information – are needed to stop unacceptable errors building up. 'The Polaris navigation system was planned on the assumption that a precision fix could be obtained at least once every eight hours.'[70] In some cases these navigational resets involved reliance on foreign bases and potential difficulties in relations with other states.

One solution to the reset problem free of international relations difficulties was to use the human navigator's old stand-by, the stars. The 'type 11 periscope' enabled 'an operator to visually locate a true star position and manually enter the information which corrects the inertial system's prediction of the ship's position'. In use 'Type 11 was a real dog. I mean it was a mechanical marvel, but it was a hydraulically-driven, hydraulically-supported periscope: it's like taking . . . sights at the top of a 40 foot pole, and you've got to remember that you've got to track and everything else while the ship is moving all over the place, and we were only too happy to get rid of it.'[71] With its 'usefulness . . . limited by marginal accuracy, cloud cover, daylight, alignment problems, and maintenance costs',[72] the Type 11 had been discarded by the time the navigation systems for the British Polaris submarines were supplied by the United States, and was finally eliminated from the US fleet in 1969.[73] Also developed was a radiometric sextant to obtain resets from radio wave emission from the sun or moon, providing an all-weather capability lacking in the Type 11, though with less accuracy.[74]

Three other sources of external fixes were concentrated on.[75] One involved surveying the sea floor with sonar and identifying distinctive features. The first Polaris submarines were to be deployed in the Norwegian Sea, and so initially only a limited area needed to be surveyed. The submarine could then navigate from one surveyed feature to another, updating its SINS at each, in just the same way that modern cruise missile guidance uses terrain mapping. So long as no extraordinary manoeuvres were required, a submarine could follow surveyed features without coming near the surface (except for communications). Of course, both this and accurate gravitational mapping required detailed surveying of future Polaris patrol areas by surface ships. This attracted the attention of the Soviet Union, and Soviet vessels began to shadow the survey ships. Even so, the true purpose of the survey ships was apparently considered too sensitive to be imparted to America's NATO allies except in most general terms.[76]

Two further solutions to the reset problem were also pursued. In addition, both helped the survey ships in the task of locating the sea-floor features they mapped. One was a more accurate version of Loran (Long Range Aid to Navigation) known as Loran-C.[77] Loran was developed during World War II at the MIT Radiation Laboratory. Time differences between the arrival of radio signals from widely spaced

49

land-based transmitters enabled positional fixes to be made. By the late 1950s Loran-C receivers were able to provide absolute navigational accuracy of about a quarter of a mile at a 1000 mile range, and were sensitive to differences of 30 to 40 feet.[78] Loran-C was actually an Air Force development which was avidly taken up by SPO's navigation branch. It was used first on the USS *Compass Island*, then for the survey ships as they mapped sea-bed features, and was available for the first Polaris submarines when they went on patrol. By 1962 Loran-C networks were operating in the North and West Atlantic, the Mediterranean, round Hawaii, and in the North Pacific and Aleutians.[79] In these areas a trailing wire antenna would be 'often deployed for continuous reception' of Loran-C so that it could 'be used continuously to monitor SINS performance'.[80]

The new Loran-C stations were built – in Norway, Italy, Spain, Turkey, Denmark, Libya, and elsewhere – without creating political controversy. In future years, however, stations designed – or believed to be designed – for FBM navigation were to lead to open political dispute in New Zealand, Australia, and Norway.[81]

Free from such political risks, and also at least in the immediate future safe from possible Soviet attack, was the third reset system. This was the world's first satellite navigation system, Transit. Scientists at Johns Hopkins University Applied Physics Laboratory were developing a technique for tracking the orbit of Sputnik using the Doppler shift in the frequency of its transmission at a ground station of known location. By reversing the process a navigational fix could be obtained from a satellite of known orbit.[82] Although not available for the first Polaris patrols, Transit would soon prove to be not only an additional source of navigational fixes, but perhaps more importantly, a major source of geodetic information.[83]

So the standard navigation equipment of the first Polaris submarines was: three SINS; an electromagnetic log which measured water speed (necessary to damp oscillations in the SINS); Loran-C receiver, Transit receiver (when developed), Type 11 periscope, and terrain matching sonar (all for updating the SINS); and two NAVDAC (Navigation Data Assimilation Computer) systems to integrate all the information.[84] Navigation data was continuously broadcast from the navigation system to the fire control system in analogue form.[85]

MISSILE

SPO's solid propulsion branch, SP-27, became the missile branch when the all-clear was given to develop Polaris in December 1956. A year earlier Lockheed Missile System Division (LMSD) had been chosen to integrate the solid propellant propulsion system for Jupiter and it was now authorized to proceed with Polaris development, replacing Chrysler Corporation which was the missile contractor for Jupiter.[86] Aerojet was chosen to develop the propulsion system, initially separately contracted directly with SPO, but from 1957 as a subcontractor to Lockheed.[87]

LMSD already had some test missiles that could be quickly brought into use for the Polaris programme. They had developed a three-stage solid-propellant ballistic missile, the X-17, to carry out reentry vehicle development tests for the Air Force.[88] Renamed FTV-3 this was used for reentry vehicle tests, the final stage firing on the descent to increase the reentry velocity of the reentry body. Other rocket motors were used to test propulsion control and termination methods. Thus the series of flight tests begun for the Jupiter S programme was continued – the first for Polaris was on 11 January 1957.[89]

The key technologies which were required for the Polaris missile subsystem included: a high impulse, large diameter solid propellant; a casing for the motors; a method of steering the missile; a means of terminating the thrust; and a light enough warhead/reentry body combination able to survive atmospheric reentry.

Developments in solid propellant technology during 1955 and 1956 had been central in SPO's successful campaign for its own missile. Two kinds of solid propellant were under development. Double base cast propellants had been developed under Office of Scientific Research and Development sponsorship in 1945. In this process small nitrocellulose grains, poured into a plastic mould, absorb a solvent containing nitroglycerine and coalesce into a solid.[90] In the 1950s cast double base propellants were used for boosting missiles such as the Talos and Terrier class missiles, which were developed under Navy sponsorship by the Allegany Ballistics Laboratory and Johns Hopkins Applied Physics Laboratory. However, the resultant propellant was very hard and inelastic and could not be case-bonded into a missile casing.[91]

In the alternative, composite propellant technology compounds such as urethane were combined with ammonium or potassium perchlorate oxidizer, allowing relatively fluid casting (followed by polymerization in place to form a rubbery solid). Because they could thus be case-bonded, these composite propellants allowed a greater amount of propellant to be loaded into a given volume, a particularly valuable feature for a volume-limited system like Polaris.[92] In late 1955 scientists working under a Navy Bureau of Ordnance contract at the Atlantic Research Corporation made an important breakthrough. By adding

51

large amounts of aluminium powder to the propellant they obtained a significant increase in specific impulse.[93] Aerojet Corporation was a leader in the manufacture of composite propellant and they built the rocket motors for both the first and second stages of the Polaris A1. Meanwhile, in the search for higher specific impulse, SPO also sponsored continuing research on castable double base type propellants with the Hercules-Allegany Ballistics Laboratory team.[94]

The propellant used for both stages of the Polaris A1 comprised polyurethane with ammonium perchlorate oxidizer and aluminium additives. Aerojet cast this composite propellant into steel cases for the first Polaris missiles. Simple in concept, each missile casing nevertheless needed to be relatively heavy to cope with the high pressures created by the burning propellant. To meet these demands whilst improving weldability a low-alloy steel was specially developed for Polaris.[95] By reducing the weight of the cases and increasing the specific impulse of the propellant, further increases could be achieved in missile range.

However, for the first Polaris, range increases were not crucial once about 900 nautical miles had been obtained – that was enough to demonstrate feasibility and consolidate the FBM programme. Methods of controlling the direction of the thrust vector and of terminating thrust were more critical, if the purported deterrence role of threatening Soviet cities was to seem credible. Without thrust vector control the missile could not be guided as required by the guidance system. The preliminary flight tests indicated that a number of approaches might be feasible. The chosen solution was the 'jetevator', invented by the former V1 scientist, Dr Willy Fiedler, who was then working for Lockheed.

The jetevator was basically a solid ring with a spherical inside surface which was hinged over the rocket nozzle. When turned into the exhaust stream it deflected the flow. The two Polaris A1 stages each had four nozzles with jetevators to provide pitch, yaw, and roll. Nevertheless, the corrosive nature of the exhaust stream, and its high content of aluminium oxide, led to considerable problems in getting the jetevators to work reliably during the static motor tests.[96] The solution was to remove the seals so that oxide build-up would not impair jetevator movement. However, this allowed more flame 'blow back' and the consequent over-heating would lead to a major problem (known as 'Hot Foot') during the flight tests.[97]

The other critical issue was thrust termination. The whole purpose of the rocket stages was to bring the payload – the warhead and reentry vehicle – to a certain velocity at a point in space where it would fall ballistically to its target. Just as the missile reached the desired velocity its second stage rocket needed to be turned off instantaneously. This was a relatively easy task in liquid-fuel missiles, but not in solid-fuel ones. One way of doing this would have been simply to blow the nozzles off, so causing a rapid drop in pressure that would extinguish the motor, but with such large motors it would be difficult to make this reliable for all the conceivable ranges and the large shock wave caused was felt likely to be too damaging.[98]

That and various other conceptual methods of thrust termination lost out to a system in which vents were opened at the front of the second stage – the escaping exhaust gases causing it to reverse acceleration at the time of separation from the payload. Six ports were built into the front of each second stage with plugs that could be pyrotechnically removed when required.

Lockheed also had responsibility for developing the payload carried by Polaris. Livermore's predicted small warhead needed a protective shield to prevent damage during atmospheric reentry. With payload weight critical because of its large effect on range, it was decided that the only way to keep the payload sufficiently light would be to integrate the warhead and reentry system.[99] Current design practice, as used in the other ballistic missile programmes, was to build the warhead and reentry shield as separate entities. Headed by Lt. Robert Wertheim, the reentry section of SP-27 coordinated this work, with Lockheed responsible for reentry body design, Livermore for warhead design, and the Naval Ordnance Laboratory, White Oak, for arming and fusing devices.[100]

Designed to be integral with the warhead – that is, to share structural and functional components[101] – the reentry body needed to be able to protect it from the rigours of atmospheric reentry. The choice had to be made between the two main technical approaches to this challenge. The approach then favoured by the Army, and used in the Jupiter IRBM, was to dissipate reentry heating by the *ablation*, or 'burning off' of the outer layers of the reentry vehicle. The Air Force, on the other hand, initially favoured *heat sink* reentry vehicles whose metallic construction simply absorbed the heat. Although they later moved to ablative reentry vehicles for ICBMs the Air Force used the heat sink type in their Thor IRBM.[102] SPO also chose to use a heat sink design for Polaris, probably because of the level of integration that Lockheed and Livermore were able to offer using beryllium (something that could not be done with an ablative design). It also looked likely to require less flight testing to validate the design. As Admiral Smith recalls:

53

> The Jupiter reentry system was an ablative cooling system, as opposed to a heat sink, and the estimates that had been made by Bothwell and later updated by Lockheed were also based on that ablative cooling assumption. There's no doubt that it's ... proven a very efficient, weight efficient method of disposing of the heat generated in reentry. However, as I saw it, at least, it has the disadvantage that the amount of ablative material cannot be reasonably validated without flight tests. ... So when Lockheed ... proposed a quite different shape, and a heat sink approach, which could much more reasonably be calculated ... I favoured that approach.[103]

A problem then with heat sink designs was 'the extreme aerodynamic heating associated with high-speed reentry of streamlined, slender cones'.[104] To avoid this most reentry vehicles at the time were blunt designs whose slower descent reduced heating, but also made them more susceptible to wind drift inaccuracy.[105]

Teller's critical warhead prediction had in fact been something of a 'guesstimate' and Livermore were unable to meet the original yield goal in time for Polaris A1 deployment (though by then, admittedly, this had been brought forward from when Teller had committed to). However, the megaton goal was not considered critical at SPO, whereas schedule was.

The Polaris design came out of a programme, code-named TUBA, already underway at the Livermore laboratory. Instigated by Livermore's first director Herbert York, this had as its objective 'the lightest-weight thermonuclear warhead we could figure out how to build'.[106] According to one of the Livermore team, the Polaris warhead was based on one major breakthrough and about four other important new ideas.[107] The greatest advance in yield-to-weight ratio came from Teller's suggestion, obvious enough in retrospect, to use highly enriched uranium or 'oralloy' in place of the unenriched uranium that was then standard for the third stage of the fission-fusion-fission design of thermonuclear devices. The weapons design mentality of the immediate post-war period – of Los Alamos, in effect – was to make the limited amounts of fissile material carefully go as far as possible; thus the practice of encasing a thermonuclear device with unenriched uranium to get a bonus of extra fission. However, if this was replaced with oralloy the yield could be that much higher for the same weight. This 'breakthrough' required no great technical expertise or ingenuity to conceive, simply a different 'mindset'.

In July 1957 the Atomic Energy Commission detonated an experimental warhead design which confirmed the general feasibility of a Polaris warhead.[108] By the time Polaris A1 was first deployed in 1960 a yield of the order of half a megaton had been achieved in the W-47 warhead.[109] This comfortably exceeded SPO's internal minimum satisfactory yield of 300 kilotons.[110]

Consequently, SPO achieved their goal of a warhead/reentry body combination weighing less than 900 pounds.[111] Whilst other services were combining warheads weighing some 1500 pounds with reentry vehicles to give total weights over 3000 pounds, Teller's promised warhead was of the order of 600 pounds, which when designed into an integral reentry body produced a total weight of about 850 pounds.[112] This was designed to be ejected from the second stage motor at the time of thrust termination by an airspring. A flare section attached to the rear of the reentry body provided 'aerodynamic damping at reentry and stabilization during descent', and contained two small rocket motors which spun the reentry body to provide stability and symmetry during reentry.[113]

However, although the Polaris payload was an innovative success, it was not without problems. Just prior to the nuclear test moratorium which began in October 1958 Livermore conducted a 'one-point' safety test on the W-47, which surprisingly gave a yield of about 100 tons.[114] Because the moratorium prevented the tests considered necessary to develop a design that was inherently one-point safe, a mechanical safing system was incorporated. This was simply a spool of wire inserted in the plutonium 'pit' which thus prevented a one-point nuclear detonation.[115] In 1963 it was discovered that this failed to operate satisfactorily in that it would stick or break when withdrawal was attempted, thus resulting in a dud.[116] A cure was devised, but doubts remained about whether it would prove fully successful after the ageing of components.[117] A further consequence of the mechanical safing device was that oil used to lubricate it led to corrosion of the plutonium pit.[118]

SUBMARINE CONSTRUCTION

Getting submarines ready to carry Polaris was the responsibility of the ship installation branch of SPO, SP-26. There were three main aspects to this work. Primarily, of course, submarines had to be designed and built. Second, all the various subsystems had to be coordinated to ensure that they interfaced correctly with each other and with the submarine platform. Thirdly, these subsystems had to be installed into the submarine.

When the missile development was accelerated in December 1957 it was decided that the long development time of an all-new FBM submarine would delay deployment. On 30 December, Electric Boat were awarded a contract for the design and construction of the first submarine, the *George Washington*, which was in fact a conversion of an attack submarine, the *Scorpion*, already under construction.[119] In essence, a missile section was inserted between the bow and stern that Electric Boat were already building.

With submarine construction already the jurisdiction of the Bureau of Ships, SP-26 had a rather different and potentially more difficult role than the other technical branches, who could deal directly with contractors under freshly instigated arrangements. Whereas guidance, navigation, launcher, and missile developments were assigned to 'prime contractors' all keen for new business and willing to match the new technology with new management approaches,[120] SP-26 had to deal with BuShips bureaucracy and the traditional management techniques of their construction companies. To make matters potentially even more fraught, nuclear-powered vessels required BuShips themselves to work together with Admiral Hyman Rickover, whose power derived not only from his technical expertise and position as head of the Navy's Nuclear Propulsion Directorate, but also from his other role as director of the AEC's Naval Reactors Branch and his strong support in Congress.

However, at this crucial stage in the submarine development Rickover's ability to interfere was minimized by the fact that the first FBM submarines were modifications of existing designs, as well as by Burke's firm control. In any case SPO were able tő convince him that his interests (getting nuclear power into the US Navy) were closely tied to the success of the Polaris submarines.[121] Indeed Rickover's technical prowess and drive made him a formidable ally in the construction of the first Polaris submarines, once the danger of him attempting to alter the design had been alleviated. Submarine work began in January 1958 using funds 'borrowed' from other Navy programmes as official funding had to wait for the FY58 Supplemental Appropriations Act which was only signed by the President on 12 February.[122] Although the construction of the first FBM submarine, the *George Washington*, was 'plagued by scores of mistakes' and 'many goofs' it was still completed at the Electric Boat yard on schedule and launched on 9 June 1959.[123] However, the schedule was only met by taking to sea an incomplete weapon system. The fire control system was not ready in time so it was simply omitted and installed some months later after the politically important launch date had been met.[124]

TESTING POLARIS

During 1957 and 1958 flight tests continued using an assortment of available rocket boosters to assess the chosen methods of thrust termination and thrust vector control, and to investigate reentry vehicle thermodynamics. A total of twenty-two of these FTV (flight test vehicle) flights were carried out.[125] In September 1958 the first of seventeen Polaris prototype AX series test flights began, with initially not very impressive results.

The first took off satisfactorily, but continued to climb vertically, apparently because of a malfunction in the autopilot programmer used in place of the inertial guidance system.[126] In the second test flight the first stage rocket malfunctioned and never left the pad, though the second stage did! AX-3 and AX-4 demonstrated erratic behaviour during the first-stage flight, caused by overheating at the base of the stage and consequent malfunction of electrical wiring. This led to an intensive investigation to understand the problem, 'Operation Hot Foot', and to corrective changes involving extra heat-shielding in 'Operation Phoenix' which had remedied it by AX-6.[127] Of the seventeen AX flights, five were classed as successful, eleven partially successful, and one (AX-2) as a failure.[128] 'Partial success' was, however, something of an SPO euphemism since any test that returned some useful data was not considered a complete failure.[129] Four of the successes reached ranges of about 700 nautical miles.[130]

In September 1959 the A1X flight tests began – using hardware very similar to that of the Polaris A1 missile later deployed. The MIT inertial guidance system was first introduced in January 1960 and from flight A1X-14 onwards the hardware flown was 'substantially the same as the production design except for the added instrumentation and range safety provisions'.[131] Forty A1X flight tests were carried out with twenty-eight evaluated as complete successes, eleven as partially successful, and only one a complete failure.[132] The main problems were failure in thrust termination (and the second stage thus bumping the reentry body) and deterioration of the second stage nozzles.[133] Ranges reached went from around 900 nautical miles in the earlier tests to around 1000 nautical miles later on. Two successful medium range tests, to about 665 nautical miles, were also carried out.[134]

A1X-31, however, was a particularly important test, the first from a submerged submarine. On 20 July 1960 it was launched successfully to a range of about a thousand miles from the *George Washington*. About three hours later a second Polaris missile was launched, again with complete success. After many set-backs SPO could breathe a sigh of relief. Admiral Burke's faith in the Polaris project had been justified. The Polaris concept was now technology, and it worked!

5 SUCCESS AND SUCCESSORS

> This is not an ultimate missile here. We are going to keep improving
> this missile as we go along, even after it is first installed in the ships,
> so we are not going to get an ultimate missile and stop.
>
> Admiral Burke.[1]

Polaris A1 became operational on 15 November 1960, when the submarine *George Washington* left Charleston, South Carolina, to patrol the
Norwegian Sea. Then on 31 January 1961 the second FBM submarine,
the *Patrick Henry*, went on patrol. Each carried sixteen Polaris A1
missiles capable of delivering a nuclear warhead over a range of about
a thousand miles to within a few miles of the intended target. Polaris
seemed to be an indisputable success.

THE SOCIAL CONSTRUCTION OF SUCCESS

Within four years SPO had developed and deployed a complex new
type of weapon system which provided a threat of potential retaliation against Soviet cities, but which itself seemed invulnerable. This
success owed much to the skill and dedication of the people who
worked on the programme. In particular SPO demonstrated great skill
in managing *both* the 'technical' and 'social' aspects of technology.
Moreover, within certain limits they were able to 'engineer' the expectations that Polaris had to meet just as well as the technology that met
them.

Schedule was paramount, with a sense of urgency generated not
only by concern about the need to counter possible Soviet developments, but also to establish a Navy right to ballistic missiles before the
Air Force achieved the hegemony it clearly desired. To meet the
schedule other system parameters could be traded off. Thus the A1
initially fell somewhat short of the 1200 mile range goal, carried a
warhead with a yield about half the 1 megaton goal, and had less than
50 per cent reliability.[2] None of these trade-offs mattered because SPO
was able to argue that Polaris A1 still provided a useful interim

deterrent capability. Likewise SPO set a pattern for future systems by agreeing to an accuracy figure as a *goal* and not as a *requirement*.

For the original Polaris this goal was 'a couple of miles CEP . . . about the size of a city' which at the start of the programme seemed to many to be 'probably . . . unobtainable' because of the then state-of-the-art of ship navigation.[3] Even a 4 mile CEP would have been considered satisfactory, but participants recollect that accuracy goals were met 'as far as we could tell'.[4] Polaris A1 probably averaged an accuracy better than 2 miles. But at the time, before the geodetic mapping carried out using Transit, knowledge of the precise location of targets was itself a major inaccuracy. For example, in 1959, before Transit, knowledge of 'the location of Australia was wrong by several thousand meters'.[5]

What mattered was demonstrating feasibility: that it could be built, that the components would function individually and collectively. Within broad limits its precise characteristics, such as accuracy, mattered less than this overall question of whether it would, in a general sense, 'work'. If the CEP of Polaris A1 had turned out to be 10 miles, or 20 miles, then it might have been judged a failure, but anything under 5 miles was quite adequate. The Naval Warfare Analysis Group's first study of the FBM, distributed in 1957 January emphasized the flexibility of performance characteristics: 'Requirements for yield and accuracy should be subordinated to early availability of the weapon.'[6]

This relaxed attitude to accuracy, as to other performance criteria that were not considered critical, helped ensure the success of the programme. SPO realized the importance of demonstrating feasibility on schedule, and avoided any unnecessary 'requirements'. To meet schedule, as Harvey Sapolsky has noted: 'Performance was a manipulatable variable in the Polaris program.'[7] Moreover, whilst SPO was developing the weapon that would provide an 'assured destruction' retaliatory threat to cities, Admiral Burke and others were developing the strategic logic that would require it. High accuracy looked to be beyond foreseeable technology in a sea-based ballistic missile and so it was not required.

However, the success of Polaris cannot be attributed entirely to the heterogeneous engineering of its proponents, highly skilled though this was. Polaris also benefited from the wider social context of the day, a context which partly lay beyond the influence of SPO and their collaborators. Polaris was also a success because its need was perceived to be so great and so urgent at the time. But the national paranoia following Sputnik was something which would probably have occurred if SPO and the Polaris programme had not existed. Similarly,

59

Senator Kennedy's exploitation of the 'missile gap' reflected his political agenda.

Nor did the success of Polaris go completely unchallenged. During its development there had been criticism from Air Force sources suggesting that the FBM concept was beyond the state-of-the-art in technology, especially in the area of submarine navigation.[8] By attacking the feasibility of Polaris the Air Force sought to counter the challenge that it constituted to their control over strategic weaponry: 'The Air Force could see a fight ahead for dollars that formerly had "Air Force" written all over them. Therefore, the Air Force missed few opportunities to remind the administration that Polaris was unproved.'[9]

But as Polaris tests progressed the credibility of the mainstream arguments against its feasibility began to weaken. Although the validity of the tests, and what they actually demonstrated, remained open to question, in practice the Air Force could not question them without raising the same doubts about its own comparable ICBM and IRBM testing. Even in the area of navigation – where the technical challenge *was* significantly different for a sea-based system – Navy demonstrations provided convincing evidence that adequate accuracy could be achieved. And, of course, Burke and SPO were promulgating a strategic doctrine in which 'adequate accuracy' to threaten urban-industrial targets was not only sufficient, but even preferable to 'pinpoint' accuracy.

By carefully differentiating their targeting doctrine from that of the Air Force, Polaris supporters thus made irrelevant such doubts raised by the Air Force about the ability of Polaris to destroy hardened military targets: 'It is still unclear, however, how efficient the low-payload Polaris will be against hardened targets, for no prototype missile has yet been fired, nor has the radically new ship's inertial navigation system – crucial to accurate firing – been perfected.'[10] By instead stressing the counter-city role of Polaris – retaliation against large, 'soft' targets – it was possible to deflect such criticism. It also left the Air Force able to justify its ICBM and bomber forces by reference to their primary counterforce mission (hence their concentration on improving ICBM hard target effectiveness from the early 1960s on), and so reduced their need to criticize Polaris. This did not stop the interservice fight over ballistic missile control and funding, but it differentiated the Air Force and Navy programmes sufficiently to allow neither side to lose out completely as they could be seen as complementary rather than direct competitors.

Indeed the attempt during 1959 and 1960 by the Air Force to obtain jurisdiction over Polaris was a tacit acceptance of its technical feasibility and strategic legitimacy. Technical criticism specific to a sea-based ballistic missile was laid to rest largely by a RAND Corporation analysis of Polaris produced in October 1958 in response to an air staff request for a 'factual and unbiased assessment'.[11] (But see below for continued opposition to *all* ballistic missiles by Air Force bomber stalwarts.) At about the same time the Air Force also decided to go ahead with a solid-fuel missile, the Minuteman, thus tacitly accepting the feasibility of solid fuel for ballistic missile use.[12] Thereafter, the Air Force's attitude to Polaris centered on the targeting issue. Burke's minimum deterrence, counter-city strategy was actively criticized as the Air Force sought to justify its own preference for counterforce.[13] But at the same time Strategic Air Command leaders sought to gain control of Polaris by proposing the integration of all US strategic forces for the purpose of coordinating targeting.

This, of course, met fierce resistance, as a 'high ranking' naval officer remarked: 'Polaris is perhaps the most attractive missile system under development. . . . Of course they want control of Polaris. But they will have to walk over a prostrate Arleigh Burke to get it.'[14] The takeover attempt did not succeed, but the Air Force move did result in the coordination of targeting into a Single Integrated Operational Plan (SIOP) in 1960. Since the Joint Strategic Target Planning Staff set up to produce the SIOP was dominated by Strategic Air Command officers it effectively settled the interservice argument over targeting.[15] The SIOP embodied the Air Force belief in a massive (and preferably preemptive) attack against the complete range of counterforce and urban-industrial targets. Air Force criticism of Polaris was now muted though the much vaunted invulnerability of Polaris was still publicly questioned by the Air Force.

In contrast to the previous decade the early 1960s saw the Air Force very much on the defensive, attempting to protect their budget share from the rationalization plans of President Kennedy's new Secretary of Defense, Robert McNamara. The main focus of Air Force/Navy competition shifted to the issue of cost-effectiveness which now came to dominate Pentagon thinking.[16] Now that the reputations of SPO and Polaris were established, Navy support for the proposed B-70 bomber was no longer forthcoming in 1961 and it was cancelled despite attempts to sell it as an alternative mobile ballistic missile basing system for the Skybolt air-launched ballistic missile.[17] Likewise the Air Force pushed the mobile Minuteman in an attempt to compete on the invulnerability issue: 'The railroad-based Minuteman . . . could elude the enemy in the event of hostilities and avoid a first strike in the same way that the Navy's Polaris missile submarines can evade detection.'[18]

The Air Force argued that their new Minuteman ICBMs would be much cheaper to deploy than Polaris. According to McNamara's own figures in 1961 the cost for each Polaris missile on station would be $9.7 million, whereas a mobile Minuteman would cost $5.0 million, and a fixed-base Minuteman only $3.2 million.[19] SPO countered this by stressing that the invulnerability of Polaris made it more cost-effective than Minuteman and that Polaris was already available, whereas Minuteman had yet to be tested. Doubts about whether the Air Force would deliver Minuteman on cost and schedule were also echoed by budget director Stans:

> we were not quite certain that the development of the Minuteman could be successfully accomplished with the level of costs estimated by the Air Force. Or whether or not the timetable could be wholly relied upon. And finally, we had no estimate of the cost of hardening the Minuteman system that we could rely upon.[20]

Polaris was also looked on very favourably within McNamara's OSD, where it came out well in the cost-effectiveness calculations.[21] Herbert York, the first Director of Defense Research and Engineering, who stayed on briefly from the Eisenhower administration, considered 'Polaris to be one of the really well run programs in the Defense Department'.[22] Although the Kennedy administration soon admitted that preelection rhetoric about the 'missile gap' was erroneous, it remained politically expedient to bolster strategic forces.[23] Polaris became a major beneficiary of this. The Air Force alternatives were considered either somewhat obsolete already (the liquid-fuel Atlas and Titan ICBMs) or unproven (the solid-fuel Minuteman). Although a Minuteman force of 1000 was approved by McNamara, this fell far short of Air Force demands, and the mobile Minuteman was first deferred and then cancelled in December 1961.

However, following the successful test flights of Polaris and of other US ballistic missiles, a different, more general challenge to their feasibility emerged. A group of critics, centered around Air Force bomber officers, began to argue that although the flight tests might demonstrate the feasibility of certain components under test conditions, they did not demonstrate the effectiveness of the system under 'real' operational conditions.

In what was apparently an attempt to settle this question, the Navy carried out a 'live' test of a Polaris A1 on 6 May 1962 – the only such test performed by a US ballistic missile. Known as 'Operation Frigate Bird' this involved launching a missile from the *Ethan Allen* over 1000 miles to the nuclear testing ground at Christmas Island. The test was considered a resounding success, and was reported to have hit 'right in the pickle barrel' exploding with a yield estimated at half a megaton.[24]

Ironically this was the W-47 warhead incorporating the faulty mechanical safing device which was later estimated to have perhaps a 50 per cent chance of producing a dud.

In any case the 'Frigate Bird' test did not entirely mollify missile critics and the Partial Test Ban Treaty signed in 1963 prevented a repeat. Public criticism of ballistic missile reliability continued through 1964 with both Senator Barry Goldwater (an Air Force reserve Major General who had 'long identified himself with the bomber faction')[25] and Air Force Chief of Staff (and former head of SAC) General Curtis LeMay voicing their doubts. However, such criticisms were difficult to sustain when many of the main critics were also institutionally committed to ICBMs. As Air Force Chief of Staff, LeMay was at the same time arguing for a force of several thousand Minuteman ICBMs. In the end the argument over whether ballistic missiles would actually work lost credibility not because tests proved that they would, but because these influential critics ceased to argue that they would not.

The success of Polaris was thus not simply a technical matter. Whether the missiles would actually work in a nuclear war was, *and is*, an issue that can always be questioned in principle.[26] It depends what is meant by 'work'. In practice, however, SPO developed an unrivalled reputation for producing what they had committed themselves to. If any US ballistic missile was going to work then SPO's impressive managerial style and avoidance of technical over-elaboration suggested that it would be Polaris. But Polaris A1 was only SPO's first step in the development and establishment of the FBM system.

POLARIS A2

The Polaris A2 was developed almost simultaneously with the A1, with the understanding that the A1 schedule was paramount. Meeting this schedule resulted in a production missile which fell short of the range and warhead yield initially hoped for, and which had low reliability.[27] It had 'worked' very effectively, in that it had demonstrated the feasibility of the concept and staked out the Navy's claim to it. But its reliability was not considered very good, as one Lockheed manager recalled:

> [the] Polaris A1 propulsion system was inherently not reliable. ...
> Polaris A1 was a vehicle that had been designed to be flight tested by engineers. It was then turned over to the Navy as a weapon. It demanded, but you couldn't give it, tender loving care in all electrical connections. And so it had electrical failures, no one failure mode predominating, that is no one area predominating, just lots of them.

... A1 was a hell of a fine weapon considering the circumstances in which it was done but it was not acceptable when it was possible to have the A2.[28]

The main changes in A2 were a new second stage to provide longer range, an improvement of the warhead design to provide slightly greater yield, and more reliable electronics. Originally the increased range was to have been achieved by increasing propellant energy and reducing inert weight throughout the missile. However, the much greater effect of improvements in the second stage, coupled with a conservative attitude to changing too much of the design at once, led to a decision to retain basically the same technology in the first stage, with an alternative second stage design. The first stage was simply increased some thirty inches over the A1 first stage to take advantage of space originally set aside for the launcher's buoyancy compensation tanks, but used the same propellant formulation and case construction as in A1.

The alternative higher performance second stage was the result of work that SPO had sponsored at the Hercules run, government-owned Allegany Ballistics Laboratory. This had come about because Admiral Raborn had wanted a backup for the original Polaris. Technical Director Levering Smith had then argued that the backup 'should be different in every respect. It should have a completely different approach to the propellant, have a completely different approach to the case, and the thrust vector control system should be different.'[29] A double base (nitrocellulose/nitroglycerine) propellant using ammonium perchlorate oxidizer and aluminium fuel was developed that could be cast into rocket cases. Full-scale development was given the go-ahead in June 1958.[30]

Hercules Powder Co. were also responsible for pioneering the development of fibre-glass as a rocket case material. This was said to have been originally stimulated by fear that a pending strike at the steel producer would jeopardize the programme.[31] Fibre-glass also appeared to offer higher strength-to-weight ratios than steel. Development of the second stage chamber for the Polaris A2 was started in 1958, with the first flight in November 1960.[32]

The alternative approach also involved a new method of thrust vector control. This sought to overcome the problems that the jetevator had experienced, to reduce the inert weight of the vector control system and minimize the loss of axial thrust in steering.[33] Out of the several concepts investigated, a rotatable nozzle design, similar to that already proving successful in the Air Force Minuteman ICBM programme, was chosen for use in the second stage.[34] Thrust termination

Length (feet)	31.0
Nominal range (nautical miles)	1500
Weight at launch (1000s of lbs)	32.5
Year first deployed	1962
No. of warheads	1
Yield per warhead (kilotons)	800
	[W-47]
Guidance system	Mk. 1
Approximate accuracy	2
(circular error probable, nautical miles)	

Figure 5.1 Polaris A-2

ports were incorporated into the second stage in a steel ring which was woven into the forward dome of the stage.

Polaris A2 was initially deployed with the half megaton W-47 warhead (known as W-47-Y1), but this was later replaced by a W-47-Y2 with a yield close to the original 1 megaton goal.[35] This upgrade was obtained during the 1958–62 nuclear test moratorium by replacing the secondary device (the fusion part of a hydrogen bomb) of the existing design, but this version of the W-47 still incorporated the faulty mechanical safing device.[36] The problem was eventually remedied by the replacement of the warhead primary in 1967 in the W-47-Y2 Mk. 3.[37]

Thus the A2 provided very similar, but slightly enhanced perform- ance as compared to A1. But whereas 'the thing that drove A1 was to get there as soon as possible, the thing that drove A2 was improve the reliability'.[38] Both were considered to have the same strategic mission, to target Soviet cities and hold them to ransom against communist aggression by the threat of retaliatory devastation. A2 was what the Navy had originally promised to provide for this purpose, but A1 allowed them to provide a lesser, but conceptually similar, capability sooner.

Flight-testing of A2X missiles began in November 1960. Out of a total of twenty-eight flight tests, nineteen were considered successes, six as partial successes, and three as failures.[39] The first successful submerged launch of the A2 was from the *Ethan Allen* on 23 October 1961, and the A2 became operational in June 1962.[40] With the increased range it was now possible for Polaris submarines deployed in the Mediterranean to threaten Soviet targets, and patrols there were announced in March 1963.[41]

POLARIS A3

With the A1 and A2 programmes on schedule, SPO had begun to consider another generation of Polaris in 1959. Initially the obvious approach seemed simply to increase the range yet further and to use a larger warhead, as was desired by a faction in the Office of the Chief of Naval Operations, who favoured attempting to match the counter-force role of the Air Force ICBMs.[42]

However, a number of factors militated against this option. Firstly, the nuclear test moratorium still prevented testing of new warhead designs, and a larger warhead was only available as an adaptation of one designed for Air Force use, or by scaling up a smaller yield design. Secondly, the Soviet Union (like the United States) had started the development of anti-ballistic missile systems which were intended to provide some defence against ballistic missile attack by intercepting them in flight. As concern grew over what was perceived to be an ABM system known as the Tallin network some provisions were made to carry penetration aids on the already deployed Polaris A2 missiles.

Lockheed was awarded a contract in November 1961 for 'pen-aids' known as PX-1 to increase the penetrability of the Mk. 1 reentry body. Twelve flight tests were carried out between July and December 1962 and 221 complete kits were produced between July 1963 and July 1964. These kits comprised six decoys, mid-course chaff, and early reentry electronic jammers.[43]

PX-1 was considered to be successful. However, problems with reliability (the batteries tended to go flat), reduced missile range, and a general unwillingness to have differing missile configurations mixed into the FBM force meant that PX-1 was only ever deployed on a few submarines.[44] Instead Polaris A3 was to provide greater penetration against Tallin type defences.

SPO's design for the Polaris A3 provided a way of meeting the original 1 megaton goal of Polaris without using warhead designs that were either untested or of Air Force provenance. Instead of the single warhead/reentry body combination carried by Polaris A1/A2 and all other ballistic missiles of the time, SPO broke new ground in developing a multiple reentry vehicle (MRV) system. The warhead used was a 200 kiloton design which the Livermore laboratory had developed and tested prior to the moratorium.[45] Rear Admiral Robert

Wertheim, then chair of the reentry Committee of the Polaris Steering Task Group, recalled how the decision was made:

> During the winter of 1959, the STG conducted trade-off studies on how best to meet the performance objectives for A3 which included longer missile range to increase submarine survivability, an increase over the A1 warhead yield (to 1 MT) and minimum vulnerability to countermeasures. In the deliberations of the STG reentry Committee ... the choice came down to a scaled-up (but untestable) version of Tuba with conventional provisions for lightweight penetration aids, and a cluster of three warheads using the tested Tuba device and deployed in a pattern which multiplied the inherent probability of penetrating ABM defences while providing the equivalent of 1 MT in effects on a typical urban-industrial area target in the absence of effective defences. The debate between the two was a spirited one, with our AEC laboratory members favoring the former and Dr Lloyd Wilson, our Lockheed member arguing for the latter. It could have gone either way, but in my mind the inability to confirm a calculated warhead performance in full scale test was an important factor in tilting the scales.[46]

So the A3 missile was designed to carry three of the 200 kiloton warheads (later designated W-58),[47] providing an equivalent mega-tonnage roughly the same as a single 1 megaton warhead.[48] The counter-city role was clear as the design of the separation of the three warheads from the missile created a triangular impact pattern that would cause the destructive overpressure considered necessary to flatten buildings – seven pounds per square inch – over an area as large as that created by a single 1 megaton bomb.[49]

A new reentry body, the Mk. 2, was developed to carry the W-58, giving a combined weight of about 300 pounds. This differed sig-nificantly from the Mk. 1, using a 'nylon-phenolic ablative heat shield' over an aluminium structure instead of a heat sink design.[50] The reason for this was that at the longer 2500 mile range of the A3, heat sink reentry bodies needed to be increasingly larger to absorb the extra heat of reentry, and consequently the lower weight (not to mention lower expense) of ablative designs became more attractive.[51] Moreover, with the Polaris A1 and A2 deployed, schedule was no longer quite so urgent and by now the ablative approach had been validated, not only by continuing SPO sponsored research and flight tests, but also by Air Force and Army developments.[52] The original choice of ablative material was pyrolytic graphite, but when it appeared that development of this would not meet the A3 timescale, nylon phenolic was chosen instead. However, the eight test flights carried out in late 1961 and during 1962 with reconfigured A2 test missiles yielded little information on the performance of the new reentry bodies. Only one flight provided data on their flight characteristics, and although this was favourable, the decision to proceed was considered to be a bit 'iffy'.[53]

In the Polaris A3 design, the Mk. 2 reentry bodies would be released simultaneously from the missile when the correct velocity was reached to take them to their target area.[54] This separation was achieved by small high-thrust short-burning solid-fuel rockets which separated the reentry bodies from the missile second stage, and spun them (for accuracy and heat distribution at reentry).[55] The second stage simply carried on till burn out and the need for a thrust termination system was thus avoided in A3. This simplified the design of the second stage, probably increasing overall reliability, and provided a significant increase in range. It may also have introduced additions to inaccuracy,[56] but these were 'consistent with other weapon system error sources'.[57]

The angle of separation of the reentry bodies from the missile, and their velocities (each was different), were determined by the intended 'impact' pattern. This was based not only on the desired overpressure level, but also on the need to avoid fratricide, whereby the explosion of one warhead might prevent the nuclear detonation of another. Thus, on their arrival at the target, the reentry bodies were separated not only in distance (by approximately one nautical mile), but also in time (by about one second).[58] Each thus arrived after the initial radiation pulse of the previous one, but all would have detonated before blast would have caused disruption.

Another consideration in the design of the A3 MRV was concern about endo-atmospheric ABM developments, which could also be alleviated by this reentry body spacing. The current American state-of-the-art in ABM interceptors, the Army's Nike-Zeus missile, like the Tallin system the Soviets were believed to be constructing, was designed to destroy or disable reentry bodies within the atmosphere.[59] The separation used by Polaris A3 was large enough to prevent what was known as 'mutual kill' a single Nike-Zeus type warhead destroying or disabling more than one warhead with the radiation blast from its nuclear detonation.[60] As a continuation of the PX-1 work, a PX-2 penetration aid package was developed for Polaris A3, and tested during the A3X flight tests. A wide variety of different decoys were developed which were to be used with chaff, but electronic jammers were not considered worthwhile. Production was kept on standby and PX-2 was not deployed.[61]

In addition to the new payload, the other main concern of Polaris A3

Length (feet)	32.3
Nominal range (nautical miles)	2500
Weight at launch (1000s of lbs)	35.7
Year first deployed	1964
No. of warheads	3 [MRV]
Yield per warhead (kilotons)	200 [W-58]
Guidance system	Mk. 2
Approximate accuracy (circular error probable, nautical miles)	0.5

Figure 5.2 Polaris A-3

was increased range, with a goal of 2500 nautical miles set. This was not a figure arbitrarily imposed on SPO, but rather derived from their studies of the advantages of the greater operating area provided by increased range and of what seemed achievable.[62] Such an increase over the 1500 mile A2 looked possible because of the potential to reduce inert weight in the missile design whilst increasing both the amount and the specific impulse of the propellant. Moreover, there was confidence that the over-designed shock protection of the launcher system would allow a heavier missile to be accommodated.

A new approach to thrust vector control which cut down on inert weight used the injection of Freon into the nozzles to deflect the exhaust stream. This was first successfully demonstrated during the second stage flight of A1X-50 on 29 September 1961.[63] It was incorporated in the design of the A3 second stage, whereas the first stage now used rotatable nozzles. Both stages were built of fibreglass and utilized denser, higher specific impulse propellant formulations.

The higher temperatures involved (over 6000°F), along with the high pressure (800–900 psi), led to difficulties with the first stage. The composite propellant developed by Aerojet for this stage was apparently more corrosive than the Hercules/Allegany Ballistic Laboratories double-base propellant used in the second stage.[64] In early tests the first stage nozzles were destroyed and it was considered necessary to reduce the propellant burning temperature, and use more substantial nozzles, thus sacrificing about 90 nautical miles in range.[65] The final A3 first stage design used silver-infiltrated tungsten nozzle throats.[66]

A new guidance system, the Mk. 2, was developed, and flight tested on A2 missiles starting in November 1961.[67] To meet SPO's range goal the missile contractor, Lockheed, wanted a much smaller and lighter system. 'SP-23 [SPO's guidance and fire control branch] wanted to separate the inertial measurement unit (IMU) and the electronics assembly (EA) to simplify the contractual structure and the shipment of the two parts. Lockheed enthusiastically agreed since this greatly simplified placement of the guidance system in the limited space in the missile.'[68] Altogether the Mk. 2 was about half the size and one third the weight of the Mk. 1. Redesign of its physical structure contributed to this with the large bar beryllium gimbals replaced by smaller spherical aluminium gimbals. The pressure from Lockheed to save weight also led to the choice of magnesium for the stable member on which the inertial components were mounted. Distortion of this magnesium due to internal corrosion was to be a source of future concern for those Mk. 2 guidance systems kept in service by the UK Royal Navy.[69] Much smaller resolvers were also used in the Mk. 2 and a higher density of electronics packaging was achieved by the first use of 'cordwood' welded (rather than soldered) construction in a missile.[70]

In addition the Mk. 2 used smaller accelerometers (16-size – 1.6 inch diameter – rather than 25-size). Moreover, the PIGAs, pendulous integrating gyro accelerometers, were replaced with PIPAs, pulsed integrating pendulous accelerometers, on all but the most sensitive thrust axis. Unlike the PIGA with its gyro wheel and internal gimbal, the PIPA consists simply of a pendulum which is held in null position by pulses sent from a signal generator to an electromagnetic torquer. A PIPA is therefore smaller than a PIGA, and is also generally acknowledged to be a simpler, easier to produce and therefore cheaper device – although one that does not match the accuracy of the best PIGAs.[71]

Nevertheless, accuracy improvements were sought in the Mk. 2 guidance system, and indeed were necessary if the missile was to be as accurate as its predecessors at the longer range.[72] But improvements in technology were incorporated only in so much as they fitted the strategic and organizational goals of the programme. Increasing the missile's range, and giving it the capability to penetrate anticipated ABM defences, seemed a natural development of a counter-city ultimate deterrent. The increase in accuracy was more a consequence of lessons learned in developing the original Polaris than a sign of a major shift to a new strategic role or any abandonment of 'differentiation' of Navy technology from that of the Air Force.

There were voices calling for just that, but they do not appear to have swayed the leadership of SPO. Thus Charles Stark Draper had argued as early as 1959, in a paper to the Polaris Steering Task Group,

70

that 'fleet ballistic missiles offer many well-known advantages, but will surely be handicapped in competition for national support unless they can be fired with accuracy levels comparable to those of land-based missiles'.[73] But, despite the desire of some in the Navy to make Polaris A3 'a warfighting machine',[74] this line of argument did not win the day. SPO did not attempt to compete with the Air Force in the accuracy stakes, and the improvements that did occur remained in the context of an assured destruction weapon. Polaris A3 was more effective than its predecessors against military targets, but only large, unhardened ones.

Two new FBM guidance technologies were developed, but not used. One, a much smaller system, called MIGIT, could have been used in a smaller missile (either for torpedo tube use or multiple packaging in the launch tube) or for reentry body guidance. The other was a strapdown guidance system 'to duplicate the Mk. 2 mission requirements'.[75] As the name implies, in a strapdown system the gyroscopes and accelerometers are held in fixed relation to the body of the missile. Mechanically this is much simpler, therefore presumably cheaper and more reliable, than the conventional stable platform design. Maintenance would be greatly simplified, as defective components could be 'unbolted' and replaced, no easy task in the complex, tightly packed gimbal structure of a stable platform.

Strapdown does, however, place greater demands on some of the guidance system components. The gyroscopes experience, and have to measure reliably, much greater rotation rates. Also much more computer power is required. In a stable platform system, the inertial components are kept in a known frame of reference physically. In strapdown, the analogous task is performed computationally. 'The lack of suitably fast computers to exploit fully strapdown advantages was the major technological barrier.'[76]

As computer capabilities improved during the 1960s, strapdown became a real option, and 'a substitution for Mk. 2 could have been made if desired'.[77] It was not. Although not (as an organization) necessarily committed to greater accuracy, SPO did not want a *less* accurate system, which might have been the case with strapdown, and there were worries about the calibration difficulties involved and a general reluctance to change unnecessarily.

A 2500 nautical miles Polaris had first become an official SPO objective in February 1959 when it was still referred to as Polaris C.[78] For a while, from May until August 1960 another programme objective was a Polaris A2 – using the Mk. 2 reentry system and guidance systems developed for the A3 – to be known as Polaris A2A.[79] Operational availability was planned for July 1964, about two years after that of the standard A2. In the end it was decided simply to go straight to the A3.

The A3X flight test programme ran from 7 August 1962 to 2 July 1964 with a total of thirty-eight flights. The main problem encountered involved failure of reentry body separation. The longest range achieved in these tests was 2284 nautical miles.[80] The first submerged launch was on 26 October 1963, and Polaris A3 was deployed on 28 September 1964, when the *Daniel Webster* began her first operational patrol.[81] Almost immediately, however, a development in the Soviet 'threat' raised questions about A3's effectiveness.

RESPONDING TO GALOSH

It became clear when the Soviet Galosh ABM system was displayed at a Red Square parade in Moscow in November 1964 and when its accompanying radars became operational, that the Soviet Union had not after all chosen to design an ABM similar to Nike-Zeus. Galosh was much larger, and clearly intended to carry a large warhead (exceeding a megaton) for interception outside the atmosphere. The Polaris penetration aids, which included chaff and decoys, were designed to cope with the wrong threat: 'they were all cut to the wrong frequencies, they were all too small to have been seen by these low frequency radars and they were spaced improperly to accommodate the large yield weapons effects ranges of the big warheads. So other than that everything was just fine!'[82]

The spacing of the Polaris A3 warheads was inadequate to prevent 'mutual kill' by exoatmospheric detonation of the large Galosh warhead.[83] Moreover, at about the same time a subpanel of the Air Force's Scientific Advisory Panel raised another potential vulnerability – the previously neglected issue of X-ray and gamma ray 'kill' of the missile booster.[84] Once considered, it became apparent that nuclear detonations outside the atmosphere could cause disabling damage to missile electronics at considerable distances. A Lockheed engineer recalls that:

> even back in the days of A3 without a post-boost vehicle, much of second stage flight is above the atmosphere, its in vacuum. We determined that someone could be setting off bombs on the moon we were so soft, that's how soft we were. Like cosmic radiation could almost drive us up the wall and so we hardened by factors of a thousand and made that whole problem go away . . .[85]

This was a particular concern for Air Force ICBMs because of what was known as the 'pindown' scenario whereby an ICBM silo field could be suppressed by periodic detonation of a single warhead high above it. In the case of the FBM submarines 'it was much harder to come up with a scenario, a credible scenario, that said that Polaris was threatened by the same thing'.[86] Nevertheless the Polaris A3 missile electronics were hardened in what was known as the 'Topsy' programme, and the original A3P missiles were replaced by the Topsy improved A3T version during the late 1960s.[87] In addition there was a modification developed for the A3 guidance system to provide some protection of the Mk. 2 guidance system electronics from the radiation effects of nuclear detonations. Intended to provide protection from both direct nuclear radiation and EMP (the electromagnetic pulse which can cause widespread damage to electrical equipment, especially from high-altitude detonations) this hardening was introduced along with the Topsy improvements.[88]

Other, more direct, responses to Galosh were developed but not deployed. Following the Pen-X committee's reappraisal of Soviet ABM defences, work began in early 1965 which was directed towards penetration of an exoatmospheric interceptor. In what was originally called 'Exo-PAC' one of the A3's reentry bodies was replaced with a penaid carrier (hence PAC). When ejected (along with the two remaining warheads) this reorientated and dispensed solid rocket powered penaids into several sectors on the null range. In other words, all these sectors (in the final version it was seven) would be positioned on a trajectory that would bring them to the same target area, one after the other.[89] Only one would contain the two reentry bodies, whereas the others would contain balloon-type decoys, and all would be masked with chaff. After releasing its penaids the dispenser would then fire another rocket motor to move it into a different sector from the reentry bodies. In addition, the two remaining reentry bodies were to be hardened to the effects of radiation in a programme known as Mark-up. The hardened reentry body was called the Mk. 2 Mod. 2 and the penaid dispenser was labelled Mk. 2 Mod. 3. In July 1965 Exo-PAC and Mark-up were combined to become the HEXO programme, and then in October this was combined with Topsy to be known as Antelope.

Antelope focused on improving survivability in nuclear environments during the launch and exoatmospheric phases of flight. Another programme, known as Impala, also included endoatmospheric penaids or 'twisters'. Impala was incorporated into Antelope in September 1966.[90] In all, sixteen test flights were carried out (including a few of Impala), mainly in the Pacific 'against' the Army's Safeguard radar at Kwajalein, with results that were considered successful.[91]

However, none of the responses to Galosh that were specifically geared towards ABM penetration were deployed.[92] Antelope, Impala, and Hexo were developed on an urgent basis, but as a backup to the next generation FBM system. As before there was little enthusiasm to begin complicating fleet operations with such modifications unless there was widespread Soviet ABM deployment. As Galosh only achieved limited deployment around Moscow, and penetration of those defences was assigned to the Minuteman ICBM and its penetration aids, it was decided that the penetration issue could be better solved with a specifically designed missile.[93] Apart from the Topsy hardening of the missile, the only other change introduced into Polaris A3 was a lofting capability to provide a steeper angle of reentry body descent.[94]

TRANSIT – THE NAVY NAVIGATION SATELLITE SYSTEM

Ironically, Project Transit, instigated to provide another source of navigational resets for the FBM submarines, was a direct outcome of the event which stimulated the acceleration of the Polaris programme – the launch of the Soviet Sputnik satellite. Whilst monitoring Sputnik's radio signal, scientists at the Applied Physics Laboratory (APL) of Johns Hopkins University had noted the Doppler effect produced. As with a train whistle the frequency of the signal recorded was higher as the satellite approached the listener and lower as it went away. It was realized that variation in the way the signal changed could be used to plot precisely the orbit taken by the satellite so long as the position of the listener was accurately known. The key insight in the development of Transit then came from Dr F. T. McClure of APL, who realized that it was possible to reverse the process. If the satellite's orbit was accurately known then the Doppler effect could be used to provide a listener with an accurate positional fix.

This was in March 1958 and by July APL was receiving the first of the funding for the development of a navigation satellite system in Project Transit. This came initially through the Advanced Research Projects Agency and then subsequently directly from SPO. As well as providing navigation fixes and geodetic information for military users, Transit would also become an extremely popular source of navigational fixes for non-military users. In 1981 about 10,000 Transit user sets were in use with about four-fifths owned and operated by non-military users.[95]

In May 1960 responsibility for Transit was formally transferred from

ARPA to SPO.[96] By then there had been two attempted satellite launches of Transit 1A and 1B. Transit 1A was launched on 17 September 1959 by a Thor Able rocket from Cape Canaveral. However, the third stage rocket failed to ignite and consequently it and the satellite reentered the atmosphere rather prematurely. Nevertheless, the data obtained during this twenty minute 'partial orbit' confirmed the predictions made for the Doppler tracking concept.[97]

Transit 1B was successfully launched into orbit on 13 April 1960. Amongst other information it provided confirmation of the earth's pear shape and highlighted the inadequacy of current knowledge of the earth's gravitational field for prediction of satellite orbits.[98] Such prediction was, of course, essential for Transit's navigational role by which receivers would determine their own position by monitoring the Doppler shift from a satellite of 'known' orbit. The technique used in Transit required a memory device carried on the satellites which was updated with its predicted orbit from the ground tracking station every twelve hours. The satellite then broadcast this information so that users could obtain their navigation fix.

It was recognized very early in the Transit programme that more accurate geodetic knowledge was required to predict the satellites' orbits with the desired accuracy. Richard Kershner, Director of the Transit programme at APL noted in May 1961 that: 'Meeting the ultimate program goals for Transit thus requires considerable improvement in the present knowledge of these factors (roughly the shape and mass distribution of the earth). This is the primary remaining development challenge of the Transit program.'[99] Thus in the early 1960s accurate geodetic mapping was the primary role of Transit, without which its 'ultimate' goal could not be achieved. Various other approaches to improving geodetic knowledge were undertaken, such as the Air Force programmes which used flashing-light beacons on satellites and laser-ranging, but Doppler tracking had the great advantage of providing data whatever the time-of-day or weather.[100] This was so successful that:

> By 1964, APL had developed a sophisticated model of the gravitational field of the earth ... that was sufficiently accurate to make possible our goal of better than 0.1 mile navigation at sea. This model was based solely on the analysis of Doppler tracking of a variety of APL satellites. At that point the gravitational-field knowledge was no longer a limiting factor in the navigation accuracy achieved at sea, which instead was dominated by orbit prediction errors caused by the inherent unpredictability of drag and the effect of errors in the estimate of ship's velocity. Continued geodetic work would not

75

contribute to our primary task of providing at-sea position fixes for the Polaris submarines.[101]

By then the first operational navigation satellite (Transit 5BN-2) was in orbit, and further launches during the 1960s established a 'birdcage' usually consisting of five or six satellites in polar orbits. Each of the early satellites varied somewhat from its predecessor as improvements were quickly incorporated. Once a design was settled on, RCA was chosen as the prime contractor to build the Oscar series of Transit satellites, the first of which was launched in 1965. When designed the expectations of component reliability led to a prediction of a mean-time-between-failure of two years and it was decided to build twenty Oscar satellites initially.[102] This, however, turned out to be rather pessimistic – the first Oscar satellite lasted thirteen years – and some would still be operational over twenty years later.

Transit thus provided the navigational reset system for the FBM system that it was originally conceived for. However, its initially unintended contribution to geodetic mapping had more profound and widespread applications. It enabled the location of targets to be 'known' with unprecedented accuracy, as could other important navigational sites. According to R. J. Anderle of the Naval Surface Weapons Center at Dahlgren in Virginia: 'Doppler observations of Navy Navigation Satellites have been used by the Department of Defense since 1963 to determine the geodetic positions of isolated sites such as LORAN-C navigation beacons.'[103] Improved gravity mapping could also feed back into gravity models developed for the guidance and navigation systems used in the FBM system.

THE POLARIS SUBMARINES

Meeting the tight schedule agreed for the interim A1 missile had required the adaptation of attack submarines to produce the *George Washington* class of FBM submarines, SSBN598 to 602. All five were initially equipped with A1 missiles and the first generation of navigation, fire control and launcher systems. Their first overhauls in 1966/7 replaced the A1 missiles with Polaris A3 and upgraded the navigation systems, redesignating the SINS as Mk. 2 Mod. 4.[104]

The first FBM submarines designed from the keel up were the *Ethan Allen* class, submarines SSBN608 to 611 and 618. These became operational between 26 June 1962 when the *Ethan Allen* first went on patrol, and 28 October 1963. Each was initially deployed carrying A2 missiles with the necessary changes in the launcher systems to accommodate them. Like the 598 class, they carried the Mk. 80 fire control system, but in the 608 class this was linked initially to the Sperry Gyroscope Company's Mk. 3 Mod. 0 SINS. These were replaced during the late 1960s with Autonetics Mk. 2 Mod. 3 SINS.[105]

The remainder of the Polaris submarines were a new larger type, beginning with the *Lafayette* SSBN616, which was launched on 8 May 1962, and began its first operational patrol on 4 January 1964. The larger size of the 616 class was not the result of any perceived military need; it simply took advantage of the lessons learnt in building the first ten FBM submarines to improve the general design and to provide more space and facilities to make the lives of the submariners more bearable on their long patrols. At the particular behest of Admiral Raborn the submarine design was extended by increasing the length of the centre section.[106] This, however, also increased the displacement of the submarines by about 400 tons over the 608 class, which seemed 'initially a bit of a problem', requiring the addition of an extra 400 tons of lead to provide ballast.[107] But, again, as in the over-design of the missile mount tubes this would eventually prove to be a fortuitous decision. The extra buoyancy provided by the larger submarines meant that they – but not the first ten – would be able to accommodate missiles that were not only larger, but also much heavier, than those of the Polaris generation.

Eight of the *Lafayette* 616 class were initially deployed carrying A2 missiles, with the other one, the *Daniel Webster*, and the *James Madison* 627 class and *Benjamin Franklin* 640 class carrying the A3 when it became ready.[108] All carried the new Mk. 84 fire control system, with the navigation system depending on which missile was carried. The submarines deployed with A2 had the same Mk. 2 Mod. 0 SINS used in the *George Washington* class submarines, whereas submarines carrying the A3 were felt to require greater accuracy. The 627 class were fitted with the Mk. 2 Mod. 2 which later had 'field modifications' to convert it to the Mk. 2 Mod. 3 installed in the 640 class and retrofitted to the 608 class.[109]

The early Polaris submarines had been authorized piecemeal throughout the last years of the Eisenhower administration, which seemed to have reached no clear decision on how many submarines the FBM force should eventually comprise.[110] By the time J. F. Kennedy became president in January 1961 nineteen submarines had been authorized, with long-lead-time funding for a further five.[111]

Within the Navy itself consensus had already been reached that something of the order of forty-five submarines was the correct number, providing a neat force structure of five squadrons of nine submarines each. With its self-proclaimed adherence to 'finite deter-

77

rence' and internal divisions over what many believed to be the financial burden of Polaris on the surface fleet, a larger force was hard to support. The first public estimate of the Navy's desired number of FBM submarines came from Chief of Naval Operations, Admiral Burke, in January 1957. In response to a congressional request he came up with the figure of forty-one, claiming later that it took him 'about one hour . . . I figured it out on the back of an envelope'.[112] Despite the public counter-city rationale of Polaris the number was apparently based 'entirely on military targets'.[113] During 1958 there were reports of some senators and Navy officers seeking as many as 100 Polaris submarines, but SPO seem to have been quite content with a lower figure. On 6 April 1959 Admiral Raborn proposed a forty-five sub-marine force.[114]

This remained the Navy position throughout 1960 and 1961. Moreover, not only was the Navy reasonably moderate in the size of its demand (as compared to the Air Force's projected ICBM force), but it also preferred to maintain a steady rate of construction at six sub-marines per year, rejecting additional funds voted by Congress in 1960.[115] When President Kennedy's State of the Union message of 30 January 1961 called for an acceleration in submarine delivery – pre-sumably as a political gesture following his campaigning 'missile gap' rhetoric – the Navy opposed it.

The Navy's projected programme of a 45-submarine force was pre-sented to Secretary of Defense McNamara on 3 July 1961. He responded in September by cutting this by four, giving a total of forty-one, but leaving the possibility open of more later. The Navy initially argued for more, even setting a new figure of fifty as a prelude to compromise, but by 1962 had agreed to settle for forty-one. Accord-ing to Dr Alain Enthoven, who was closely involved in the relevant decisions, the choice of forty-one was: 'simply an historical accident. There was no precise calculation of the necessary number of missiles. The Administration had inherited a program of 19 [Polaris submarines] then added ten, and then six and six, for forty-one.'[116]

The construction of these forty-one submarines over a period of about seven years was a considerable achievement, given the disparate organizations involved. SPO coordinated the activities of BuShips, and its Nuclear Power Directorate headed by Admiral Rickover, and four shipyards: two private companies, Electric Boat and Newport News Shipbuilding and Drydock Company; and two Navy yards, Ports-mouth Naval Shipyard and Mare Island Naval Shipyard.

What made this all the more extraordinary was that BuShips and Rickover's Nuclear Power Directorate both had formal control over parts of the programme; BuShips over the submarine construction and Rickover over the nuclear reactor.[117] But the great scope for bureaucratic wranglings and internecine power struggles interfering with the Polaris programme was not exploited.

At least in part this stemmed from a unanimity of purpose that Polaris was necessary, indeed vital, not just for the nation, but also for the Navy. Of course, not everyone shared the latter belief, and some even doubted that the former required such a rate of submarine construction. But such dissent had little power in the relevant organizations at the time, and CNO Burke was very effective in imposing unanimity when required.

Rickover's main concern was to put his nuclear reactor designs to sea. The *Nautilus* had demonstrated the feasibility of his technical dream, and now only a few years later he had the opportunity for its large-scale application. Without the Polaris programme he would have had to struggle to find such an eager user for what was a relatively expensive technology (at least in terms of initial capital outlay).

Thus, although initially concerned that Polaris might divert resources from his reactor work,[118] Rickover soon came to see that their common purpose, to combat Soviet military developments, could also have mutual benefit. Rickover's potential for disruptive interference remained, of course, and was recognized by CNO Burke from the very start. When describing the attributes that led him to choose Raborn to head SPO, Burke even went as far to as to emphasize that: 'In other words I didn't want a Rickover in there.'[119] 'Under unwritten orders from Admiral Burke, Raborn and [the Chief of BuShips, Rear Admiral] Mumma excluded Rickover from all the preliminary studies.'[120]

Rickover first received official information on the intended Polaris submarine design on 16 April 1957 when it reached the Nuclear Propulsion Directorate.[121] It was to be a single screw design using the S5W reactor being developed for the *Skipjack* and *Thresher* class submarines. Rickover objected to this, arguing instead that a twin-screw reactor design should be used, but he was overruled, and thus kept out of Polaris design details. In other instances too, Rickover found himself forced to concede, for example, when he attempted to restrict the operating depth of the *Ethan Allen* class submarines because he doubted the adequacy of some of their components, or when he was held to be delaying recruitment of FBM submariners with his tortuous interviewing technique (which involved him personally interviewing all officers).[122]

79

FBM COMMUNICATIONS

Communication with the FBM submarines was obviously an important part of the technological system. Even a last-resort retaliatory deterrent needs to be told to unleash its vengeance. Indeed the report of the Steering Task Group in the spring of 1957 described command and control communications as a potential 'Achilles heel of the entire Polaris operation'.[123] However, unlike the other FBM technologies, communications was not assigned to a technical branch of SPO.

Instead, jurisdiction over FBM communications was shared between SPO, the Bureau of Ships and the Director of Naval Communications.[124] SPO tolerated this arrangement, it seems, for two reasons. Firstly, it was a political compromise which enrolled other parts of the Navy into supporting Polaris. Certainly, if SPO had attempted to assert dominance over communications it could have involved a damaging dispute. Secondly, although communications were important in the long term for the operational deployment of Polaris, they were not so vital to the short-term demonstration of its feasibility. SPO was thus not too unhappy to leave those problems to another part of the Navy. Their more pressing concern was to build a missile that could be fired from submerged submarines.

It was also the feeling at SPO that a sophisticated communications system was not essential to the deterrent mission of Polaris. A two part FBM communications programme had been set up, and the first part, aimed at the development of a reliable and secure system, indicated that a basic system was not difficult to achieve, though it would be expensive. The second part of the programme was orientated to long-term research and development of more exotic and survivable solutions to the evident weaknesses of the basic approach – mainly that it was vulnerable to sabotage or attack, that it might take quite a while for all the submarines to receive the message and that you could not be sure that they had.

Earlier submarine voyages – such as the round-the-world trip of the *Triton* – had already indicated that an antenna raised to the water's surface could receive radio transmissions.[125] By using very low frequency (VLF) radio waves (14 to 30 kilohertz) it was possible to receive messages over great distances. In early 1959 messages sent from a Navy VLF transmitter at Annapolis were said to have been received some 6000 miles away, by a submarine in the Mediterranean.[126] Beginning in the late 1950s six major US VLF transmitters were constructed at Annapolis, Maryland; Cutler, Maine; Oso, Washington; Wahiawa, Hawaii; Yosami, Japan; and North West Cape, Australia.[127] These consist of very large antennas with power outputs of the order of a million watts.[128] Supplemented by a further twenty-one low frequency (LF) transmitters they have been the main method of communication with the FBM submarines since the first one went on patrol in 1960.

The main problem with VLF and LF is their limited penetration of water. VLF only penetrates to depths of about 9 metres and LF to about 5 metres.[129] To remain contactable submarines must therefore have an aerial continuously deployed near the surface. Two types of aerial can be used for this. One has an antenna buoy at the end of a long cable, which is deployed some 6–9 metres below the surface, whilst the submarine can remain at a depth of about 45 metres. However, submarine speed is limited to about 4 knots. In the other method a trailing buoyant wire antenna about 550 to 640 metres long is extended behind the submarine which can then travel at around 10 knots, but is restricted to a depth of around 15–18 metres.[130]

In addition to these limitations, both forms of antenna also increase the vulnerability of the submarines to detection. The trailing buoyant antenna is also only bi-directional and so limits submarine movement when monitoring a particular VLF transmitter. The buoy antenna was plagued by unreliability problems in its early use by Polaris submarines.[131]

Nor does the VLF system provide complete assurance that messages will be received in a timely fashion, or indeed at all. In 1972 Rear Admiral Samuel Gravely revealed that 'one of our problems is that some of our messages never get delivered'.[132] For this reason the basic VLF and LF transmitters have now been complemented by other higher frequency systems, in the high (HF) and ultra-high (UHF) bandwidths, able to take advantage of a wide range of US communications systems. These require an antenna to be raised above the water surface, thus risking detection, but provide much greater data transmission rates than the lower frequency systems. In operation FBM submarines would normally monitor VLF, but progressively move to higher frequencies if no messages were available.[133]

Finally, one radio frequency, despite some apparent advantages, has become publicly controversial and had its development delayed for many years. The extremely low frequency (ELF) bandwidth was recognized in the late 1950s as a potential communications system for submarines. Amongst its apparent advantages are much lower attenuation than VLF by the atmosphere (so providing longer range) and by seawater (so penetrating much deeper), and low susceptibility to jamming. The disadvantages are that data rate transmission is very low and that producing the long wavelength requires a correspondingly large transmitter with very high power output.[134]

ELF research began in 1958 and feasibility was demonstrated in 1962,

Table 5.1. *History of ELF proposals*

Year	Project name	Location	Antenna length	Antenna cables	Power input	Estimated cost
1968–75	Sanguine	Wisconsin	10,000km	buried	800 MW	$2–300m
1975–78	Seafarer	Wisconsin	3900km	buried	20 MW	$590m
1978–81	Austere ELF	Wisconsin/ Michigan	45 plus 210km	buried	2.4 MW	$455m
1981–	Project ELF	Wisconsin/ Michigan	45 plus 90km	above ground	2.6 MW	$260m

Source: M. Spaven, 'ELF: Surviving the Traumas – Part 2', *Jane's Defence Weekly*, vol. 4, 1194

but after a succession of increasingly modest schemes, an operational ELF system has only just been adopted by the US Navy. During this period ELF developments have been cancelled once by a US President, once by the Chief of Naval Operations and once by the legal action of the State of Wisconsin.[135] Local environmental opposition to ELF seems to have focused on the potentially harmful effects of the low frequency radiation, though given the comparative absence of opposition to the smaller VLF transmitters, the initial concern may simply have been the sheer size of the original ELF proposals. Each successive ELF proposal has been clearly shaped by these concerns as size and power output have been reduced. A modest, scaled-down version of ELF eventually became operational in October 1989.

Moreover, although sponsored and funded by SPO through its feasibility demonstrations, and despite its apparent advantages ELF was not a programme that initially found much support in SPO. SPO considered the basic VLF system to be adequately survivable to ensure retaliation. The great expense and potential local opposition involved in constructing an ELF antenna embracing about 40 per cent of the state of Wisconsin also weighed against it.[136]

Other communications developments were also delayed because of doctrinal disagreement within the Navy over the role of the FBM force. Whilst the first part of the FBM communications programme had concentrated on constructing the basic system, the second was devoted 'to seek exotic solutions to weaknesses revealed in the basic systems'.[137] In particular it was desired to develop communications systems which were more survivable and which would provide more prompt message transmission.[138]

But in SPO prompt retaliation was not considered necessary for an 'assured destruction' deterrent. The rhetorical question asked was:

'Does the threat of nuclear destruction deteriorate over time?'[139] Others, who favoured a counterforce role for the FBM force, saw prompt response as an important feature of communications. A delay in receiving the command to fire might mean the targets (enemy missile silos) would be empty by the time the Polaris missile reached them. Similarly, limited nuclear war, counterforce targeting scenarios (such as advocated by Secretary of Defence McNamara in 1962), required communications systems that would remain operational during a nuclear exchange; they had to be very survivable.

This disagreement over the FBM communications requirements led to a stalemate in the long-range programme investigating the development of the more exotic concepts. The cumulative cost of the programme grew whilst little was actually deployed. A 1964 review of the programme was aptly titled 'Where did the $100 million go?'[140] Eventually FBM communications research was completely separated from SPO in 1967, and a Special Communications Project Office was established.[141] This was directed to provide 'effective communications at all times for the National Command Authorities and Commanders in Chief to the deployed FBM forces . . . during and after heavy nuclear and electronic jamming attack'.[142]

Eventually, in 1969, a more survivable system was deployed, which had been under development since 1962. Known as TACAMO (from 'take charge and move out') this consisted of twelve EC-130 aircraft equipped with VLF transmitters using long trailing antennas. By circling tightly the several mile long antenna is held vertical.[143] In 1972 the Special Communications Project Office described TACAMO as 'the only operational survivable element that the Navy has today and most likely will have until the latter part of the 1970s'.[144] Although intended to provide at least one aircraft continuously on patrol in both the Atlantic and Pacific this goal does not seem to have ever been achieved.[145] Indeed, despite general acknowledgement that it provided the most reliable form of communication in a nuclear war environment, the TACAMO programme became a victim of the Navy's obsession with ELF. In 1978 Congressional testimony the Navy's Director of Command and Control and Communications Programs recalled:

> We got into trouble in this [TACAMO] system by permitting it to gracefully degrade, numbers wise, during the years when the Department of Defense was viewing the very hard Sanguine (ELF) system as the keystone of surviving communications to our deterrent forces. During those years, we drew down TACAMO assets in one command to keep a 24-hour airborne capability in another, and with the change in concepts shifting from the very hard Sanguine to the

soft and less survivable Seafarer system our planning and budgeting had hardly kept pace with the ravages of time and accidents.[146]

THINKING ABOUT THE NEXT GENERATION

Hardly had development of the A3 been approved in September 1960 than consideration of another generation began. Lockheed, the missile contractor, began to push the idea of an A4 missile during 1961, with longer range the main selling point. SPO, apparently, were not immediately enthusiastic, seeing no pressing need for longer range at that time.[147] However, in response to guidance from the Office of the Chief of Naval Operations, SPO put forward in November 1963 a proposal for a new larger diameter missile, by then known as the Polaris B3, which was to carry either three larger warheads or one much larger warhead than A3.[148]

This new missile was to take advantage of increased launch tube size gained by reducing the thickness of the shock protection system. The possibility of significant increases in missile size was first pointed up by work done in Westinghouse's systems analysis group, which was tasked by SPO to consider ways of carrying Polaris missiles on surface ships and trucks for the proposed NATO Multilateral Force.[149] The idea of equipping a NATO force with perhaps as many as a thousand US nuclear missiles, probably either Polaris or Pershing, came under serious consideration in 1960.[150] Truck mounting, with the missile held horizontal, was the biggest problem. The stowage launch adaptors used in the original Polaris launcher were unsuitable for holding the missile in a horizontal position and the sheer weight of the heavy machined launch tube was considered impracticable.

Westinghouse's group came up with a much lighter approach, in which the missile would be enclosed in foam padded resin reinforced fibreglass panels with heavy duty zippers up the sides which would be undone after the missile was loaded into the launch tube. The foam/fibreglass combination supported the missile in all orientations and its resilient flexibility obviated the need for a heavy machined launch tube. The launch tube itself could also be cushioned by foam rather than the liquid springs used in the first Polaris launch system, the Mk. 17. The need to cut down on weight also led to consideration of a lighter method of ejection to replace the compressed air system. Two small solid propellant rockets fired sequentially were to provide the pressure required to eject the missile from the launch tube.

Two demonstration trucks were in fact built, but the multilateral force never transpired. Westinghouse, however, informed SPO of these launch system advances: 'We pointed out to the Navy that a design could be produced to take existing missiles and develop a launching system with a substantial space saving.'[151] Thus in 1961 SPO had the choice of revising the design of the remaining FBM submarines to make them smaller, or keeping them the same size but squeezing perhaps twenty or twenty-four missiles into the same size submarines. SPO's first thought, however, was: 'You mean we could put a bigger missile [in the submarines]'.[152]

But with the Polaris A3 development only just started there appeared little immediate justification for another generation of FBM. Instead it was decided to incorporate some of the launcher system improvements into Polaris submarines of the same size and capacity, while retaining the possibility of back-fitting a larger diameter missile in the future. The new launch system, known as the Mark 21, was first introduced into the *James Madison*. The major difference was the use of polyurethane foam to replace the thirty or so liquid springs by which the launch tube was suspended in the submarine mount tube. The liquid springs on which the launch tube rested were retained, as were the stowage launch adaptors holding the missile in the launch tube. Also, starting in the *Nathan Hale*, the compressed air ejection system was replaced by one using solid propellant generated steam.[153]

However, the Mk. 21 still only accommodated a 54 inch diameter missile. Extra space remained available in the mount tube which meant that the next generation FBM could be bigger, with longer range or greater payload or both. But for the next few years its exact design would be contested, taking even longer to decide than its final name. The only thing that was not in doubt was the missile's eventual development. As Stanley Burriss, general manager of Lockheed Missile and Space Company, put it, 'the question is not "if" it is needed, but "when."'[154] And, he might have added, 'what for'?

6 POSEIDON

> Most of us saw the role of Poseidon as not different from the role of its predecessors, namely providing an absolutely dependable, reliable deterrent, and most of us were sceptical about the need to dig out hard targets as an essential element of deterrence. We went along with it to the degree necessary in order to keep the program. The nature of democracy ... is that you're constantly making compromises with conflicting constituencies, and we had to serve the reigning constituency even if we, sometimes we felt they were a little nutty.   Admiral Wertheim.[1]

Polaris A3 was generally seen as a logical extension of the FBM role established by the A1 and A2 missiles – deterrence by the threat of devastating counter-city retaliation. Although some people had favoured more emphasis on enhancing counterforce capabilities, the A3 payload was clearly 'disoptimized' for such a purpose, except against soft, spreadout military targets. SPO had taken care to exploit the success of the Polaris programme and to emphasize continuity and a moderate approach by retaining the Polaris name for the A3, which was almost entirely a new missile. As thoughts turned to the next generation, again this was initially thought of as another Polaris, be it A4, A3A or, as it was later known, B3.

Lockheed, keen to maintain their workload after A3, were first to suggest another generation of Polaris. Lockheed studies during 1961 proposed a new Polaris that could provide ranges in excess of 3000 nautical miles, but SPO were unenthusiastic.[2] By early 1962, the emphasis had switched to increasing payload over the same range in what was called Polaris A3A.[3] This was to be a 66 inch diameter missile, the increase from the standard Polaris diameter of 54 inch being made possible by the changes in launch tube technology developed for a possible multilateral force role. The main payload options considered were either an MRV design like A3, but carrying three 600 kiloton warheads, or a single large warhead.[4] The larger warheads reflected the desire of some Navy planners, apparently endorsed by the CNO

Admiral Anderson,[5] to compete with the Air Force by attempting to rival the counterforce role of ICBMs: 'Suffice it to say that they were doing what a military staff would be expected to do – go out and clobber the enemy. The enemy being the Air Force!'[6] Although submitted by SPO the proposal for a Polaris A3A came about 'in response to guidance and direction from the Navy's planners'.[7]

The Navy proposal to fund development of Polaris A3A drew the following response from Secretary of Defense McNamara:

> The Navy has proposed the development of a Polaris A-3A missile. The proposed program would have 368 A-3A missiles and 288 A-3 missiles in submarines by FY 1969 at an additional cost of $1.6 billion. The A-3 missile has approximately 300 lbs. available for decoys; the A-3A has approximately 920 lbs. available for decoys at the same ranges. Although I believe that further development of a more advanced Polaris missile may be desirable, I do not believe that the extra capabilities offered by the A-3 [sic] missile, by comparison with the A-3, are worth the cost of development and procurement. Therefore, I recommend that the Navy proposal be disapproved.[8]

With the missile gap now acknowledged to be in favour of the US, Polaris A2 being deployed, and A3 almost ready, there was little pressure for urgent development of another FBM generation. What mattered more was to ensure that the next generation itself would not become obsolescent quickly, as in some ways was perceived to have happened with Polaris. Two issues in particular troubled Harold Brown, McNamara's Director of Defense Research & Engineering (DDR&E), with the A3A proposal. First, there was the question of accommodating an increased missile size by removing some of the shock protection that had turned out to be over-designed for the original Polaris. Rather than rushing to develop a 66 inch diameter missile, Brown told SPO that he did not 'want a still larger missile coming around a few years from now'.[9]

The second issue which bore heavily on ensuring a new missile's enduring utility was the nature of the payload it would carry. On the one hand there was concern about Soviet ABM developments, on the other the question of what types of target should be given priority in the design. As SPO Director Rear Admiral Galantin (who succeeded Raborn on 26 February 1962) noted: 'The range is not as valuable to the submarine system as it is to a fixed system, so it's the payload and how we would slice it . . .'.[10]

Various reentry system configurations were evaluated during the first half of 1963, for what was now a 74 inch diameter missile concept known as Polaris B3.[11] The 74 inch missile would take full advantage of

87

the launcher system advances, use up all the extra space created by the original 'over-design' of the system, and still require relaxation of the original 'spec' that promised survival in a depth charge environment.[12] In November 1963 Brown indicated that SPO should 'proceed with the definition of a Polaris follow-on (known initially as the B-3) that would enhance FBM penetration of defended urban-industrial targets'.[13] Brown had also authorized the Air Force to proceed with development of a new reentry vehicle in late 1963, with the proviso that it should be a joint Navy–Air Force development. The reentry vehicle, known as the Mk. 12, was authorized for development by the Reentry Systems Division of General Electric Company in March 1964.[14] The Mk. 12 was designed to carry a warhead of about 150 kilotons, allowing several to be carried by the next generation FBM.

For a while SPO and Lockheed reluctantly based their studies around this reentry vehicle. Firstly, the possibility of carrying six Mk. 12s in an MRV arrangement was considered, but the simple ejection method used in A3 did not allow a separation for six reentry bodies that was considered useful. Then, in early 1964, Lockheed carried out a trade-off looking at three methods, again with the baseline of six Mk. 12s, that might provide a greater warhead scatter for urban-industrial destruction. 'Mailman' was an adaptation of technology that the Air Force was currently developing for its Minuteman ICBM.[15] A platform or 'bus' containing both a guidance system and some method of propulsion would carry *all* the reentry bodies, releasing them one at a time to achieve the desired pattern over the target. This, however, would require a change in guidance from the implicit Q-guidance so far used in Polaris to one based on explicit 'knowledge' of where it was. The second possible method, known as 'Blue Angels', would retain the Q-guidance. To do this, however, required each reentry body to have its own separate guidance and propulsion system.[16] Third, and least seriously considered, was 'Carousel', in which the missile was to have been spun so that the reentry bodies could be scattered out by centrifugal force.

SPO's guidance branch engineer initially retained a preference for staying with Q-guidance to avoid the in-flight computational complexity that explicit guidance required.[17] However, 'Mailman' was generally considered the more elegant solution and was favoured at Lockheed and by SPO's leadership because it did not tie the Navy to using the Air Force's Mk. 12 reentry vehicle. At least in principle, the 'Mailman' approach could be pursued without an irrevocable commitment to the Mk. 12; the bus could carry other passengers.

Service pride was not the only issue here. A joint development with the Air Force threatened to reduce SPO's control over the programme, and raised the possibility that the resulting technology would not be optimized for their requirements. Ever intent on limiting potential threats to their independence, SPO's leadership seized upon a suggestion made by two members of the Polaris Steering Task Group, Carl Haussman of Livermore nuclear weapons laboratory and Lloyd Wilson of Lockheed. They proposed using a small warhead/reentry body design that Livermore had failed to 'sell' to the Air Force.[18]

While OSD still strongly favoured the use of the Mk. 12, SPO promoted study of the small reentry body, which would become known as the Mk. 3.[19] Thus it was decided that the new missile would use a MIRV (multiple independently targetable reentry vehicle) system. Originally adopted to facilitate a shotgun effect against a single city, this technology also allowed warheads to be delivered to separate cities many miles apart. Some, however, questioned whether the Navy should continue to restrict its mission to targeting cities.

Within the office of the Chief of Naval Operations there were those who favoured an explicit shift to a counterforce capability. Rather than combating potential developments in Soviet ABM defences they preferred the new missile to provide the FBM force with a significant hard-target capability and so directly challenge the Air Force's counterforce monopoly. This viewpoint became centered in the *ad hoc* 'Great Circle Group', headed by Rear Admiral George Miller, which Secretary of the Navy Paul Nitze set up in 1964 as a part of the Navy's Long Range Objectives Group.[20]

Most Navy officers, however, were indifferent to the technical characteristics and strategic mission of the FBM, but highly sceptical of the need for yet another generation so soon after Polaris A3. It was widely believed, and with good reason, that Polaris had been paid for out of Navy funds which otherwise would have gone to the traditional surface fleet.[21]

Along with the indecision over its technical specification and strategic rationale, this Navy resistance further delayed the initiation of a new programme. However, the basic concept of the Polaris B3 was decided during 1964. In July 1964 Secretary of the Navy, Paul Nitze, noted 'the fact that the B3 Polaris missile can give us the option of the same high accuracy that land-based missile systems have'.[22] Although the exact nature of the payload to be carried remained undecided, SPO was officially instructed in November 1964 to proceed with a MIRVed Polaris B3 with guidance improvements to provide greater accuracy.[23]

In December McNamara's draft memorandum for the President noted:

> I recommend the inclusion in the FY 1966 budget of $35 million to begin development of a new POLARIS B-3. We intend to initiate a project definition for this missile during FY 1965. The B-3 would incorporate improved accuracy and payload flexibility permitting it to attack a single, heavily defended urban/industrial target, or a single hardened point target, or several undefended targets which might be separated by as much as 75 miles.[24]

However, the delay had already led SPO to take an unprecedented step in broadening its scope beyond its single-mission dedication to the FBM system. In June 1964 SPO accepted responsibility for the Deep Submergence Systems Project (DSSP), which was instigated in response to the loss of the nuclear submarine, the *Thresher* in 1963. As Sapolsky has noted this served a dual purpose for SPO:

> Since the technologies involved in deep ocean research were somewhat related to the technologies involved in the FBM system and since some Special Project's Office contractors and part of its technical staff were interested in exploring the opportunities such research presented, DSSP provided both a means to keep the FBM team together until Poseidon was approved and a possible follow-on to strategic missile work.[25]

POSEIDON C3: NEW NAME, SAME DIFFERENCE (OF OPINION)

On 18 January 1965 President Johnson announced the development of the next FBM generation, and gave it special emphasis with a new name. The B3 was now called Poseidon C3, the change in name apparently inspired by the president's desire to rebuff criticism that his administration was failing to develop new strategic systems. The president's announcement also stated that the new missile would 'double the payload of the ... Polaris A-3. The increased accuracy and flexibility of the Poseidon will permit its use effectively against a broader range of possible targets and give added insurance of penetration of enemy defenses.'[26] The public emphasis on counterforce was clear as he predicted that 'its effectiveness against a hardened target will be some eight times greater than the latest version of *Polaris*'.[27]

That Poseidon was to be a MIRVed missile had been decided, but this one technology meant different things to different people, both in design and in its implications for nuclear strategy. Whilst its development in the Air Force stemmed from a desire to increase accuracy and came to stress the ability to hit a greater number of widely separated *military* targets, the concept had developed in the FBM context as a means of dispersing reentry bodies over a single urban-industrial target and of defeating Soviet ABM defences.[28] But in the Navy too, hard target kill capability was becoming a central, and as it turned out, divisive issue.

As early as 1962 the Chief of Naval Operations had expressed interest in a hard target capability for the FBM.[29] This was a departure from the Polaris tradition, but SPO was becoming increasingly incorporated into the formal naval hierarchy. In 1963 SPO ceased to report directly to the Secretary of the Navy, instead coming under the aegis of the Chief of Naval Material, who in turn was subordinated to the Chief of Naval Operations in 1966.[30] Moreover, Defense Secretary Mc-Namara's new nuclear strategy – which emphasized the more selective use of counterforce targeting and the initial withholding of attacks on cities – could be taken as implying the desirability of a hard target MIRV for Poseidon. SIOP-63 moved away from the all-out 'wargasm' of the first SIOP, providing options for holding back, and so increasing the potential utility of survivable forces like the FBM.[31]

The hard target issue translated into two tightly related questions: how accurate should Poseidon be, and how large should its warheads be. Ultimately, the dispute came to bear on the issue of accuracy, but at first it was warhead size that was more controversial. In addition to the Mk. 12 and Mk. 3, there was a third candidate reentry body. Also under development by the Air Force, this was the Mk. 17, which was intended to carry a large multi-megaton warhead to provide high hard target kill capability. Initially the Office of the Secretary of Defense (OSD) 'expected to use the Air Force Mark 12 and agreed with some Navy planners that a Mark 17 option should be available to provide greater counterforce capability'.[32] SPO, on the other hand, preferred larger numbers of the smaller Mk. 3 as a way of guaranteeing the retaliation mission, even against improved ABM defences, and also to avoid using a reentry vehicle designed for Air Force use.[33]

At stake in this disagreement within the Navy was not just the virtues of counterforce *per se*, but also the wisdom of a more direct confrontation with the Air Force, rather than a policy of differentiation: 'There were advocates in the Office of the Chief of Naval Operations ... who [felt that] anything the Air Force could do the Navy also needed to do.'[34] This view was centred particularly in the Great Circle Group (in 1967 the Great Circle Group became the Office of Strategic Offensive and Defensive Systems).[35] The Great Circle Group sought a Navy role in a 'warfighting' nuclear strategy and advocated the use of the Mk. 17 on Poseidon. They were suspicious of SPO. Ted Greenwood reports that 'one Naval officer associated with long-range planning for the Polaris force in the middle 1960s even suggested that SP had made a deal with the Air Force not to try to gain counterforce capability'.[36]

However, the appearance of Galosh in November 1964 greatly strengthened SPO's preference for the Mk. 3 reentry body. After considering various configurations, the Mk. 12 was eliminated from the options during 1965. It was not seen to offer any great advantage over the Mk. 3, which, being smaller, could be carried in larger numbers.[37] SPO's preference was for large numbers of the Mk. 3 as a way of guaranteeing the retaliation mission, even against improved ABM defences, and also to avoid using a reentry body designed for Air Force use.[38] Uncertainties in assessing potential Soviet ABM capabilities strengthened the conclusion that 'the best decoy is one that weighs as much as and looks just like, and therefore might as well be, a warhead'.[39] However, OSD still agreed with some Navy planners that they should retain the option to carry the large Mk. 17 to provide greater counterforce capability, and so a two Mk. 17 configuration continued to be assessed. Although this would have used the same Poseidon guidance system, it required some unique post-boost vehicle technology to carry the reentry bodies.[40]

SPO were put under pressure on accuracy as well as on warhead yield. This pressure came not only from Great Circle Group counterforce proponents, but also from the Office of the Secretary of Defense. Secretary McNamara, and his Director of Defense Research and Engineering, Harold Brown, pushed SPO to increase accuracy. Admiral Levering Smith recalled this interchange with Brown:

> after agreeing on all the other elements of the system, he told me, 'Well, it is fine, I can agree with these objectives, and I think I can get approval of them, but I cannot get approval of the system unless you put in an accuracy improvement, I cannot sell it to McNamara.' . . . Mr McNamara's general thought in this regard, as was expressed by Dr Brown to me at the time, was that it would cost very little more to try to improve the accuracy at the same time that you are doing all the rest of the development.[41]

A key adviser to Secretary McNamara recalls that 'it was certainly intended to give Poseidon a significant probability of destroying hard targets'.[42] Studies carried out under Glenn Kent during 1963 and 1964 had convinced OSD that useful 'damage limitation' – the destruction of at least some enemy missiles in their silos during a conflict – could be achieved if US forces comprised enough accurate warheads to assign one to every Soviet silo. Thus any accuracy improvement was considered worthwhile so long as it was not too expensive.[43]

This meant improved guidance and more work for the Instrumentation Laboratory, whose sheer size became a matter of concern to the MIT authorities in the 1960s. MIT Vice President James McCormack investigated whether the Instrumentation Laboratory should be allowed to take on the Poseidon contract, and how important their contribution would be:

> Apparently, it was in fact Secretary McNamara who insisted on extending the program to incorporate the best that can be had in the guidance system, especially as regards accuracy ... Admiral Smith was most informative along the following lines:
> (1) In the Navy's earlier concept, the requirement for a longer-range missile could have been satisfied by a lesser improvement to the guidance system, the development of which would accordingly have most likely been assigned to an industrial contractor, as a logical further development of the Polaris guidance system.
> (2) With Mr McNamara's insistence on getting all of the accuracy possible ... the services of the Instrumentation Laboratory definitely came to be required.[44]

Why was SPO not intent 'on getting all the accuracy possible'? First, as with Polaris, Smith and SPO preferred to avoid rigid technical requirements that had to be met come what may, agreeing instead to goals which could, if necessary, be traded off against other system characteristics. Admiral Smith formally could not refuse to accept an accuracy requirement, but by (perhaps realistically) doubling the development cost estimate, he ruled out such a choice. In effect, 'the Technical Director of the Special Projects Office [Levering Smith] agreed to take on the task of providing increased accuracy for Poseidon only if the specific missile accuracy desired were treated as a development goal rather than a development requirement'.[45] To accept a stringent accuracy requirement, and then fail to meet it, would have been very damaging to the reputation of the FBM programme, a reputation carefully built upon the capacity to keep promises.[46]

The second reason for lack of enthusiasm for greatly enhanced accuracy was, again, 'differentiation' – the conviction that the FBM programme was best served by having a mission and identity distinct from the Air Force programmes, and a desire to avoid 'copycat' competition with these. The third reason was a deep commitment to the retaliatory deterrence, assured destruction strategy. This may originally have been shaped by the organizational logic of differentiation, but it was now deeply felt by many in SPO.

By January 1966 the baseline Poseidon characteristics had been agreed, very much in line with SPO's preferences. The main legitimation for Poseidon was to be possible Soviet developments in ABM defenses and not in ASW (anti-submarine warfare), and so the missile's range was to be about the same as Polaris A3. To counter the ABM 'threat' each missile would carry a large number of the small Mk. 3 reentry bodies. Concerns over the discrimination capabilities of Soviet ABM systems were obviated by the large numbers of small warheads or 'armed decoys' as they were known. Flexibility in numbers of reentry bodies carried and the spacing of their deployment from the bus was seen as providing a hedge against changes in this threat. Moreover, by 'off-loading' some of these warheads it was also possible to increase range if Soviet ASW did come to be considered threatening. Nominal 'compatibility' with the Air Force Mk. 17 reentry body was still required – the only success of the Great Circle Group's campaign.[47] The immediate question of accuracy, and thus the pressure from the Office of the Secretary of Defense, was resolved by an agreement to aim for about 50 per cent increase over A3,[48] but as a 'goal', not a 'requirement'.

POSEIDON GUIDANCE

As noted earlier, there had been some resistance to dropping Q-guidance in SPO. According to the then head of FBM guidance at the Instrumentation Laboratory, the feeling was that: 'we had a horse that ran right in the proper direction and why change it?'[49] But the decision to use the 'Mailman' concept required a move to an explicit guidance formulation. With this the missile constantly 'knows' its position and velocity and recomputes the trajectory required to bring it to its target. This required more onboard computational capability, which Q-guidance had deliberately avoided in Polaris, but by the mid-1960s this was not a limitation. Indeed, the Instrumentation Laboratory's successful Apollo development of an explicit guidance system using a general purpose computer had already undercut the supporters of Q-guidance in that organization. Computational advances also made the use of strapdown guidance appear feasible and it was considered for 'multi-manoeuvrable buses' each carrying a strapdown system slaved to a main guidance system in the missile.[50]

This approach was not developed, however, and strapdown was again not considered suitable for the missile guidance. With a manoeuvring bus deploying reentry bodies onto various trajectories the amount of reorientation of the system was considered likely to lead to poor accuracy with strapdown.[51] Instead the Poseidon Mk. 3 guidance system was a traditional stable platform design, an evolutionary development from the Mk. 2.

With the more complex trajectory flown in a MIRVed system, no one axis would be as dominant as previously, and so the extra difficulties and expense of retaining one PIGA (pendulous integrating gyro accelerometer) were judged to be not worthwhile. Instead three 16-size (1.6 inch diameter) PIPAs (pulsed integrating pendulous accelerometers) were used together with three 25-size Mod. 3 IRIGs. Although similar to their predecessors in basic principle, these devices incorporated 'evolutionary' improvements achieved through continuing work at the Instrumentation Laboratory. In particular the PIPAs were improved by 'more than an order of magnitude' by reducing bias and scale factor errors as a result of going to permanent magnet torquers, and by changing the method of torquing.[52]

Because of the move to an explicit guidance formulation, the simple digital differential analyzer type of computer was no longer adequate. Instead a general purpose computer was used, drawing on the Instrumentation Laboratory's Apollo work.[53] Its integrated circuits were small-scale integration (SSI) with a total gate count of about 5000 (as opposed to 400 for Mk. 1 and 800 for Mk. 2).[54] 100K of read-only-memory (ROM) was used for permanent storage of certain programs, such as guidance formulations, and a 12K plated wire random-access-memory (RAM) stored variables that were read in prior to or during flight.[55] The plated wire memory was chosen because it was the only radiation hard memory then available.[56]

Whereas gravity was implicit in Q-guidance, explicit guidance required a gravity model of the earth. A simplified but adequate technique was developed which used an assumption of a spherical earth, but with 'offsets' precalculated for particular trajectories. Like the Q-terms in the Mk. 1 and Mk. 2 guidance systems these offsets were computed at the Naval Surface Weapons Center at Dahlgren and carried by the submarine fire control system to be read in to the missile computer prior to launch.[57] Also for the first time the general purpose computer provided the capability for in-flight error compensation. Reflecting the concern raised by Galosh of vulnerability to nuclear detonations the Mk. 3 guidance system was 'hardened' against the effects of radiation.

STELLAR INERTIAL GUIDANCE, HARD TARGET KILL AND THE MK. 4 GUIDANCE SYSTEM

Advocates of a hard target kill FBM were not content simply to have Poseidon designed for 'compatibility' with the Mk. 17 reentry vehicle. They sought actual deployments of Poseidon equipped with the heavy, counterforce Mk. 17 as well as the light Mk. 3. SPO resisted, arguing against a mixed force:

> The Mk. 17 was going to be expensive, it was going to require a logistical nightmare ... a specially configured missile assigned to special targets as opposed to submarines which could go on patrol with the flexibility to be targeted from one kind of a target to another without having to worry about what you had in the tubes.[58]

The argument against the 'mixed force' was not, however, the only resource SPO was able to deploy against the Mk. 17 reentry vehicle, for warhead choice began to interact with a crucial new issue in guidance system design. Corporate engineers – outside the existing SPO/Instrumentation Laboratory circle of guidance specialists – began to argue for a radical departure from existing guidance system design. Simple in principle, but with considerable technical and political ramifications, their idea was to supplement the missile's inertial guidance system with information derived from star sightings, taken while the missile was in flight.

This option had not been considered in the early days of US ballistic missile programmes, and in the early 1960s many continued to deem it infeasible – an attitude reinforced by the failure of early tests.[59] Further tests, in the Stellar Acquisition Flight Feasibility (STAFF) programme (which used 'spare' Polaris A1 missiles), were considered successful, but still led to no production contract from the US Air Force, who supported the early stellar-inertial work. The proponents of stellar-inertial, located above all at the Kearfott Division of the General Precision Corporation (now a division of Singer), thus had to turn to the Navy.

Just as the Air Force work was coming to an end, Kearfott engineers came up with a radical change to stellar-inertial guidance that was to be of great significance. It had originally been believed that sightings on two stars were necessary, as in classical navigation by the stars. Kearfott's new argument – known as the 'Unistar principle' – led to the conclusion that one 'optimum' star sighting could give as much relevant information as two. This greatly simplified the mechanical design of a stellar-inertial system at, apparently, little or no cost to accuracy.

What Kearfott could offer the Navy, then, was a technique that promised a considerable increase in missile accuracy. Their argument was that the star sight could drastically reduce the importance of the error sources – uncertainty in initial position and azimuth that had seemed to condemn submarine-launched missiles to be *inherently* less accurate than those fired from fixed silos on land.

Initially stellar-inertial guidance met with considerable scepticism. A key figure in 'selling' it was Marvin Stern, a former Deputy Director of Defense Research and Engineering in McNamara's Pentagon, who had then become President of Kearfott. Armed with the Unistar concept he 'went down . . . badgered the people in the government and . . . sold this concept'.[60] Still, despite 'considerable encouragement' from Harold Brown's successor as DDR&E, John Foster,[61] SPO was not enthusiastic. Although he jokingly referred to the Unistar concept as 'Mexican arithmetic' Admiral Smith was nevertheless convinced by Stern that it would indeed work.[62] Whether it would work was one issue, whether it was actually needed was another.

SPO did not wish to complicate the guidance system to provide extra accuracy which Poseidon's strategic role, in their view a secure counter-city retaliatory deterrent, did not require. What accuracy goals they did have seemed attainable with an all-inertial system. However, the pressure exerted from the Office of the Secretary of Defense eventually told. A key SPO figure who was in the office of DDR&E between 1962 and 1965, Captain (later Rear Admiral) Robert Wertheim, was convinced personally, and played an important role in SPO's conversion. SPO then pressed the Instrumentation Laboratory to consider it for FBM application.

Some people there 'were very much opposed to it'.[63] A senior figure in the Instrumentation Laboratory's FBM management recalls the reasons:

> First of all . . . there was a certain degree of the 'not invented here' aspect of it. But also there was a concern here at the Lab. that it was an unnecessary complication. . . . the guidance system is enough of a pain in its most simple form that you really don't want to complicate it. . . . then the other concern that I always had and I still have is that . . . there's a possibility of a high altitude nuclear explosion making the stellar system inoperable.[64]

The Instrumentation Laboratory had a great investment in developing more and more accurate inertial components, a line of technological development which seemed threatened by stellar aided guidance. People there argued that by further refining all-inertial technology one might be able to match the accuracy of stellar inertial without the necessary penalties of weight increase and complication involved in the latter:

> Dr Draper took the gyro out of his pocket and said if you have a good enough gyro you wouldn't need a [star-sensor] . . . [Draper and the people at the Instrumentation Lab] didn't think one should gimmick it by adding these crazy things called stellar sensors, that's like putting a band-aid on an inertial system.[65]

One engineer at the Instrumentation Laboratory remembers 'having tunnel vision myself talking with my boss at the time about a star-tracker: "Well, the system has been pretty good so far. We don't need to improve it with a star-tracker, necessarily".'[66] But eventually the Instrumentation Laboratory was persuaded ('If the guy with the money says he wants it you convince yourself quite easily that you agree with him'.)[67]

Despite their lack of enthusiasm for hard target capability, SPO, apparently paradoxically, began to highlight this potential attribute of stellar inertial guidance. The reason, it seems, was the continuing battle against the Mk. 17 reentry body. In 1966 Lockheed, the missile contractor, did a study for SPO which concluded that with stellar-inertial guidance the small Mk. 3 warhead would have sufficient hard target capability to make the large Mk. 17 reentry body unnecessary: 'The Mk. 17 program . . . was made to disappear by the prospect of still further accuracy improvement which made it possible to show that even with the small yield warheads . . . you could, potentially at least, threaten damage to moderately hard targets.'[68] Stellar-inertial guidance – even in conceptual form – thus enabled SPO to solve the 'mixed force' problem, by cutting the ground from under the feet of the proponents of the Mk. 17. It was the final nail in the Mk. 17's coffin, providing a 'technical' argument to cancel a programme that by now (thanks in part to Avco's over-energetic advocacy) had few influential supporters. It also avoided a substantial loss of market for Lockheed. Like all previous FBM reentry bodies, the Mk. 3 was designed and built by Lockheed, while the competitor Mk. 17 was developed by Avco Corporation.

But having helped 'kill' the Mk. 17, stellar-inertial guidance was allowed to languish. The lingering resistance at the Instrumentation Laboratory led to various counterproposals over how the concept should be implemented. For example, the Instrumentation Laboratory favoured positioning the stellar sensor telescope on the outside of the Inertial Measurement Unit case, whereas Kearfott had proposed that it be on the stable member: 'As a matter of fact, when we did get involved, pushed by the Navy . . . we had a counterproposal instead of a telescope that would sit on the stable member inside, we were proposing to add on the outside a case-mounted stellar tracker.'[69] Because of these disagreements development of a stellar-inertial Mk. 4 alternative guidance system for Poseidon did not really get under way for a couple of years,[70] while the all-inertial Mk. 3 guidance system proceeded apace.

The plan was to fit the first Poseidon missiles with the Mk. 3 guidance system and later ones with the Mk. 4. In its final form the Mk. 4 was 'a cludged-up Mk. 3 with the stellar sensor telescope mounted on the stable member and the addition of a fourth gimbal to allow the telescope to be elevated to the chosen star line prelaunch'.[71] This could take a star sighting following the boost phase (after the two rocket stages had burnt out and separated), prior to deployment of the reentry bodies. The image of the star would pass through a telescope and mirror system to the signal plate of a photoelectric 'vidicon' tube. Comparison of the actual star position with that predicted (from a star map) provided the information to correct the guidance system for errors in initial launch position and azimuth knowledge.

Navy testimony to Congress in 1968 clearly refers to the Mk. 4 development and its apparent intended purpose: 'During the past year the decision was taken to develop [deleted] to increase the accuracy of Poseidon. When these improvements are completed, Poseidon will be effective both in the assured destruction role and in attacks against hard targets.'[72] Then in January 1969 the new administration of President Nixon took over. That seemed at first to enhance the Mk. 4's prospects. Charged with cutting the defence budget, Nixon's Secretary of Defense, Melvin Laird, was looking for cheap ways of toughening up the defence posture. One possibility, suggested to him by stellar-inertial proponent John Brett of Kearfott, was to speed up the development and deployment of the Mk. 4 guidance system.[73] Laird liked the idea and presented it to Congress in March 1969:

> The increase of $12.4 million for the development of an improved guidance system for the Poseidon missile will advance the initial operating capability (IOC) of that system by about six months. . . . This is an important program since it promises to improve significantly the accuracy of the Poseidon missile, thus enhancing its effectiveness against hard targets.[74]

Paradoxically, though, this success was to backfire on the proponents of stellar-inertial guidance. As its political visibility increased, stellar-inertial guidance became openly controversial. The Instrumentation Laboratory's doubts about whether it really was a 'sweet' technology never surfaced in the public domain. But Congressional critics, assuming that stellar-inertial guidance *would* enhance accuracy, began to question whether this was actually desirable.

Key figures in the opposition – in effect, the first Congressional challenge to a 'technical' feature of an FBM system – were Senator Edward W. Brooke of Massachusetts and his aide, Alton Frye. A moderate, Black Republican, Brooke had campaigned actively for

Richard Nixon in 1968, taking the view that this was the best way to 'maintain influence in a Nixon Administration'. Until 1973, he enjoyed 'cordial access' to the President.[75] Both through his personal rapport with Nixon, and in the Senate, Brooke campaigned against hard-target kill capability.

In the climate of the time, in which the public rationale for US possession of nuclear weapons was dominated by the idea of mutually assured destruction, this forced the administration onto the defensive. Thus a lengthy letter from Brooke to Nixon on 5 December 1969 seeking reassurances 'that the United States will not seek a capability to disarm the Soviet Union', led, after consultations between the White House and Department of Defense, to a reply from Nixon on 29 December asserting: 'There is no current US program to develop a so-called 'hard-target MIRV capability.'[76] Reality was then brought into line with this assertion by cancelling the Mk. 4 stellar-inertial guidance system, and the following summer John Foster, still Director of Defense Research and Engineering in the new administration, probably referred to this when he testified that: 'We had a program of investigation along these lines and last year I cancelled it. My purpose was to make it absolutely clear to the Congress and hopefully to the Soviet Union, that it is not the policy of the United States to deny the Soviet Union their deterrent capability.'[77] Thus, as one of Lockheed's FBM team put it, the Mk. 4 programme 'was desalinated'.[78] The ease with which this Congressional pressure ended the Mk. 4 programme reflects, as Ted Greenwood notes, the ambivalence about it in SPO.[79] Foster, too, recalls that he personally was influenced by the argument of SPO Director Levering Smith that too much accuracy in the FBM force was strategically destabilizing.[80] By contrast, the Air Force's Advanced Ballistic Reentry Systems (ABRES) programme also had funding for hard-target aspects of it curtailed at the same time, but the Air Force easily circumvented this restriction.[81] SPO seemed to take almost the opposite view, that the Mk. 4 was a non-essential pro-gramme which provided them with some buffer funds which could be redirected to more critical areas if required.[82] Current Poseidon miss-iles still bear testimony to the seriousness with which the Mk. 4 star sensor was considered (a 'trap door' through which the star sighting was to be taken remains).[83] However, SPO's approach to it was prag-matic and contingent. If the Office of the Secretary of Defense wanted stellar-inertial guidance (and was prepared to pay for it), that was fine, especially as it helped to bury the Mk. 17 reentry vehicle. If then enthusiasm and funding for the Mk. 4 guidance system dried up, that was fine too. SPO's programme managers had quite enough to do meeting their goals with Poseidon as it was. Technologists intrigued by the new challenge of stellar-inertial guidance, advocates of a hard-target FBM, and, of course, Kearfott would, however, all have another chance with the next generation FBM, which was already on the horizon.

DEVELOPMENTS IN NAVIGATION TECHNOLOGY: THE TRANSIT IMPROVEMENT PROGRAMME AND THE ELECTROSTATICALLY SUPPORTED GYROSCOPE

However, as the Mk. 4 stellar inertial guidance system programme was cancelled in 1968, another programme was being initiated to provide improvements in FBM submarine navigation. But, in contrast to the hard-target rationale of the Mk. 4, the improved navigation programme was justified on the grounds of increasing navigation reset intervals and availability, and hence submarine survivability, and so did not excite Congressional opposition to accuracy improvements.

The Improved Navigation Program covered a variety of developments aimed at enhancing various aspects of FBM navigation. These included the development of the 'phase-shift' Loran-C transmission method whereby on-board caesium-beam atomic clocks allow the synchronization necessary 'to provide range-range operation from two stations in addition to the normal three-station hyperbolic time-difference mode'.[84] When it became operational in 1974 this provided a large increase in the geographic availability of Loran-C navigation resets.

Another major development was a new generation of Transit satel-lites known as TIPS (Transit improvement program satellites). The first experimental improved satellite (known as TRIAD or TIP-1) was launched in September 1972.[85] The improvements were touted as providing greater radiation protection and longer useful life in the event of the loss of ground station control.[86] The major innovation was a drag compensation system (known as DISCOS, for disturbance compensation system), which 'is a device that compensates for the effects of aerodynamic drag forces and solar radiation pressure which act on the satellite in orbit, thus permitting the satellite to follow an orbit influenced solely by the gravitational field of the earth'.[87] The concept used is theoretically quite simple, and had been known for many years. A proof mass unsupported within the DISCOS unit is shielded by the unit from atmospheric drag and solar radiation and so experiences only gravitational forces – it follows a purely gravitational orbit. The DISCOS control system senses the motion of the proof mass relative to itself and responds to maintain their separation using Freon 14 cold gas thrusters – thus allowing the satellite to emulate the gravitational orbit of the proof mass.

DISCOS, along with an onboard general purpose computer to compensate for predictable drift in the satellite's reference oscillator, provides the capability to maintain accurate navigational broadcasts for over a week, as compared with the previous Oscar satellites which require orbital determination updates every day or so.[88] It may also provide somewhat more accurate navigational fixes as compared to the best offered by previous Transit satellites, but the primary rationale seemed to be extension of accuracy in case of loss of ground stations.

However, although TIP satellites were tested during the 1970s, the first of the production 'Nova' satellites was not launched until 1981.[89] Other Transit improvements were introduced in 1975 when the gravity model used for orbit determination was changed (from the one originally developed by the Applied Physics Laboratory to the new World Geodetic System 1972),[90] providing greater accuracy,[91] and when a technique was introduced to allow reduced exposure of the FBM submarine's BRN-3 antenna for navigational fixes.[92]

Another development which came to be funded under the improved navigation programme, the electrostatically suspended gyroscope (ESG), would, like the TIP satellites, only find operational deployment in the 1980s. The ESG was in many ways directly analogous to the stellar-inertial guidance system. But while decisions about Poseidon guidance became explicitly political, decisions about SINS technology remained firmly 'inside the black box', treated as merely technical. Yet the nature of developments in guidance and navigation technology was remarkably similar. There too evolutionary improvement of existing technology was challenged by a radically different technology whose proponents promised greatly enhanced accuracy. There too these proponents came from outside the traditional circle of suppliers to the FBM programme. There too the challenge failed, at least for the time being.

The challenge was right to the core of existing SINS technology: the gyroscopes. Because they had to keep the SINS stable platform in accurately known orientation for far longer than did missile guidance gyroscopes, these were crucial. Their design had stabilized to a 'paradigm' involving both flotation of the can containing the rotor in fluid and self-activating gas bearings for the rotor to spin on. The challenge involved doing away with conventional bearings altogether. It emerged from work done in the early 1950s by Professor Arnold Nordsieck of the University of Illinois. Nordsieck sought to construct the 'ultimate gyroscope' by supporting the gyro rotor in a vacuum in an electrostatic field.[93]

In the mid- to late-1950s, SPO supported exploratory studies of Nordsieck's concept at Honeywell and General Electric, 'with a view to the possible use of ESGs in Polaris submarines'.[94] The potential advantages were clear. The electrostatically suspended gyroscope was canvassed in the early 1960s as having drift rates of the order of 0.0001 degrees per hour.[95] In that period, a gyro with 0.01 degrees per hour drift was considered good, and though SINS gyros would certainly have been considerably better than that, the ESG could be put forward as a major possible improvement.

What was at stake was not simply the technology at the core of the SINS, but the organization that would supply it. Although Autonetics, which was consolidating its position as the sole SINS supplier, had begun studying the ESG in 1959,[96] the early running on the technology was made by Honeywell. Though Honeywell had, and has, an involvement in the manufacture of inertial components for ballistic missile guidance systems, it was an outsider to the SINS programme. As a supplier of inertial components, but not systems, Honeywell seems to have been concerned to enlarge its involvement through developing innovative technologies.[97]

But despite the promise of greater accuracy, the ESG 'for years seemed destined to remain only a cumbersome laboratory curiosity'.[98] Simple and elegant in concept, actually producing ESGs in any quantity proved to be extremely difficult. A completely spherical ball is best for purposes of suspension, but difficult to make. The Honeywell ball had to be machined to within 5 millionths of an inch, and 'during fabrication the hollow sphere is formed with a slight elongation along its spin axis such that it will become perfectly spherical when rotating at high speed'.[99]

Sphericity was not the only problem. Without physical contact between ball and case, reading out the ball's orientation (which was the point of the whole exercise) was tricky. The Honeywell gyro, and a research gyro developed at the University of Illinois in the early 1960s, used optical sensors to track a special pattern on the surface of the ball.[100] And of course there was the fear of what would happen if there was an interruption of power supplies when the ball was spinning. Without the supporting electrostatic forces, the ball would 'crash' and disintegrate. Because the gap between the ball and the walls of the cavity in which it was spun was tiny (of the order of a hundredth of an inch), sudden shock or vibration could also cause a catastrophic 'touch down'.

Honeywell never succeeded in getting its ESG adopted by the Navy. Although advanced in the early 1960s as 'pinpoint for Polaris launching', neither the Polaris nor Poseidon programmes made use of it. This was not because it failed to meet accuracy goals in performance terms. One report from the time noted that: 'Such [electrostatically suspended] gyros manufactured by Honeywell have been undergoing tests aboard the USS *Compass Island* for several years with very gratifying results. Performance specifications have been exceeded ...'[101] However, the ESG had to compete with evolutionary improvements of the more familiar SINS technology.[102] SPO's judgement at the time was that the ESG performance was 'modestly better' than the projected performance of improved SINS. But it 'would cost a lot of bucks' to get that modest improvement.[103] As Poseidon was retrofitted to the FBM submarines various improvements were made to the navigation systems, but conventional SINS remained at their heart.

The argument against the ESG was thus not dissimilar to the argument against stellar-inertial guidance. The proponents of the ESG, however, do not seem to have been effective 'heterogeneous engineers' like the proponents of stellar-inertial guidance. Here, apparently, there was no lobbying of high officials, no engineer feeling the need to 'join the power structure' (i.e. the Department of Defense) to secure the technology's acceptance, as one key corporate proponent of stellar-inertial guidance decided was necessary as a result of the failure to get it incorporated in Poseidon. Quite possibly as a result, the advocates of hard-target kill did not seize on the ESG to push for its early deployment, and Congressional doves were never given cause to oppose it. It remained a 'technical' technology, not a 'political' one.

But it did not die either. Like stellar-inertial guidance, the ESG was eventually to find success. Interestingly, though, it was to find success in a different design, and produced by a different corporation. Honeywell, its key proponent, never secured a place in submarine navigation.

BUILDING POSEIDON

The debate over the technical characteristics of Poseidon was centred on those technologies that were seen as defining its operational capability. Whether it would continue to be seen as an extension of the counter-city role attributed to Polaris, or, as some desired, as a counterforce system, came to rest on the twin attributes of warhead size and system accuracy that traditionally define 'hard-target kill capability'. But of the principal technologies that determine accuracy in a mobile system – guidance and navigation – only one became openly controversial. Guidance improvements were publicly touted as a means of enhancing hard target kill and thus attracted criticism. Navigation developments, on the other hand, did not attract the advocacy of counterforce proponents and continued to be justified on the widely favoured grounds of improving submarine survivability.

Other subsystems of Poseidon were less contested. The payload was to be delivered to a range that was nominally the same 2500 nautical miles as Polaris A3, depending on how many warheads were carried. At the maximum loading of fourteen warheads the range was about 1800 miles,[104] but by offloading warheads this could be increased to at least 3000 miles. Although some advances were made in structural weight savings and improved propellant performance, much of the increased payload capability stemmed simply from Poseidon's larger size. As in Polaris A3, Poseidon's two stages both use fibre-glass chambers with what is known as 'composite modified double base' propellant.[105]

Compared to A3, the Poseidon propulsion development was considered a conservative technological step.[106] In the only significant compliance by SPO with the new defence procurement regulations developed under McNamara, the Poseidon propulsion became the first major FBM subsystem to be competitively tendered.[107] Hercules Powder Co. collaborated with Thiokol Chemical Corporation in a 'joint venture' to produce both stages, with Hercules responsible for the entire second stage and the fibre-glass casing for the first stage into which Thiokol loaded their propellant. Aerojet, who had built Polaris propulsion systems, also tendered for both stages, but were squeezed out on cost.

Development of Poseidon propulsion proceeded without any serious problems, but, later, after deployment, began to encounter unexpected failures. After several years' investigation this was finally identified as due to age-related cracking of insulator rubber. The transition from the storage state of the missile in the launch tube to the high pressure following ignition led to failures which were found to be related to the missile storage temperature. This was largely eliminated by increasing the missile launch tube temperature, thus stopping the rubber insulators from becoming so brittle. What made this failure particularly intriguing, however, was that SPO had two manufacturers of the insulators, which provided markedly different failure rates:

> Both of them made these insulators to the 'identical process' – I use that in quotations – best we could tell they were identical, everything we specified they were identical. Obviously we didn't specify enough.

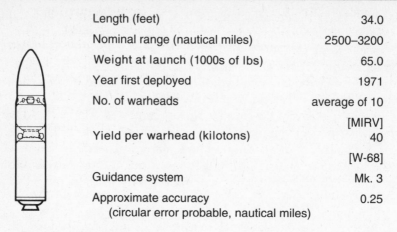

Length (feet)	34.0
Nominal range (nautical miles)	2500–3200
Weight at launch (1000s of lbs)	65.0
Year first deployed	1971
No. of warheads	average of 10 [MIRV]
Yield per warhead (kilotons)	40 [W-68]
Guidance system	Mk. 3
Approximate accuracy (circular error probable, nautical miles)	0.25

Figure 6.1 Poseidon C-3

> The problem developed in the one insulator fairly early in its life and eventually developed in the other one, but a lot, lot later. And we never could figure out . . . what was different about the two processes as they actually did it that created this problem.[108]

Thrust vector control in both stages is provided by single moveable nozzles, which are actuated by hydraulic pistons using fluid pressurized by gas generators. With the introduction of the MIRV bus for deployment of the reentry bodies, second stage thrust termination was again considered necessary (both for range control and also as a means of separating the bus from the booster). Instead of the prebuilt plugs used in Polaris A1 and A2 the thrust termination vents in Poseidon were simply blown out pyrotechnically through the homogeneous fibre-glass chamber.

This thrust termination is intended to leave the 'bus' travelling at the approximate velocity for it to release the individual reentry bodies onto trajectories that will take them to their intended targets. To reorient the bus so as to drop reentry bodies onto different trajectories requires a propulsion system of some sort. Whereas the Air Force Minuteman III MIRV system uses liquid fuel engines for this purpose, the Navy preferred to avoid liquid propellants for submarine based systems. Instead they choose to use solid propellants, which are considered safer, but more difficult to mechanize. Whereas liquid engines can be turned on and off precisely, solids burn at a constant rate once lit and cannot be stopped and started easily.

In the Poseidon bus a gas generator burns continuously feeding eight pairs of opposing nozzles, each pair of which has a valve that can be commanded to vent in either direction. This manoeuvring and the release of reentry bodies is controlled by the guidance computer, through a steering logic developed by close collaboration between Lockheed and the Draper Laboratory. Thus the bus which carried the reentry bodies could release them on to trajectories covering targets spread out over a 'footprint'. Both range and the crossrange width of this footprint depended on the number of reentry bodies carried. A full payload of fourteen reentry bodies provided a range of about 1800 nautical miles and almost no footprint crossrange; it provided no real MIRV capability. Ten reentry bodies allowed 2500 nautical miles range and 150 nautical miles crossrange, and a loading of six reentry bodies gave a maximum range of 3000 nautical miles and a crossrange of 300 nautical miles.[109]

Development of these reentry bodies was fraught with difficulties. Like the Mk. 1 reentry vehicle of the Polaris A1/A2, the Poseidon Mk. 3 was a heat sink design made of beryllium, but with an ablative graphite nosetip. It also incorporated a shell – intended to provide additional protection from X-ray deposition caused by ABM nuclear detonations – which peeled off during reentry.[110] So important was hardness considered that the Mk. 3 reentry body is said to be four times 'harder' than any reentry body developed, then or since.[111] This level of hardness was seen as necessary because otherwise the large numbers of reentry bodies and the low energy of the bus solid propulsion meant that the spacing between the reentry bodies was insufficient to avoid multiple kill by a single ABM detonation.

An initial concern during development was ensuring that the reentry body design would not suffer from the phenomena known as spin-up and spin-down. Reentry bodies are spun so that the effects of atmospheric reentry are symmetrical, and to limit loss of accuracy. Spinning is particularly important in ablative designs where uneven ablation would alter the aerodynamic characteristics of the reentry body and so severely reduce its accuracy.

The Poseidon Mk. 3 is a very small reentry body and the asymmetries that occur as it deforms during reentry are especially significant.[112] In its development phase asymmetry-induced torques resulted in the occurrence of spin-up and spin-down. As one Lockheed manager put it: 'It would take a banana shape and that would cause a trim ... [and it] would end up either rolling up or down.'[113] This was a serious concern as spin-up can lead to the destruction of the reentry body and spin-down through zero greatly reduces system accuracy. However, recognition that the reentry system was the greatest innovation in Poseidon led to a supplemental flight test programme using Athena boosters starting in September 1966, and this resolved these concerns.[114]

With this problem solved (essentially by shifting the reentry body centre of gravity) there was still a further upset much later in the programme. The reentry body carbon nose tips had worked well during prototype flight testing, but when the programme moved into its production phase apparently identical nose tips started to break up in flight tests, especially those conducted over longer ranges:

> These graphite nosetips had worked perfectly up throughout the development of Poseidon without exception. We never had a failure in a development flight test and we went into production, we started our testing and . . . lo and behold we started getting failures. A few, not large numbers, but a small percentage of the nosetips of the reentry bodies broke up in flight. And this presented a tremendous challenge to us because what in the world was going on. Something had changed and we examined the graphite with great care using every non-destructive test means we could to find out what was different about the graphite that had gone into the production nose-tips and the ones that we had used in the development flight testing. We could find nothing other than the fact that they were produced in different facilities. It turned out that the manufacturer, who was Union Carbide, had used an R&D facility, a small furnace, for graphitizing the nosetips in the processing and when we'd gone into production, very much larger numbers, they had shifted to their production facility and we concluded that the control of the thermal gradients and the temperatures in the large production furnaces was just not, could not have been the same. We couldn't find any other reason for this statistical variation in quality.[115]

In 1973 a three-year modification programme was instigated to remedy the design and replace already deployed reentry bodies.[116] A further problem, this time with the actual warhead (the W-68), was also to require remedial action some time after deployment.[117]

DEPLOYING POSEIDON

Despite the development problems Poseidon was deployed only two months behind schedule. At the end of March 1971 the *James Madison* went on patrol, its Polaris A3 missiles replaced by Poseidon during its first overhaul. Conversion of Polaris submarines to carry Poseidon mainly involved changes in the navigation, fire control, and launcher subsystems.

The submarine SINS were improved to provide better performance with the Mk. 2 Mod. 3 upgraded to a Mk. 2 Mod. 6 configuration. This used a redesigned Inductosyn package for heading readout so as to reduce the transmission error, and the SINS G7B gyroscopes were selected to a higher standard:

> G7B gyros were screened during factory selloff tests. These tests included the final drift test, self-induced vibration test, and output axis hysteresis test. If the gyro met specified performance criteria for these tests, it was designated a C-3 gyro for use on the MK 2 MOD 6 SINS. If the gyro exceeded the C-3 criteria, but met a less stringent set of criteria, it was designated an A-3 gyro for use on the SINS installed in the submarines still carrying Polaris A-3 missiles.[118]

Other new hardware included a considerably more powerful computer based on the Univac CP-890 to replace the NAVDAC, and a new Loran-C receiver, the AN/BRN-5 to replace the original AN/WPN-3.[119] Other improvements 'included use of survey maps for compensation of vertical deflections due to gravity anomalies, use of a Kalman filter for optimal estimation of SINS errors from a history of position fixes, improved inertial heading determination and self-calibration, implementation of at-sea calibration of the electromagnetic log . . .'.[120] The Mk. 88 fire control system used in the submarines that were converted to carry Poseidon was an 'evolutionary' improvement of the Mk. 84 used for Polaris A3.

In the launcher system the developments that had originally 'discovered' the extra tube space that made Poseidon possible were taken advantage of. The Mk. 21 launch system originally installed in the submarines to hold Polaris A3 missiles had been designed so that modular replacement allowed for relatively simple upgrading to the Mk. 24 system for Poseidon. The heavy launch tube and stowage adaptors used for Polaris were replaced with a thin launch tube taking up almost all the space in the submarine's mount tube. Padding replaced the stowage launch adaptors in holding the missile snug in the launch tube.[121]

CONFLICTING INTERESTS: 'FOLLOW-ON' AND COUNTERFORCE

Poseidon was the outcome of a number of influences, some of which were conflicting. SPO as an organization needed a new missile development to justify its special status. With the Polaris A3 development due to finish in 1964, there was a danger that a delay in starting development of another FBM generation would at best lead to the break up of the expertise that SPO had assembled (both internally and in its contractors), and at worst might lead to the dissolution of SPO.

But Poseidon cannot be explained simply as the inevitable product of a follow-on imperative.[122] SPO and Lockheed certainly were keen that there should not be too long a gap between FBM generations, but other aspects of the FBM programme, such as maintenance of existing systems, were both considered important at SPO and a source of work for Lockheed. Moreover, whatever the incentives pushing organizations to ensure rapid 'follow-on', they still need to be sanctioned by Congress and the Department of Defense. In the case of Poseidon, neither of these were simply to present SPO with a 'blank cheque' to build what it wanted. Indeed Poseidon was the first FBM system to be consciously subjected to a Congressional cut when the Senate Defense Appropriations Subcommittee refused to allow more than two Polaris submarines to be converted to accept it.[123] The Office of the Secretary of Defense (OSD) was supportive of a new generation, but wanted to ensure that the next FBM would provide some extra capability. As it was, the delay in authorization of Poseidon which stemmed from OSD's directed redesign led to SPO taking on the Deep Submergence Systems Project as 'a means to keep the FBM team together until Poseidon was approved'.[124]

In particular, SPO found the rest of the Navy very unresponsive to the idea of replacing Polaris with another generation missile. The costly Polaris programme was widely perceived in the Navy as having used funds that would otherwise have gone on more traditional missions. To many these missions seemed rather more pressing than the development of another generation FBM. Such resistance was only overcome during 1964 when Secretary of the Navy, Paul Nitze persuaded CNO Admiral McDonald that the Poseidon programme should go ahead.[125]

The follow-on to Polaris was, then, neither easy nor particularly swift. Even after a decision to proceed was made, the actual design remained contested for several years. Many who were supportive of a new missile, particularly those in the Great Circle Group, continued to press for technical characteristics orientated towards counterforce. More importantly, counterforce was also seen as desirable by McNamara's OSD and accuracy improvements were sought in the FBM for this purpose, as for some time, was the possibility of carrying larger warheads.

However, although SPO's autonomy was cut back during the 1960s skilful heterogeneous engineering maintained the programme's continuity without significant compromises. Accuracy remained only a goal, and not a requirement. Stellar-inertial guidance was used as a argument against the Mk. 17 heavy warhead, and then itself dropped. In its final form Poseidon's technology reflected more SPO's concern of

ABM penetration than that of those who desired to rival the counter-force role of the Air Force. SPO's leadership thus maintained the aspect of the FBM programme it considered most important, its ability to meet the promised goals – particularly that of an assured retaliatory deterrent – and therefore its differentiated role as compared to the Air Force.

The outcome was a weapon system whose accuracy/yield combination was considered inadequate for the destruction of hardened targets, such as missile silos. But although it never achieved the counterforce capability that some had desired for it, Poseidon provided more such capability than Polaris. As well as the traditional FBM targets – large, vulnerable urban-industrial areas – Poseidon now could also be directed against a range of smaller, soft targets, including non-strategic military installations, R&D centres and other important industrial facilities away from cities. Indeed the legacy of a forty-one boat fleet, combined with the decisions over Poseidon's payload, almost demanded such targets be included in the nuclear warplan, the single integrated operational plan (SIOP). With all but the first ten FBM submarines to be converted to Poseidon, the increase in targeting depended on how many warheads each missile carried. To provide extra range, Poseidon was initially deployed carrying considerably less than the maximum fourteen warheads per missile allowed in SALT – perhaps as few as six per missile – giving a sixfold increase in targets as compared to the Polaris missiles replaced.[126] Although delivering less equivalent megatonnage than the Polaris it replaced, a six-warhead Poseidon could cover extra targets. When the limited nature of Soviet ABM developments became apparent, these extra warheads provided a capability which 'required' the addition of many marginal targets to the SIOP.[127]

Poseidon, thus, left a contradictory legacy. Although SPO's autonomy was much reduced during the 1960s, it nevertheless managed to avoid serious setbacks to the programme. But Poseidon did leave SPO's image of technical and managerial competence tarnished. The long, drawn-out development period, the demanding nature of the MIRV technology, and increasing limitations on SPO's independence all served to highlight difficulties. But although there were serious problems which continued to impair reliability even after Poseidon became officially operational, these were not unprecedented in the FBM programme. SPO and its contractors (which remained virtually the same from Polaris to Poseidon) did not suddenly become poor technologists. What changed, most crucially, was the world in which they operated. Unlike with Polaris, SPO could no longer command unlimited funding whilst remaining able to shift performance goals to meet achievement.[128] SPO became subject to increasing interference from the Navy leadership, from the Office of the Secretary of Defense, and from Congressional scrutiny. The special powers granted by Burke to Raborn for Polaris dwindled,[129] as SPO no longer came to be considered 'special' – indeed its name was changed to Strategic Systems Project Office in 1967. The change in name reflected official subordination under the Office of Strategic Offensive and Defensive Systems (Op-97).[130]

Developed in the Cold War atmosphere of Sputnik and the 'missile gap', Polaris was seen as a desperate 'need', and Raborn's skill was to ensure that no-one forgot that. But for Poseidon, with the US nuclear arsenal already well exceeding the Soviet Union's in the mid-1960s, the 'need' was unclear (the potential ABM 'threat' never materialized), internally contested, and difficult to rally public or Congressional enthusiasm for. SPO no longer commanded priority.[131]

With SPO's dominance reduced, Poseidon became the first FBM to be seriously contested, not only within the 'establishment', but also in public where its MIRV development attracted much criticism. Also, while SPO was able to avoid a commitment to a hard-target Poseidon, and to retain the emphasis on assured destruction, the final outcome was an FBM force which fell a little short of providing the one (hard-target kill), but exceeded 'requirements' for the other (assured destruction). To many, especially those within the Navy connected with targeting, this increased the desire to make any future FBM have 'genuine' hard-target kill capability. Navy officers assigned to the Joint Strategic Target Planning Staff (JSTPS) soon tired of Air Force taunts about the Navy's 'firecrackers' – Poseidon's 40 kiloton warheads.[132]

But even as Poseidon began to enter service, counterforce advocates were to have another chance as the next FBM generation was planned. Preoccupied with rectifying Poseidon's problems, SPO would again have its authority challenged, but this time, on many key issues it would be the loser.

7 STRAT-X, ULMS, AND TRIDENT I

> I considered that we'd better surrender to Rickover so that we wouldn't have to surrender to the Russians.   Admiral Zumwalt.[1]

While Poseidon development was still underway, and its final nature not yet completely decided, consideration began of another generation of fleet ballistic missiles. Ironically, the path that leads to Trident II – the first Fleet Ballistic Missile in which hard-target kill capability would be a clear requirement – began with a study based on the criteria of a different era. That study was called Strat-X, and embodied the cost-effectiveness orientation of the 'systems analysis' of the McNamara era, and its emphasis on 'assured destruction'.

STRAT-X AND ULMS

The Strat-X study was a response by Robert McNamara's Deputy Director of Defense Research and Engineering, Lloyd Wilson, to Air Force pressures in the mid–1960s for a new, very large ICBM, provisionally called WS-120A; it may indeed have been initiated precisely to kill the Air Force missile.[2] Starting in late 1966, Strat-X was carried out by the Institute for Defense Analysis, and was submitted in August 1967. Its task was specified, in part, as follows:

> Strat-X is to be a technological study to characterize U.S. alternatives to counter the possible Soviet ABM deployment and the Soviet potential for reducing the U.S. assured-destruction-force effectiveness during the 1970s. It is desired that the U.S. alternatives be considered from a uniform cost-effectiveness base as well as from solution sensitivity to various Soviet alternative actions.[3]

Various strategic nuclear weapons systems were compared using criteria based on 'assured destruction'. How, it was asked, could the US most cost-effectively ensure the retaliatory 'delivery' to the Soviet Union of sufficient 'equivalent megatons' to deter it – and do so on the assumption of possible Soviet developments such as ultra-accurate ICBMs and anti-ballistic missile defenses?

113

Both the Navy candidates – one submarine and the other surface-based – did well in this competition for the most cost-effective 'assured destruction' weapon system, and the Navy was instructed to continue studying them, but the surface-launched missile system (SLMS) was dropped in 1968.[4] The submarine concept, known as ULMS or under-sea long-range missile system, comprised a large (443 feet long, 8,240 tons displacement),[5] but not very fast, submarine carrying up to 24 missiles of 4500 to 6500 mile range held in canisters external to the pressure hull.[6] The use of canisters was primarily an artefact of the way the study was conducted.[7] A common missile (80 inches in diameter and 50 feet long) was to be used by everyone to ensure valid comparisons between different basing modes. Since the characteristics of this missile were also being decided during Strat-X, the use of canisters allowed submarine design to go ahead simultaneously. In retrospect, however, it was also possible to rationalize how canisters could provide some launching advantages: 'Missiles may be released from the submarine at all speeds and depths up to the maximums, and missile firing may be delayed to avoid backtracking of trajectory so that submarine survivability is not inhibited by missile launch constraints.'[8]

An advanced development objective for ULMS was established by Chief of Naval Operations, Admiral Thomas Moorer on 1 February 1968, with Admiral Smith of SPO named as the project manager in March. Then in July, reflecting the interest in a possible surface-launched system, Admiral Smith's responsibility was increased to include all Navy strategic systems (not just FBMs) and the Special Projects Office was renamed the Strategic Systems Project Office (SSPO).[9] During 1967–69 SSPO carried out preliminary studies to define the ULMS technology based on the concepts used in Strat-X.

In particular, Admiral Smith and SSPO sought to keep research and development costs low by utilizing as much existing technology as possible. The long range of the missile would be obtained simply by increasing the volume of propellant used – the missile envisaged was to be about twice the volume of Poseidon – and the submarine size would grow accordingly.[10]

The reactor envisaged to power the new submarine was an existing concept which had been tested in the attack submarine *Narwhal*. This again would help to reduce the cost and uncertainty involved in the development of new technology, especially when responsibility for that development would lie outside of SSPO's control, in the hands of Admiral Rickover, head of the Navy's Nuclear Propulsion Directorate. In addition, the *Narwhal* reactor was a natural circulation design which at low speeds used convection rather than pumps to circulate the water coolant. At the normal cruising speeds of an FBM patrol this was expected to make it significantly quieter than a conventional forced circulation design. This accorded with Admiral Smith's desire to minimize the noise (and other observable characteristics) of the ULMS submarine so as to enhance its survivability against developments in Soviet anti-submarine warfare. However, because the *Narwhal* was only about a third the size of the proposed ULMS submarine, its 17,000 shaft horsepower (shp) reactor would only allow a top speed of about 18–19 knots, making it about 4 knots slower than the Polaris/Poseidon submarines.[11] But a high top speed was not considered an important attribute of an FBM submarine in Strat-X, nor by Admiral Smith.

Instead SSPO's ULMS design reflected the emphasis on cost-effectiveness and survivability through low observability. The Strat-X concept of externally carried encapsulated missiles was dropped in early 1969 in favour of bare launch from vertical launch tubes, as in the Polaris/Poseidon submarines. Although the extra missile length allowed by external canisters meant that option was favoured by some missile designers, the final decision of Admiral Smith was that the advantages did not merit changing the tried and tested method used before.[12] As usual Admiral Smith also sought to ensure that SSPO would be able to deliver what it promised on schedule. In particular, the choice of an existing reactor design not only greatly reduced the time and expense of a new research and development programme, but also reduced SSPO's reliance on others.

But, in marked contrast to Polaris, the development of the next generation FBM submarine was to be a divisive and contested battle, the outcome of which would affect the nature of FBM technology for many years. In this struggle, issues which might usually be considered simply 'technical' aspects of the design of the new submarine became entwined in a struggle over the future role of the FBM involving both domestic and international politics.

THE TRIDENT SUBMARINE DEBATE

The submarines that carried Polaris and Poseidon had been uncontroversial. But ULMS reopened the issue that SPO had successfully closed with the choice of a modified existing attack submarine design to carry Polaris – the potentially deeply problematic relationship with Admiral Rickover, 'father' of nuclear propulsion.

Rickover became aware of the ULMS plans early in 1970 when SSPO asked his nuclear propulsion directorate for information on the weight and size of the *Narwhal* reactor. He immediately objected, arguing that the ULMS submarine should be able to reach a top speed of at least 24 knots. Above this speed active sonar had failed to operate effectively in tests, and so even though Soviet attack submarines would be faster (and so able to outrun a 24-knot submarine), they would be 'blinded' in chasing at such speeds.[13]

To meet the 24 knot 'requirement' Rickover instead proposed powering each submarine with two 30,000 shp reactors of a design that was still to be tested. Although many remained sceptical of the argument for speed (the 'blinding' effect was based on limited data) Admiral Smith was put under considerable pressure by the Office of the Chief of Naval Operations to reach an agreement that would allow the submarine design to be settled. With SSPO's technical authority already being questioned for the first time in the Poseidon programme, and with its autonomy much reduced from the days of Polaris, Admiral Smith chose not to fight a divisive battle with Rickover which might further delay and endanger the ULMS programme.

Despite his personal misgivings Admiral Smith was forced to concede that his area of expertise was the missile system, whereas that of Rickover 'was basically shipbuilding in its various aspects, particularly propulsion'.[14] This logic compelled Admiral Smith to accept that once he had set the missile characteristics, and most importantly their weight, then Rickover should design the submarine. This agreement led, by March 1970, to a 'compromise' which very much favoured Rickover. The ULMS submarine was to use his favoured twin natural circulation reactors to give the submarine a top speed of 26–27 knots. To accommodate these large reactors, as well as the large 6000 mile missiles (in launch tubes nearly three and a half times the volume of Poseidon) required a huge submarine with a 50 foot hull diameter and displacing about 30,000 tons.[15]

But this was far from the end of the matter. When the Deputy Secretary of Defense David Packard learnt about the proposed submarine in September 1970 he 'rejected the idea of such a large submarine emphatically and categorically'.[16] It became clear that approval of ULMS would require some compromise towards Packard's preferences, which were made clear to the Navy: 'Minimum detectability as well as minimum cost will be given top priority in OSD reviews.'[17]

ULMS now became a more pressing concern for the newly appointed Chief of Naval Operations, Admiral Elmo Zumwalt. In October 1970 he revitalized the ULMS Steering Group which worked out a smaller, less expensive ULMS submarine design, basically by scaling down the Smith/Rickover compromise. Recognizing the necessity of maintaining Rickover's support, the new design retained his favoured 30,000 shp reactor, but used only one rather than two. Although it still had a displacement over one and half times that of the latest 640 class Polaris/Poseidon submarines, it was dubbed the 'Super-640', apparently in an attempt to minimize the difference. It also differed significantly from the Strat-X concept in that the missile tubes were only about 10 per cent larger in volume than Poseidon's.[18]

Zumwalt himself favoured repeating the first Polaris submarine construction method by simply adapting the latest attack submarine design, the 688 class, and installing a missile section into it. Since the 688 design was already developed (including the reactor) this option eliminated much of the research and development costs, and seemed to offer considerably cheaper submarines, which was Zumwalt's main concern. However, Zumwalt decided that Rickover's support was the critical factor in determining the feasibility of the ULMS submarine. What would be the optimum design in 'technical' and strategic terms was something over which there was considerable disagreement, but one 'design factor' was indisputable – the potential of Rickover to block the programme. Zumwalt needed to enrol his support for ULMS: 'it was clear to me that Rickover would never support anything that didn't have his huge . . . new reactor in it. It was clear to me that he would have been willing to take any delay to get it.'[19]

The Super-640 satisfied Rickover, but had the unintended consequence of undermining the rationale for developing *any* new submarine. When faced with the prospect of a submarine which could only accommodate launch tubes not much bigger than Poseidon's, SSPO set about investigating whether they could meet Strat-X's range/payload goals with a smaller missile than previously envisaged. By abandoning the commitment to minimize research and development it seemed possible to develop a new missile which could provide longer range. Moreover, it might be possible to develop this so that it would not only fit the Super-640 tubes, but also those of the existing submarines, currently carrying Poseidon. Known as EXPO (extended range Poseidon), or C3D, this offered the prospect of deferring submarine construction altogether.[20] Retrofitting EXPO to existing submarines would increase their searoom and thus survivability against any short-term developments in Soviet anti-submarine warfare capabilities.

A Defense Science Board Strategic Task Force reviewed the ULMS issue in late 1970, early 1971, and also concluded that Poseidon submarines should be retrofitted with a longer range missile.[21] EXPO gained the support of Admiral Smith because it obviated the need for the Navy to rush into development of new submarines based on

117

hurried studies and a possibly premature assessment of Soviet developments. Rather than the Navy pushing the development of the ULMS submarine so vigorously, Smith felt that the impetus for such a major programme should come from above. If more submarines were needed in the meantime then why not simply build a few more of the 640-class and equip them with either Poseidon or EXPO missiles?[22]

Not surprisingly EXPO found little favour with Rickover or Zumwalt. Zumwalt's concern over what he called 'the tremendous growth of the Soviet threat' was the reason why he was prepared to give in to Rickover over the Super-640. Zumwalt wanted to start construction of a new submarine as soon as possible. To him the EXPO option was 'just peeing around', as he put it at a meeting of the ULMS Steering Group on 27 January 1971.[23] Viewing EXPO as 'a way of defeating construction of a new submarine' he made it quite clear at that meeting that the Super-640 decision was final – OSD was not even to be informed of the EXPO option.[24]

In March 1971, apparently in response to a Rickover proposal, Zumwalt set up a new office to manage the ULMS programme and appointed Rear Admiral Harvey E. Lyon – considered by many to be a Rickover protégé – as ULMS project manager, or PM-2. Zumwalt felt this necessary to coordinate ULMS development because 'it was evident that Levering Smith and Rickover could not talk to each other in a reasonable way'.[25] But in effect it meant that Admiral Smith, as PM-1, was subordinated to the role of missile developer. From the highpoint of SPO's autonomy during the development of Polaris, the office, now SSPO, had lost much of its control over the development of ULMS.

Following the establishment of PM-2, the Electric Boat Division of General Dynamics Corporation was awarded an initial contract for submarine design and the ULMS Ship Acquisition Project was set up to oversee it. ULMS characteristics were worked out for submission to OSD with initial operational capability (IOC) to be in 1979 or 1980. Particularly significant was growth in the size of the missile – by about 6 inches in diameter and 4 to 5 feet in length – without any change in mission requirements.[26] Unlike the earlier design, which was not that much larger than EXPO, the new dimensions meant a larger submarine would certainly be required. Similarly, the reactor size was increased from 30,000 to 35,000 shp, perhaps to help avert any suggestions that an existing 30,000 design (forced, not natural circulation) already deployed in attack submarines be used to save research and development costs.[27]

Still Deputy Defense Secretary Packard remained sceptical. On learning of the EXPO proposal – apparently via a civilian staffer in SSPO who felt no particular loyalty to or fear of Zumwalt's injunction to suppress it[28] – he began to favour an approach very similar to Admiral Smith's. He would commit to ULMS development, but on a delayed time-scale with IOC no sooner than 1984, and in the meantime suggested that EXPO development – with an IOC of 1978 – would provide interim cover to ensure FBM submarine survivability.[29]

Packard's proposal formed the basis of one of the options presented in a twenty-page Development Concept Paper (DCP no. 67) that was prepared by OSD and the Navy and released on 7 September 1971. It presented five options 'for maintaining the deterrent effectiveness of our sea based forces':[30]

1 Do nothing (cancel ULMS and extended range Poseidon).
2 Extended range Poseidon, IOC about CY [calendar year] 1977.
3 ULMS, with IOC about CY a) 1979, b) 1980, c) 1981, and d) 1982.
4 ULMS, IOC about 1981, but with a parallel development of an extended range Poseidon missile to permit the option of deploying extended range Poseidon in about CY 1977.
5 Extended range Poseidon missile, with IOC about CY 1977, followed by ULMS with a delayed IOC (about CY 1983).

To all concerned options 4 and 5 were considered the only real alternatives.[31] Option 4 would give 'the Navy' (not SSPO, of course) what they wanted – a firm commitment to ULMS with only token reference to EXPO development, but not necessarily deployment. Option 5 embodied the preferences of Packard and Admiral Smith. Attached to the DCP were recommendations from other interested parties, which ranged from that of the Joint Chiefs of Staff (who favoured the option 3, ULMS only approach which gave 'the Navy' what it wanted at the least cost to the defence budget) to that of the Assistant Secretary of Defense for Systems Analysis (who favoured immediate engineering development of EXPO, but wished to keep the whole question of ULMS design, and indeed of whether to choose ULMS at all, under review for several more years).[32]

A week later on 14 September, OSD released a 'Secretary of Defense Decision' on ULMS, said to have been drafted by Packard.[33] This was presented as approving a modified option 4 from the DCP, but in substance was nearer to Packard's original preference, option 5. The term EXPO was diplomatically dropped, but emphasis was given to the development of a missile with 'a range as near to 4,000 miles as possible while being compatible with the present configuration of Poseidon boats'.[34] This missile, referred to as ULMS I, was to have an

119

IOC of 1977, whereas ULMS II would be a longer-range 'optimized missile design for deployment in a new submarine'.[35] No exact IOC was set for either ULMS II or the new submarine, whose characteristics still remained to be defined:

> The parameters of the new boat which are affected by the missile characteristics should not be established until work on the missile program has established range, performance and size parameters for the new missile. Development of subsystem improvements, propulsion, quieting, etc., can and should proceed in parallel with the new missile development. The objective of the ULMS program should be to bring in a new force of reasonable cost in the early 1980s.[36]

Whereas quietness was to be given 'first priority' in the submarine design, no mention was made of speed or power requirements.[37] Although EXPO was repackaged as ULMS I, the decision seemed to be a blow to Rickover and Zumwalt and a satisfactory outcome for Admiral Smith and SSPO.

But this decision did not last long as international (and domestic) politics now came to play a role. In October 1971 Packard and Secretary of Defense Melvin Laird were persuaded by President Nixon that US FBM force development should be accelerated to allow him some leverage in the SALT negotiations with the Soviet Union.[38] As well as providing a 'bargaining chip' to use against the Soviet Union in SALT (and possibly later negotiations), an initiative in FBM submarine construction was also considered useful to mollify possible 'hawkish' right-wing and service opposition to SALT ratification.[39]

The quickest way to begin increasing US FBM forces was, of course, either to build more 640-class submarines or to convert attack submarines already under construction, but these options were known to be unacceptable to key Navy factions, and especially to Admiral Rickover. Attempting to impose them on a recalcitrant Navy would be unlikely to mollify anybody. Instead Packard agreed to reshape his ULMS package.

He first consulted with Rickover, who on 31 October replied affirmatively to Packard's inquiry about the feasibility of accelerating the ULMS submarine construction schedule. According to Rickover, the lead ship could be ready by late 1977, and beginning in 1978 construction could proceed at the rate of three a year.[40] Packard then instigated a Navy study to compare the options for accelerating FBM submarine construction, and to provide justification for the one he had already chosen, ULMS acceleration.[41] As recalled by an SSPO source: 'The study was a sham. Packard had already made up his mind. We were simply going through the motions. We all knew what the answer was.'[42]

But OSD was not simply imposing the president's wishes on the Navy. The FBM acceleration issue also provided an opportunity to strike a blow against the interference of Kissinger's National Security Council (NSC) in military matters. Kissinger had set up the Defense Program Review Committee (DPRC) in the National Security Council in an attempt to gain some control over the Department of Defense.[43] Secretary of Defense Laird sought to minimize the role of the DPRC, and in this case National Security Council staff were unable to obtain details of the studies that were circulating in the Pentagon.

Thus the favoured approach at the White House – which was apparently to build more Polaris/Poseidon type submarines – was simply ignored by OSD. On 26 December, without consultation with the president, Laird ordered ULMS acceleration.[44] This was leaked to the press on 12 January 1972 presenting the President with a *fait accompli*, which realistically could not be challenged. To do so would not only involve publicly contradicting the Secretary of Defense, but also taking on the powerful factions of the Navy, including Zumwalt and Rickover. The Navy backed up their claim that ULMS submarines could be ready virtually as soon as extra Polaris/Poseidon submarines by drastically shortening the ULMS development time, almost literally overnight. A staff member of the Trident Ship Acquisition Program Office recalled what happened over a weekend in early January 1972:

> The delivery date on that Monday was December 1977; on the preceding Friday it had been December 1981. In that one fell swoop, they [the Office of the Chief of Naval Operations and the Navy Secretariat] had taken ... the program parameters and what have you, and for political reasons, which were obviously SALT, had [changed] them.[45]

Aware that Packard was now determined to back an accelerated ULMS programme, the ULMS Project Office was able to set the design to suit its priorities. This included a missile tube sufficiently larger than the Super-640 version to make it completely unable to fit an existing or modified Polaris/Poseidon submarine. The ULMS submarine was to have a 42 foot hull diameter, would displace 18,700 tons (compared to the Super-640's 14,000), and have a reactor of 35,000 shp (compared to 30,000 in the Super-640).[46] On 15 May 1972 ULMS was renamed Trident.

The number of missiles to be carried by each submarine ended up being set at twenty-four or half as many again as in the original FBM submarines. Navy parametric studies supported the obvious conclusion that the more missiles per submarine, the cheaper the deployment cost per missile. But, according to Admiral George Miller (head of Navy strategic planning since the Great Circle Group was set up and an advisor to Strat-X), the decision to go for twenty-four was 'arbitrarily made, just to make the expensive sub look more cost-effective'.[47] Just how arbitrarily he did not reveal. In fact, the Navy studies had settled on twenty tubes, but in a press announcement Secretary of Defense Laird mistakenly said twenty-four and this it remained.[48] However, although more missiles per submarine was more cost-effective, it also, to some, raised the worry that the Navy was putting all its eggs in too few baskets, should Soviet anti-submarine warfare improve. For example, Admiral Smith of SSPO 'would have favoured a smaller submarine than the Trident – wouldn't have put as many missiles in it'.[49]

It was this fiercely contested result of bureaucratic intrigue that was presented to Congress for funding. There too the FBM programme no longer commanded unquestioning support. Poseidon had already raised some doubts, and although the general principle of eventually building new FBM submarines was not in question, many opposed the administration's acceleration plans as being too hasty. Ironically, the administration now found it necessary to put pressure on some of the 'hawks' whose expected reaction to SALT it had originally intended to placate by ULMS acceleration. In both 1972 and 1973 tied Senate votes on amendments to cut Trident funding were only overturned after intensive lobbying of key conservatives – John Stennis in 1972 and Barry Goldwater in 1973 – by the administration and the Navy.[50]

Despite the tenuous consensus in support of Trident, funding was approved. However, some of the recommendations of the Research and Development Subcommittee of the Senate Armed Services Committee were taken up by the new Secretary of Defense, James Schlesinger:

> The Secretary of Defense has restructured the program, consistent with the actions of Congress, but has gone even further. He has adopted the recommendations made by the Research and Development Subcommittee last year [1973] to slow the pace of submarine construction from three to two per year, and has approved the backfit of Poseidon submarines with the C–4 missile, beginning in fiscal year 1979, now planned for ten submarines. Previously, this was approved only as an option for initiation in the early 1980s.[51]

This decision to make a firm commitment to backfit the Trident I missile into existing FBM submarines was very much inspired by the wishes of Admiral Smith of SSPO, who did not want the deployment of that missile to be limited by any delays in the Trident submarine construction which lay beyond his control.[52] It turned out to be a very prescient decision.

BUILDING THE TRIDENT SUBMARINE

Throughout the late 1970s the Trident submarine programme was dogged by delay, cost overruns, and litigation. While it was originally hoped that the first Trident submarine, the *Ohio*, would be delivered in December 1977 it in fact began sea trials only in June 1981.[53] Compared to the success story of the original Polaris, the Trident submarine construction was a public relations disaster.

Many of the problems stemmed from the decision to accelerate Trident construction, that Rickover had assured Packard about in late 1971, and that had led the delivery date to be advanced four years over one weekend. Although widely disliked within the Navy, Admiral Rickover was respected for his technical competence, and had cultivated many admirers in Congress. He not only assured Congressional doubters that the first Trident submarine could be delivered within the new schedule – in time for the expiry of the SALT Interim Agreement in 1977 – but also committed the Navy to unusual costing arrangements.

First-of-a-kind lead ships, with the *exception* of nuclear-powered ships, would normally be built under some kind of cost-plus contract. With so many uncertainties in the design of a lead ship it was generally considered unreasonable to insist that a fixed price be met. Typically a cost-plus contract would provide for all relevant costs to be reimbursed with the addition of an incentive fee, the size of which depended on how nearly the target cost was met.[54] Admiral Rickover, however, was a firm believer in fixed-price contracts which committed the government to pay the fixed price agreed on (usually providing a greater profit margin to the contractor than cost-plus arrangements), but in which the contractor bore at least some of the financial risk involved.[55] He argued that the Trident submarines would be similar in nature to those built for Polaris, and that many of the new components, such as the nuclear reactor, would be supplied as government-furnished equipment (GFE). Construction would therefore be a fairly straightforward task, involving little risk.

The Trident acceleration was thus 'sold' to Congress in 1972 on the understanding that delivery by 1977 was a simple matter, which could be achieved as cheaply as possible by a competitively tendered fixed-price contract. But this view was not held by the only shipyards capable of building the submarine – General Dynamic Corporation's Electric Boat Division at Groton, Connecticut and the Newport News Shipbuilding and Drydock Company (a subsidiary of the Tenneco Corporation) in Virginia. The Navy received their bids on 5 November 1973 and neither complied with the terms outlined in the Navy's RFP (request for proposals). Newport News offered delivery in May 1981 under a cost plus fixed fee contract. Electric Boat were prepared to attempt delivery for April 1979 and wanted a cost plus incentive fee contract.[56] Neither, of course, were acceptable to the Navy and Rickover, who had been promising delivery by December 1977 under a fixed-price contract.

In fact both shipyards already had problems building the Navy's latest nuclear-powered attack submarines, the 688 class. Newport News was having great difficulty with the first five 688 boats, and when a second buy of eleven submarines was tendered in 1973 their bid was considered too high by the Navy.[57] Newport News had other work, including merchant shipbuilding, and so did not need the financial risk of bidding low. Electric Boat, however, had only one product, submarines, and only one customer, the Navy. They too had problems with the 688. The ambitious new chairman of General Dynamics, David Lewis – after considerable pressure from Rickover – had 'undercut' Newport News on the bid to build the second eleven 688s.[58] This was in October 1973, just before the Trident bids were due, and the shipyard was already committed to build many submarines at a price and schedule that it would not be able to meet. Then in December, following their unacceptable cost-plus Trident bid of November, Rickover persuaded Lewis to resubmit their bid as a fixed-price contract. The risk of construction uncertainties causing a large overrun would, Rickover reassured Lewis, be catered for by simply making the fixed-price sufficiently high.[59]

After prolonged negotiations between the Navy and Electric Boat it was agreed to settle on a fixed price contract with a target price for the first submarine of $285,400,000 but with an unusually high ceiling price (up to which the Navy would still pay at least 85 per cent of the overrun) of $384,400,000.[60] Electric Boat also promised to make its 'best efforts' to deliver by December 1977 and guaranteed delivery by April 1979 but in neither instance was there to be any penalty for being late.[61] Electric Boat was in fact less than candid about its ability to meet the demanding specifications of the new submarines on schedule.[62] The contract, which offered the prospect of more work than Electric Boat could (literally) cope with, was signed on 25 July 1974.

To save its face, and Rickover's, the Navy had played on the ambitions of Electric Boat's management to push them into a cosmetic contract which seemed to meet the fixed-price, competitively tendered, December 1977 delivery date promised to Congress. In reality it met none of these, and despite repeated attempts to suppress Electric Boat's difficulties, the non-delivery of the *Ohio* on the promised schedule inevitably brought the Trident programme into disrepute. In the late 1970s Electric Boat found itself committed to building too many submarines, too quickly. Expectations of increased productivity, which had encouraged lower bids, simply could not be realized. The *Ohio* was eventually delivered in October 1981 after the construction schedule had been officially extended six times.

TRIDENT I C4

Admiral Smith's worst fears had come true and had justified his concern in arguing for a Trident I missile small enough to be backfitted into the majority of the existing FBM submarines. Although largely excluded from the Trident submarine programme, SSPO retained jurisdiction over maintaining the existing FBM fleet and over missile development. In line with SSPO's preferences, Trident I was to be a realization of the EXPO concept, providing extra range within the size constraint presented by the existing FBM submarines.

In March 1971 the Navy still apparently viewed the FBM as an essentially urban-industrial weapon, referring to 'the assured destruction role that we are building ULMS for at this time'.[63] Assured destruction was the criterion on which Strat-X had been based and it was the role which was considered paramount at SSPO. Others, however, including some in key positions, favoured increasing the counterforce capability of the sea-based portion of US ballistic missiles.

One of these was John Brett, Under-Secretary for Strategic Systems, who was responsible for transforming Packard's vague direction into a more detailed specification for Trident I or, as it was labelled in SSPO's characteristic nomenclature, C4. Brett could not, of course, impose a specification unilaterally. But he was well-placed to intervene – for he was a former Kearfott engineer, a protagonist of Kearfott's stellar-inertial system, who felt that the US badly needed a significant counterforce capability. He also appreciated – following the cancellation of the stellar-inertial accuracy enhancement of Poseidon – that Congressional opinion needed to be taken seriously.

The strength of the anti-counterforce lobby in Congress meant that it would be unwise to push the C4 as a hard-target killer. The specifications of C4 could, however, be set in such a way that enhanced navigation and guidance capability was still required, but on 'assured destruction' grounds rather than 'counterforce' grounds. A longer range missile – which provided more sea-room for the submarine to patrol in and so would alleviate concerns about Soviet anti-submarine warfare developments – required improved navigation and guidance capability simply to prevent deterioration in accuracy. Similarly the ASW 'threat' could be taken as necessitating the capability to operate for much longer periods of time, up to several weeks, without resort to navigational resets – again necessitating enhanced navigation and guidance. The navigation and guidance specifications for the C4 thus were set as follows: system accuracy of C4 at 4000 nautical miles should be as good as Poseidon at 2000 nautical miles, and submarine navigation should be able to operate for periods of thirty days without external reset.[64] In Brett's opinion, this left no option but that Trident I would require stellar-inertial guidance.[65] It also meant that under the best possible circumstances, at shorter ranges and soon after a navigation reset, C4 accuracy would be considerably better than Poseidon. Up to this point SSPO, whose main concern was longer range, was considering simply modifying Poseidon's Mk. 3 guidance system, even at some loss of accuracy.[66]

Warhead size, however, raised the hard-target issue in a way that was harder to 'fudge'. As with Poseidon, the supporters of hard-target capability in the Offices of the Secretary of Defense and Chief of Naval Operations wanted a larger-yield warhead than Poseidon Mk. 3's 'small' 40 kilotons. As before, SSPO was unconvinced, seeing little reason not to use basically the same reentry body and warhead as on Poseidon.[67] This time round SSPO had a powerful 'technical' argument to mobilize against a very large warhead: the missile design required to get the longer range from the same size. A third-stage rocket motor was added for the first time, and instead of it being below the post-boost vehicle containing the guidance system and warheads, as was conventional, the third-stage motor went effectively to the top of the missile, with reentry bodies and guidance system, etc., arranged round it. Reentry body size was limited by the size of this annular ring, and this in turn limited the maximum yield warhead possible with the current state of technology. SSPO's view was that there was little to be gained from moving to a slightly larger warhead, especially given the expense. Their original design of what became Trident I, known as C3D, was to have carried ten Mk. 3 reentry bodies to a distance of 3000 nautical miles.[68] The range could have been extended by carrying fewer reentry bodies.

However, too many influential actors opposed the Mk. 3 reentry

body and its 'small' warhead. This time hard-target advocates commanded more power in the Office of the Secretary of Defence, and
they found strong support from the Department of Energy's nuclear
weapons laboratories which were unwilling to see any new strategic
system deployed without a new warhead. These opponents were also
able to deploy an additional 'technical' argument against the Mk. 3,
since it seemed the case that the heat sink design would be unsuitable
for some trajectories at the longer ranges considered for C4 (which has
a nominal range of 4000 miles).[69] It still seemed a high price to pay for
marginal advantages (since the flexibility to fire over all conceivable
trajectories was not required) and only a small yield increase, but in
the end SSPO went for a new reentry body and somewhat larger
warhead, reportedly because 'they recognized the political benefit of
agreeing with OSD'.[70] Compared to the Poseidon's typical loading of
ten 40 kiloton warheads, Trident I has a maximum loading of eight 100
kiloton warheads.[71]

With the decision to build a new warhead/reentry body combination, OSD's hard target advocates now were able to get not only
higher yield, but also a reentry body with a higher ballistic coefficient
and hence less accuracy loss due to dispersion.[72] To survive at the
ranges desired and also have a high ballistic coefficient necessitated
the choice of an ablative design for the Mk. 4 reentry body. Various
alternative designs were tested during 1974 and 1975 using surplus
Atlas and Minuteman missiles. The final choice – based very much on
the technology used in the Air Force Mk. 12 reentry vehicle – has 'a
tape-wrapped carbon phenolic (TWCP) heatshield bonded to a thin-
wall aluminium substrate for the shell and a graphite nosetip'.[73] The
longer range of the missile, fewer reentry bodies carried, and more
efficient bus propulsion system meant that nuclear hardness was less
critical as the reentry bodies would be more widely spaced out and so
less vulnerable to multiple kill by an exoatmospheric ABM. Also, after
the problems that had occurred with production of the Poseidon
nosetips, particular attention was given to the graphite production: 'So
critical was graphite quality, and so difficult to inspect the end
product, that a separate factory, a computer controlled facility, was
built for its exclusive production where processes could be completely
controlled.'[74]

Whereas Poseidon's modest range goal had required only a relatively conservative approach to propulsion, the perceived need to
provide more sea-room to counter developments in Soviet ASW (and
also reduce the need for potentially problematic reliance on overseas
FBM bases) pushed the Trident I missile design. Almost twice the

127

Length (feet)	34.0
Nominal range (nautical miles)	4000
Weight at launch (1000s of lbs)	73.0
Year first deployed	1979
No. of warheads	8 [MIRV]
Yield per warhead (kilotons)	100 [W-76]
Guidance system	Mk. 5
Approximate accuracy (circular error probable, nautical miles)	0.12–0.25

Figure 7.1 Trident C-4

range was desired from a missile of about the same size and weight. The four general ways possible to do this were followed: decreasing inert weight in the missile (which included a reduction in payload); increasing the volume available for propulsive energy; increasing the usable energy per unit volume; and increasing the delivered impulse per unit usable energy.[75]

This approach led to the development of lighter components throughout the missile, including the guidance system, electronics, the post-boost vehicle or 'bus', and the chamber cases. Weight reductions in the bus stage provided a significant range increment and led to the choice of graphite-epoxy composite material, which in 1973 became available in a suitable form.[76] In designing the 'bus' some accuracy was traded off against reduced weight:

> In designing for range, the 'bus' structure was designed to be of minimum weight for structural integrity with adequate margin. The optimized graphite cone structure, as an outcome, had vibrational modes which added a statistically bounded, but not exactly pre-dictable on a body-by-body basis, increment to deployment velocity. This increment of course translates to an addition to the CEP [circular error probable] ... While neither large nor affecting performance relative to the goal, this deployment inaccuracy was nevertheless identifiable and could have been traded for less range.[77]

Because of the critical effects of weight savings in the 'bus' the type of propellant it used was the object of some debate. There were some who suggested that the savings in weight (though not volume) pro-vided by moving to liquid propellant, as used in Air Force designs, outweighed any safety concerns. SSPO disagreed, placing the highest priority on system safety, even at some loss of range. Instead, a solid propellant system was retained, though one which allowed a means of 'throttling'. This was 'a solid propellant gas generator which burns slower at lower pressure when less thrust is needed as when changing attitude, when no change of velocity vector is needed, or when making vernier changes, but burns rapidly at a higher pressure when high thrust is needed to change the vehicle velocity vector'.[78]

The bus structure takes the form of a squat cone through which a third rocket stage protrudes. The addition of this third stage, small though it is, provides a greater addition to range than simply increasing the propellant carried in the second stage by the same amount. However, situating the third stage through the post-boost vehicle made thrust termination and separation more problematical. Venting the third stage to provide thrust termination would have been difficult without inflicting high shock levels on the equipment section, flying it out the front would expose the vehicle to high heat and force levels, and backing it out seemed to be difficult to test when the third stage could have differing amounts of fuel left. The solution devised was elegant. With what was called a general energy management system (GEMS), the guidance computer would shape the missile trajectory to use up all the propellant in the third stage. This obviates the need for a thrust termination system, which not only eliminates that potential source of reliability and accuracy reductions, but also increases maximum range (since thrust termination adds dead weight to the system). As all the fuel is used it leaves a constant weight third stage motor case thus simplifying its separation from the bus. Testability was then designed in: 'By sizing the thrust ejecting the empty third stage from the post vehicle to accelerate at one g, this new feature could be easily ground tested rather than depending primarily on flight testing.'[79]

Another consequence of the third stage positioning, along with the desire to utilize the launch tube volume to the full, was an unusually blunt nosed missile. The extra aerodynamic drag experienced during the boost phase would have reduced the range achieved and this concern led to the development of an aerospike to reduce drag. Self-contained, to avoid interface problems, the aerospike extension is powered by a small solid propellant gas generator triggered by the acceleration sensed as the missile is ejected from the submarine.[80] The optimum length for the aerospike was derived from experimental data; indeed, in 1984 there was 'still no theoretical means of predicting spike effects'.[81] The aerospike is said to add 300 nautical miles to the missile's range.[82]

Meeting the range goal also required major technical advances in the first and second stage motors, to increase propulsive impulse whilst reducing inert weight. Again the 'joint venture' of Hercules and Thiokol won the competitive tender against rival bids from Aerojet, for the first two stages, and United Technology Corporation, for the third.[83] The propellant chosen for all three stages was a development of the composite double base type which permitted a higher level of solids (the fuel and oxidizer), thus giving both greater density and specific impulse.[84] Meeting the 4000 mile range goal may have led SSPO to push the motor designs too far, however.

Particularly alarming was an unexpected and unprecedented second stage motor detonation during a static test firing in May 1974. For over a year this became the focus of the development programme, as 'extensive analysis, laboratory experimentation, and large-scale motor tests were conducted to gain an understanding of the mechanism involved'.[85] The apparent cause was failure of the motor casing at the high pressures involved, leading to shear of the propellant away from the chamber wall and break up of the propellant. This rapid formation of a large propellant surface area in a confined space then initiated the detonation.[86]

Even with a less than complete understanding of the mechanism, SSPO set in train corrective measures aimed at generally improving the uniformity and quality of components, and changing the propellant formulation to make it less energetic and less frangible. In so doing they gave up some range to ensure the safety of the system. As Admiral Levering Smith testified to Congress in 1976: 'the solution to the detonation mechanism that we have identified resulted in our adopting a somewhat less energetic propellant with some loss of range'.[87]

But solution of the detonation problem did not end the propulsion difficulties that were to contribute to the poor public image that the Trident programme also acquired from the submarine construction delays. Following deployment of the missile in 1979 there were a number of first stage motor failures during test flights which led Undersecretary of Defense for Research and Engineering, Richard DeLauer, to describe their performance as 'lousy'.[88] A defect was identified as causing the failures and in 1984 a programme to replace 'suspect' motors was begun, and changes were made in propellant processing and in first stage insulator thickness. These changes were considered to provide a greater performance margin against such defects.[89]

Despite these propulsion difficulties Trident I achieved its range

130

goal. However, they did make inert weight reductions throughout the system more critical, as 'the performance loss associated with the use of less energetic propellants than originally intended increased the need for greater performance contributions by all other areas'.[90] A newly developed material, Kevlar, had been chosen for the chamber cases of the three rocket motors because of its high strength-to-weight and modulus-to-weight ratios. Weight reductions were stressed throughout the missile, including in the guidance system. A light-weight version of the Mk. 4 reentry body was developed and first tested in late 1975.[91]

Weight-saving also shaped the design of the missile electronics, as did compactness, low-power operation, radiation-hardness, and reliability. For example, the relative compactness of electronic components went from a density of 16 equivalent parts/cubic inch in Poseidon to 480 parts/cubic inch in Trident I (Polaris A3 had 4 parts/cubic inch).[92] The combination of characteristics desired by Lockheed proved to be harder to manufacture than expected, and some of the intended components were unavailable for the early test missiles.[93] These difficulties with electronics and propulsion led to delays which caused the Trident I IOC (initial operating capability) date to be adjusted twice, first by six months, and then by five.

TRIDENT I GUIDANCE

As intended by John Brett, the Mk. 5 guidance system developed for Trident incorporated a star sensor mounted on the stable platform of the inertial measurement unit, together with the gyroscopes and accelerometers. This stable member was held in a four gimbal system rather than with three as in Poseidon and Polaris. This allowed one gimbal to be used for optical alignment with the SINS whilst another could be devoted to elevation of the star sensor through the vertical plane of the predicted star, something which could not be so simply mechanized with three gimbals. In general this removed the problem of gimbal lock[94] which had to be carefully avoided with a three gimbal system. This gives the C4 much greater ease of reorientation during MIRVing, when reentry bodies are dropped off onto different trajectories.

The proponents of stellar-inertial guidance at Kearfott and elsewhere saw its adoption as enhancing system accuracy. But it is important to note that the design of the Mk. 5 guidance system for Trident C4 did *not* unequivocally prioritize accuracy. Thus, the accelerometer chosen for the Mk. 5 guidance was essentially the PIPA used in

131

Poseidon's Mk. 3 system with a few modifications, 'largely things that made it more producible'.[95] It was considered by SSPO to be good enough to meet the accuracy goal and light enough to meet the range goal, and so the extra cost of developing a new accelerometer was judged to be not worthwhile:

> we chose to stay with the accelerometer because we didn't have to go out and re-invent the thing ... Staying with the accelerometer certainly simplified the job ... Inertial components ... are always difficult to do whenever you start to design some new ones. Not just the design and development, but also getting the production system up to speed. Start-up costs, start-up problems – they're always tremendous.[96]

Producibility concerns also played a role in the selection of the gyroscope for the Mk. 5 guidance system, where Kearfott, whose overall Unistar stellar-inertial concept had been adopted, also turned out to be successful. For the first time in the FBM programme, Draper floated gyroscopes were abandoned, with SSPO instead favouring Kearfott 'dry' tuned-rotor gyros. In this, the spinning rotor was supported on a shaft direct from the motor, in a sort of 'mushroom' or 'umbrella' set-up. This support is not rigid, and is so designed that at the rotation speed of the gyro wheel, the 'spring' effect of the support is exactly counterbalanced by a 'negative spring rate' of the rotor. This 'cancelling out', tuning, effect means an effective decoupling of the gyro wheel from its support.[97]

Kearfott and also Litton, the other main supplier of inertial navigation for the military aircraft market in the United States, both developed major dry tuned-rotor gyro programmes in the 1960s. The technology was less labour-intensive than floated gyro technology for a given level of performance, and thus less expensive, at least at American wage levels. And because it was analogous to a 'free' gyro rotor, the dry-tuned device could detect rotations about two axes – it was a 'two degree-of-freedom' gyro. So only two dry tuned-rotor gyros were needed in an inertial system, not three as with the one degree-of-freedom floated instrument.

Nevertheless, despite their apparent advantages, dry tuned-rotor gyros might well not have been introduced to the FBM programme had it not been for Kearfott's 'plain flatout aggressive salesmanship'.[98] Together SSPO guidance branch SP–23 and the Draper Laboratory considered the trade-offs. As guidance design agent for SSPO, Draper Laboratory's conclusion was that either gyro approach would meet the system goals, and a Draper design would probably be more expensive though less risky.[99]

It was in Kearfott's favour that two of their gyros would be smaller and lighter than three Draper instruments, an important consideration in C4, where weight savings were vital to stretch out the range to almost double that of the same-sized Poseidon. This made room for the stellar sensor, which because of its ability to compensate for errors elsewhere in the system, helped undercut the argument that Draper gyros were more accurate than the dry tuned-rotor design. In the end 'the Kearfott gyro was selected on the basis of producibility and cost and . . . demonstrable accuracy adequate for the job'.[100]

The Mk. 5 guidance computer was an evolutionary development from that of Mk. 3, with the addition of a stellar subsystem. The stellar update computation and corrections had to be made very rapidly at the start of the post-boost or 'bus' phase, in order to maximize the amount of bus fuel left for deployment of the reentry bodies. To do this the computer has virtually 100 per cent throughput during the stellar update, and so this 'sizes' its computational power. The Mk. 5 computer has about 200K of PROM (programmable read only memory) which stores the guidance equations and steering laws, and about 48K of plated wire RAM (random access memory) for parameters read in prior to launch. Components are largely small and medium scale integration (SSI and MSI).[101]

As in Poseidon the guidance computer uses a simplification of a spherical earth with presets calculated by fire control to take account of variations in gravity from launch point to launch point. Stellar-inertial guidance complicated the work of fire control. The star sighting provides only two error values (vertical and horizontal errors from that predicted from a star map), but these two values are used to correct not only for launch point errors, but also guidance system gyroscope drift. Whereas the former, prelaunch errors can be corrected once and for all, the latter must be propagated throughout guided flight. To achieve all this required the development of much more complicated fire control software. The stellar sighting could not correct for errors in initial velocity or for gravity anomalies that the inertial sensors could not distinguish from velocity errors. To minimize the impact of this, SSPO identified 'areas where the gravity anomalies were known to be very bad and just stay[ed] away from them'.[102]

The Mk. 5 guidance system never became as controversial in the formal political system as the cancelled Mk. 4 stellar-inertial option for Poseidon. Some funding was apparently cut by Congress from Trident I stellar inertial guidance funding in 1974 and 1975, but this had little impact on the programme.[103] Whereas Mk. 4 had been specifically touted as a hard-target kill enhancing technology, the emphasis in

133

Trident I was on longer time between navigation resets and hence greater submarine security – features quite compatible with an 'assured destruction' role.

THE MK. 500 EVADER

What did temporarily re-ignite the hard-target controversy was an alternative reentry body, the Mk. 500 Evader. Unlike all previous FBM reentry bodies this does not simply fly on a ballistic trajectory after being released by the bus, but can perform preselected manoeuvres once within the atmosphere. It was developed in response to a request from the Office of the Secretary of Defense in 1973:

> provide reasonable assurance that a possible later decision to initiate engineering development for service use of a manoeuvering reentry vehicle would not require reengineering of the Trident weapon system. . . . include sufficient flight tests of an advanced development prototype MARV to demonstrate compatibility with the C4 missile and the Trident weapon system.[104]

Some at SSPO considered the Mk. 500 development an unnecessary waste of their time, but so long as the funding was readily forthcoming, SSPO's leadership 'strongly favoured its development to a stage that development and production could be accomplished as quickly as ABM deployment'.[105] Its official rationale was as a hedge against possible Soviet ABM developments – particularly the upgrading of surface-to-air missiles (SAMs) – which were the subject of disputed analyses from various parts of the intelligence community:

> To gain the increased full payload range [with the C4], it was necessary to give up some of the maximum possible ABM exchange ratio which would only be of value should the then proposed ABM treaty be abrogated. As a hedge against such a contingency, advanced development of a manoeuvering, evader reentry vehicle capable of being carried by the missile was included in the program.[106]

By developing the Mk. 500 system, the manoeuvring reentry body and associated penaid dispensers, SSPO could design the main C4 configuration without any compromise for penetration (except that it should be compatible with the Mk. 500 system). Thus, so far as SSPO and Lockheed were concerned, the Mk. 500 was just as useful in helping them evade what they saw as probably unnecessary penetration requirements for the main C4 Mk. 4 reentry body as it was for penetrating Soviet defences. This was important because the range objective for C4 required as light a reentry body as possible, but the lightest reentry body designs are not those which are most easy to mimic with decoys. So the Mk. 4 could be optimized for lightness rather than similarity to decoys.

The Mk. 500 comprises a bent-nosed reentry body containing a simple guidance system.[107] Once within the atmosphere the bent nose causes aerodynamic lift which is controlled by rolling the body by shifting an internal weight (in fact the electronics package). This was a relatively rudimentary approach to the task of developing a manoeuvring reentry body, best suited for evasion, with accuracy a secondary consideration. Indeed some loss of accuracy compared to the baseline Trident Mk. 4 reentry body was considered acceptable, though studies did suggest ways in which the Mk. 500 could be used to improve accuracy. (By effecting a 'tuck' as it reached the target – so descending vertically onto it – the Mk. 500 could reduce the loss of 'accuracy' due to variations in the timing of the warhead fusing.)[108] At the time, during the mid–1970s, it was viewed by some as an attempt to gain hard-target kill capability, and provoked some opposition in Congress.[109] But as no attempts were made to deploy the Mk. 500, the controversy petered out.

The Mk. 500 was flight tested five times on Minuteman I boosters between March 1975 and January 1976 with all flights reported to be successes.[110] Compatibility with the C4 missile was then demonstrated in a further test in June 1977.[111] With the general feasibility of the concept thus demonstrated, the technology was put 'on the shelf', though in practice this meant that deployment would involve an estimated lead-time of three and a half years to manufacture the Mk. 500.[112] Further work on the concept led to testing of an 'improved evader' during 1978 and 1979 and an 'advanced evader' in 1981 and 1982. In these designs the fixed trim of the bent-nosed original Mk. 500 was replaced with noses that allowed variation in trim, and thus presumably better control of the flight path.[113]

SINS AND THE ESG MONITOR

The introduction of a star-sensor complicated the relationship between submarine navigation (the province of the branch of the SPO known as SP-24) and missile guidance (SP-23). From a situation of relative independence, their work became much more closely related. The star-sensor permitted a degree of *post hoc* correction of errors in the information about launch position and heading that the missile guidance system received from navigation through the fire control system. According to a former SSPO technical director:

Partitioning of the task became more difficult in that accuracy, unlike reliability, did not partition linearly. Even with exhaustive co-ordination, the accuracy performance of one branch could not be divorced from that of the other, and management visibility into subsystem activity to a level beyond that desired by the branches became essential. Additionally, the process was affected by intra-organisational politics, budget realities and the capability and ambitions of the contractors.[114]

Another problem area was the introduction of a fully digital link (rather than analogue 'synchros') between navigation and fire control/guidance, which was delayed because it was difficult to agree the form of the link. Should the navigation computer have to 'broadcast' data several times a second, whether or not that information was being used, as those responsible for missile guidance would have liked, or ought the rest of the system, as those responsible for navigation preferred, have to 'request' data from navigation, with the answer possibly being delayed?[115]

The star-sensor's ability to correct for navigation errors reduced the demands on SINS accuracy, though improvements were still sought here to achieve longer reset intervals. Despite claims from advocates of the electrostatically supported gyroscope that 'preliminary test data indicated a quantum improvement in performance with a system using ESGs over one using conventional SINS gyroscopes',[116] SSPO proceeded conservatively. An evolutionary modification of the existing Autonetics SINS, the Mk. 2 Mod. 7, was chosen. However, the ESG did now find a place in the Trident submarine (and the Poseidon submarines retrofitted with Trident I missiles), as a 'monitor' over-seeing the two SINS. The ESG Monitor did not directly provide navigational information, but was used to update the SINS periodic-ally. The same overall accuracy of SINS output could thus be main-tained, while increasing the time intervals between external resets, and thus decreasing the vulnerability of the submarine to anti-submarine warfare. Using the ESG as a monitor allowed the introduction of a new technology and its benefits while avoiding reliance on its success. SSPO, as ever, were concerned to minimize the risk of failure.

The ESG that went into FBM submarines was, however, not Honey-well's; the successful device came from Autonetics division of Rockwell International, the traditional SINS supplier. Two aspects of this are particularly interesting. The first is the difference between the two designs. Though Honeywell's large, hollow ball was believed by its proponents to maximize accuracy, the successful Autonetics design employed a small, solid ball, that was significantly easier to make. So 'producibility' – always a critical factor with inertial components – won out over apparent theoretical accuracy. Secondly, it appears that this was exacerbated by a Honeywell management decision. At a crucial point, Honeywell shifted ESG production from their traditional site in Minneapolis to the new facility they were developing in Florida:

> We told the corporation what was going to happen to them – that they were going to move down there, half of their people weren't going to go, and this [ESG production] was an artistic thing . . . They could produce them, but it wasn't something you could put on the production line. You had people who had techniques, etc. . . . They moved down to Florida and nothing worked. Half the people didn't move, wouldn't move, some of them retired, everything we said happened with spades. Eventually they were in deep [trouble] . . . [Autonetics] persuaded us that since Honeywell was falling on their face, we ought to give them a chance, and we decided that we would. And they funded much of that chance themselves, and the answer is we had a time when we wanted to see the Honeywell thing on the [USS] *Compass Island* [the ship used for testing navigational equipment], and when that time came Rockwell had the one there and knew how to run their thing and . . . Honeywell delivered one a few months late and they hadn't the slightest idea what to do with it . . .[117]

TRIDENT I DEPLOYMENT

Once the initial development problems – especially in the propulsion and electronics areas – were overcome, the Trident I flight test programme, carried out between 1977 and 1979, was considered very successful.[118] So much so that the number of flight tests was reduced from thirty to twenty-five.[119] With the first Trident submarine well behind the 'promised' December 1977 delivery date, the decision to backfit Trident I into existing FBM submarines seemed to have been proved wise.

In retrospect it seems that many, including some at SSPO, would now question the urgency of Trident I deployment.[120] The potential advances in Soviet anti-submarine warfare do not seem to have been realized, and the extra sea-room allowed the submarines by Trident I's range increase over Poseidon has been a hedge that was not needed. At the time, however, SSPO's leadership clearly believed that Trident I deployment was an urgent matter. Although the Trident submarine programme was out of SSPO's control, the backfitting of Trident I remained its responsibility.

Because of the problems that the main shipyards were experiencing with Trident and 688 attack submarine construction, SSPO decided to take the precaution of arranging to backfit some Trident Is by alternate means. Six existing FBM submarines – following the normal procedure – were backfitted from Poseidon to Trident I during their scheduled second overhaul, starting in March 1979 with the *Simon Bolivar* at Portsmouth Naval Shipyard.[121] However, the other six of the submarines to be backfitted were done under 'emergency' conditions, with shifts working twenty-four hours to complete the backfitting at temporary pierside installations.[122] The same urgency guided SSPO's unusual efforts to maintain peak production rate of the C4 by stockpiling critical materials in advance. Lockheed, for example, bought enough rayon (over 3 million pounds) for use in booster nozzles and reentry bodies because dropping demand for rayon car tyres had led to a sharp fall in the supply of the synthetic material.[123] Other critical materials, such as molybdenum, had lead time delays of over a year.

Accommodating the Trident I missiles – with their blunter noses and increased weight – in the 'Poseidon' submarines required the development of a new launcher system, largely based on that used for Poseidon.[124] Fire control was also upgraded from the General Electric Mk. 88 to a Mk. 88 Mod. 2 version. A major change with the Trident I missile was that 'the alignment and erection loops were closed within the guidance system'.[125] Whereas in previous missiles these tasks were directly performed by fire control, they are now done by fire control loading a pre-flight software program – the platform positioning and initial velocity program – into the guidance computer. Azimuth is still established with an optical alignment system, however, though the missile's stellar correction makes this less crucial than before. A new computer (known as the Trident digital control computer) selects a suitable star and calculates the correction matrix necessary for the missile's stellar update. The last of the twelve backfitted submarines, the *Casimir Pulaski*, went on patrol in June 1983.

TRIDENT I AND NUCLEAR STRATEGY

With its emphasis on longer range and extended submarine navigation reset interval it would seem that Trident I simply reflected traditional concerns with maintaining the potency of the 'assured destruction' threat. But, of course, there was never a consensus that this was the only role that the US FBM force should be capable of. Just as with previous systems there were advocates of greater counterforce capability, even against hard targets. On the other hand, SSPO itself and Congress – particularly the Senate Armed Services Committee *ad hoc* Subcommittee on Research and Development – were still sceptical of efforts to increase the hard-target kill capability of US strategic forces.

Still, advocates of greater counterforce capability were not without influence, both within the Office of the Secretary of Defense and within the Office of the Chief of Naval Operations. C4's larger warheads were partly an outcome of their pressure for greater flexibility to hit harder targets than Poseidon could. Similarly OSD's accuracy goal, whilst not a strict requirement, pushed SSPO towards stellar-inertial guidance and accuracy greater than SSPO might otherwise have deemed necessary. As originally conceived in Strat-X, ULMS emphasized cost-effective delivery of equivalent megatonnage in the face of a Soviet first strike and Soviet ABM defences. But as ULMS evolved into Trident I its counterforce utility became enhanced.

Just how far this could go was limited, however, by the size constraint which had in effect been strongly advocated by Admiral Smith. By insisting that Trident I should be small enough to be backfitted into the existing FBM submarines, he effectively (though most likely inadvertently) ruled out the use of very large warheads. With the missile volume available the range goal made a third stage seem unavoidable and this then left an annular space for reentry bodies too small for the very large warheads that some would have liked to see deployed on FBMs. With regard to accuracy improvements, Admiral Smith was again cautious, claiming that it still was not possible to promise to meet a requirement for high accuracy. High accuracy could not simply be bought by building a stellar-inertial guidance system. It required considerable investments in instrumentation and modelling to understand and validate what was happening, as well as very expensive improvements in other aspects of the system, such as submarine velocity knowledge and gravity and sea-bed terrain mapping.

Nevertheless, C4 appears to have turned out more accurate than the original goal.[126] Although perhaps an exaggeration, a 1984 report claimed that 'during 1983, the Navy's tests achieved consistent 750-foot CEPs with Trident I, twice as good as the 1500-foot goal'.[127] This makes Trident I a significant threat to all but the hardest Soviet targets. But to many this intermediate capability seemed of limited value:

> There was no point in going to intermediate accuracy because it wouldn't do any good. That was the C4. The C4 got intermediate accuracy and we built a new warhead and so what? It didn't provide a capability that bridged a new set of targets. It was still only useful against soft targets and pretty useless against hard targets. And it turns out that there are soft targets, then there's a small number that are slightly hard, 50 to 100 psi, and then you start going thousands of

139

psi – bunkers, command bunkers and silos – and there's very little in the middle. You just don't waste money building systems tailored to these intermediate targets and that's what happened. C4 ended up being useful against a set of these intermediate targets that don't exist in any significant numbers. . . . if you want to use it against a hard target, you've got to use several, and when you use several you have terrible targeting problems.[128]

But by the time C4 was deployed, the pendulum would have finally swung all the way towards hard-target counterforce. It would become offically stated US policy and an Improved Accuracy Program, set up in 1974 at Secretary of Defense Schlesinger's instigation, would undermine SSPO's arguments against committing themselves to a high accuracy requirement. The next FBM, Trident II, would have a stringent accuracy requirement and a relatively large yield warhead – a combination that would widely be seen as providing the capability to destroy very hard targets.

8 THE IMPROVED ACCURACY PROGRAMME AND TRIDENT II

> If the TRIDENT submarine is now seen as a vehicle to sell a larger payload missile, rather than as a vehicle to assure the invulnerability of the sea-based offensive force, we will have lost a great deal of credibility . . .
>
> Admiral Smith.[1]

The ULMS 'decisions' of the early 1970s, and particularly the final design of the submarine, were made on the assumption of the eventual development of a large Trident II missile. Although other factors – particularly Rickover's desire to build new large reactors and 'the Navy's' (not SSPO's) desire to justify new FBM submarines – drove the larger size of the Trident submarines, they were justified on the basis of the need to carry the large Trident II, which itself was characterized as a continuation of the Strat-X missile concept.[2] There was little doubt that a Trident II would make full use of the extra launch tube volume, but what remained to be decided was exactly when, and what capabilities the missile would possess. In the original ULMS conceived in Strat-X, long range had been considered an important attribute and originally Trident II was to have a 6000 mile range, as opposed to the 4000 miles of Trident I.[3] In the late 1960s and early 1970s extra range provided an uncontroversial way of justifying the new missile. However, by the time it came to be developed, the emphasis would have shifted from enhancing range to enhancing accuracy, an attribute which was earlier considered not especially important by many, and even destabilizing by some.[4]

THE IMPROVED ACCURACY PROGRAMME

Throughout the 1960s SPO had resisted pressure to meet increased accuracy 'requirements' for the FBM force. Requests from the Office of the Secretary of Defense and from the Office of the Chief of Naval Operations met a standard response, which embodied a distinction that epitomized Admiral Smith's approach. SPO would attempt to meet accuracy 'goals', but measurement and understanding of FBM inaccuracy was not good enough to promise to meet 'requirements'.

Following a 1972 request from Chief of Naval Operations, Admiral Zumwalt, SSPO director Levering Smith estimated that he would need $1·5 billion to assure an improvement in FBM accuracy.[5] This led to SSPO asking Johns Hopkins University Applied Physics Laboratory to 'investigate ways to determine a demonstrably precise' error model to allow better understanding of FBM test results.[6] Then in late 1973 the new Secretary of Defense, James Schlesinger, 'asked the Chief of Naval Operations for a presentation on possible improvements of accuracy of the sea-based strategic system'.[7]

Schlesinger, like Robert McNamara in the previous decade, was an activist secretary. An economist by training, Schlesinger had headed the strategic studies division of the RAND Corporation, and there had come to favour 'limited nuclear options' – relatively small-scale, selective nuclear targeting, designed to exert political leverage. This was also the main thrust of a review of nuclear strategy which had been conducted during 1972 and 1973, and which Schlesinger then adopted and promoted. Known as National Security Decision Memorandum 242, and signed by President Nixon in January 1974, the resultant new policy marked a radical departure from the previous *declared* policy of assured destruction. In fact, the Single Integrated Operational Plan for targeting nuclear forces did allow some relatively limited options during the 1960s, but NSDM 242 went much further in providing preplanned options for small-scale nuclear strikes against military targets.[8]

Although Schlesinger argued that the flexibility of NSDM 242 could be achieved with the existing arsenal, he considered greater accuracy, and greater confidence in accuracy figures, to be desirable. He 'just kept pushing for improved accuracy' in the fleet ballistic missile programme.[9] As before, SSPO's leadership was unwilling to commit itself to a stringent accuracy requirement 'because they still had essentially no ability to correct for excess errors if tests of the developed system showed that the requirements had not been met. They lacked the ability to measure the magnitude of error contributions and the understanding to extrapolate errors to other than test conditions.'[10] Schlesinger was impatient with this, as Admiral Smith recalls: 'I remember a couple of sessions with him personally when I was trying to show that we were unable to explain the fall of shot. He rolled up his sleeves and said "OK, I'll explain it for you". And we sat down with the raw data a couple of hours each time.'[11] The improved accuracy programme (IAP) emerged from these discussions. Secretary of Defense Schlesinger's Posture statement of 4 March 1974 noted that: 'We plan to undertake an advanced development program which will define our capability to improve and measure the accuracy of our SLBMs and which, if implemented by retrofit, could lead to improved accuracy in the future.'[12] SSPO again avoided any strict requirement for accuracy improvement in Trident I, but committed itself to undertake a programme involving three broad areas of development: accuracy error model analysis, instrumentation, and component development. In January 1975, SSPO received further direction from the Director of Defense Research & Engineering to: 'Restructure the accuracy improvement program to accommodate funding adjustments and to be compatible with providing an improved accuracy capability for the Trident II missile with IOC in FY [deleted]. Incremental accuracy improvements in the Trident I missile should be pursued when cost effective.'[13] Whilst explaining the IAP in Congressional testimony Admiral Smith outlined the inadequacies of previous FBM accuracy assessment methods:

> Those methods are influenced by the fact that in the current weapons system, C-3 and C-4, accuracy is a goal. It is not stated as a requirement. We did not propose in the C-3, and we have not to this point proposed as a part of the Trident C-4 program, the funding of a high confidence assessment method.
>
> The accuracy assessment is approached basically by the direct or splash assessment, the limited subsystem error assessment, and limited modeling techniques.
>
> This has resulted in low statistical confidence because of the small number of test flights, the limited variety of operational conditions available to us, and the limited subsystem error measurement capability.[14]

The basic objectives of the IAP were to:

> Gain an understanding of SLBM error sources and their relationships. Based on this understanding, assess the accuracy improvement potential of:
> improved components
> advanced system concepts
> Conduct advanced development of promising:
> improved components
> advanced system concepts.[15]

A major part of the IAP was the development of new instrumentation methods to provide more information about the sources of error both in the submarine position and velocity prior to launch and during the missile flight (see Table 8.1).[16] The velocity and position

143

Table 8.1. *Improved accuracy programme instrumentation and data collection*

Data gathering system	type of data	Phase	Error estimates affected
LONARS	SSBN position	Patrol, prelaunch	Navigation errors, combined system errors at launch
VPRS	SSBN position and velocity	Patrol, prelaunch	As above
Shipboard data recording	Navigation, fire control, and guidance prelaunch outputs and interfaces	Patrol, prelaunch	Navigation errors, fire control errors (align, erect), presetting errors, system errors at launch
SATRACK	Range and Doppler shifts relative to GPS satellites	Boost, post-boost	System errors at launch, guidance errors
In-flight missile telemetry	Guidance and flight control system outputs	Boost, post-boost	Guidance errors, system errors at star sighting, system errors at reentry body deployment
Telemetry from instrumented reentry bodies	Reentry body acceleration and orientations, radar tracking at reentry	Post-boost, deployment, reentry	Deployment velocity errors, reentry errors, system errors at atmospheric reentry
SMILS or MILS	Location of impact	Impact	System errors at impact

Source: Topping, 'Submarine Launched Ballistic Missile Improved Accuracy', 3.

reference system (VPRS) comprises sea-bed mounted transponders in the ocean areas used for operational test launches and provides more accurate data on the submarine's position and velocity at launch. A specially calibrated Loran-C system provides position data for 'demonstration and shakedown operations' missile launches off Florida.[17] For determining missile position and velocity during flight, radar improvements at the eastern test range were supplemented by a satellite tracking system, known as Satrack. Satrack emerged from the 1973 accuracy evaluation study done by the Applied Physics Laboratory for SSPO, which 'indicated that a satellite-based system could meet the major objectives of SLBM accuracy evaluation at the system flight test level'.[18] This was based on the Navstar Global Positioning System satellites, and used a similar principle – comparing time delays of signals sent to the missile from various satellites and a test ship and then retransmitted back (at a different frequency). Satrack was available in mid–1978 for the final Trident I development missile launches from Cape Canaveral and for the submarine-launched tests beginning in early 1979.

During flight, telemetry is broadcast from the missile guidance system, reporting its values for velocity and orientation, and the stellar sighting results and correction. In addition some of the reentry bodies carry an inertial sensing system which provides telemetry on both the accelerations imparted when deployed and also those experienced during reentry. The final stage of instrumentation comprises the missile locating system (MILS) and the sonobuoy missile locating system (SMILS) which use acoustic sensors to provide data on impact location.

When the Trident I flight tests began these instrumentation systems were used to validate improved accuracy error models which had been developed meanwhile.[19] At the same time, in addition to developing more sophisticated error modelling and investigating improved components, there was also appraisal of a range of different ways of improving accuracy.

Three main ways of improving accuracy were considered. One was to take advantage of the emerging satellite navigation system, the global positioning system, which offered extremely accurate position fixes, by placing GPS receivers on missiles. However, GPS suffered from concerns about its vulnerability, both operationally in a nuclear war, and programmatically, in the battle for funding. Although all the services expected to benefit from GPS, none were especially keen to provide the funding for it and the resultant lack of a firm commitment to the system has allowed technical problems to cause delays in deployment of a full satellite constellation. Mid-flight updates from GPS were considered likely to provide accuracy as good as improvements to a stellar inertial system, but the potential vulnerability to countermeasures, and to the availability of GPS counted against it.[20]

The second approach to accuracy improvement was to move to 'homing' reentry bodies, which would use some method of electromagnetic recognition to take a precise 'fix' in the target area. This offered the 'highest accuracy potential', but it too was susceptible to countermeasures and was the 'least developed technology' of the three. A particular objection concerned its 'testability . . . our ability to conduct flight tests over land'.[21] For obvious legal and political reasons, US ballistic missile tests are conducted primarily over water, and impact is by 'splash down' in areas such as Kwajalein Atoll. A homing reentry body would have to 'recognize' terrain features, and there was thus a major question mark over whether it could be adequately tested without politically difficult overland testing.

The third way was further development of the stellar-inertial guidance technology used in C4. What were considered incremental improvements in this technology offered 'a rather significant improvement potential in accuracy on the order of [deleted] feet, CEP at the 4,000 nautical mile range. ... in order to achieve this kind of system accuracy, we are going to have to improve accuracy essentially across the board in almost all areas of the system, navigation, fire control, guidance, geodesy, and the like ...'.[22] Of these, the two biggest errors identified in the IAP were in submarine velocity and in the stellar sensor system.[23]

The improved accuracy programme ran from 1974 to 1982, and cost of the order of $600 million over the period.[24] It provided the means by which the various options to improve accuracy could be assessed. Most of the funding of advanced development went to the stellar-inertial guidance technology – basically improving the techniques and components used in the Trident I Mk. 5 guidance system. Following this approach there was confidence within SSPO that accuracy of about 500 feet CEP over a range of 4000 nautical miles could be achieved. Work on mid-course and terminal updates was largely restricted to 'paper studies and investigation'.[25] Although improvement of C4 accuracy was dropped as an explicit aim of the IAP, there was some feedback that could be incorporated in software changes, notably in compensating for accelerometer errors.[26]

It was not surprising, then, that with the next FBM system, Trident II D5, it was decided to stay with stellar-inertial guidance. As so often before, SSPO preferred, if possible, to deal with familiar technology and familiar organizational relationships.

TRIDENT II D5 – DECISIONS

Given the survival of the Trident submarine programme, it was difficult to envisage the C4 as other than an interim missile. The much bigger submarine made possible much bigger missiles, and from the inception of the programme a second, big missile, a Trident II, was projected. During the 1970s the date for Trident II IOC was shifted around, from as early as FY 1982 to FY 1987.[27] After denying funding for Trident II initial studies in 1975 and 1976, Congress finally gave the go-ahead in 1977. The issue then was what to do with the extra volume available in a Trident submarine missile tube.

Various options were considered through the mid-1970s: C4 with better accuracy; a long C4 with a new first stage to give increased range (thus known as C5); a 'stepped' missile using an 82 inch first stage with 74 inch upper stages that retained some commonality with C4; a D5

146

missile with third stage protruding through the reentry bodies (as in C4); or a 'clear deck' D5 reverting to two stages to provide more space for the payload.[28] Out of these options the 'clear deck' D5 was initially favoured.[29] SSPO's preference was to use such a missile simply to carry the Mk. 4/W-76 payload developed for Trident I. A baseline number of fourteen Mk. 4 reentry bodies could be carried to the same range as Trident I, and there was also considerable flexibility to increase range by offloading.[30]

Indeed initially, in the early 1970s, SSPO's tentative accuracy goal for Trident II had been 'to achieve at 6000 nautical miles the CEP of POSEIDON at 2000 nm'.[31] Then came the pressures from other branches of the Navy – including PM-2 (the Trident Project Office) and OP-21 and from the Office of Secretary of Defense which culminated in the improved accuracy programme. Increasingly, improved accuracy came to be seen as important to provide higher counterforce capability for the FBM. In a May 1976 memorandum to the Secretary of the Navy, Deputy Secretary of Defense, W. P. Clements, Jr, referred to 'the ability of the FBM forces to respond to the guidance provided by NSDM 242 and the NUWEP'. Along with the relative invulnerability of the submarine, he noted:

> the potential for increased throw weight in a follow-on to the Trident I missile, encourages consideration of options to expand our SLBM capability against the full spectrum of the target system. Towards this objective, improvements in communications and in payload, including [deleted] and weapon system accuracy in a follow-on to the Trident I missile would enhance the utility of the FBM weapon system. . . . It is therefore requested that the Navy develop an overall plan, including a plan for the development of a Trident II missile with an IOC in the 1980s, for increasing the utility of the FBM weapon system. Increasing SLBM throw weight should not be pursued as an objective independent of substantial accuracy improvement.[32]

Such pressure for accuracy improvements in the FBM system was not new, of course. Since at least the early 1960s there had been pressure from the Office of the Secretary of Defense to increase FBM hard-target capability via accuracy improvements. But such pressure had only produced a grudging response. Accuracy improvements were made, but did not receive the highest priority, and hard-target capability did not increase significantly. Throughout the 1960s and 1970s the FBM force remained differentiated from the Air Force ICBMs, in both perceived capability and in doctrinal attitudes. Whereas counterforce was the byword of Air Force planning, the Navy remained wedded to deterrence by retaliation. But by 1976 things were beginning to change – future FBM needs were now considered to include the ability to 'strike hard targets to hedge against dependence on ICBM's'.[33]

This represented a significant change. Not only would hard-target kill capability come to be a central feature of FBM design, but it would do so as a clearly perceived substitute for Air Force ICBM hard-target kill capability. But this did not, it seems, come about due to the efforts of those Navy strategic planners who had long wanted to challenge Air Force dominance of the counterforce missions, nor simply because the technology was now available. Trident II came to be seen as a substitute for the Air Force MX ICBM more by default, because of difficulties which threatened that programme, rather than because of advocacy by the Navy.

What happened was that the various strands of US nuclear policy came together to form a powerful consensus around the desirability of US possession of significant hard-target kill capability, but during the same period in the late 1970s it became evident to many that MX might not be able to satisfy this 'requirement'. The reasons for this highlight just how broadly 'technical' issues must be understood.

THE SHIFT TO COUNTERFORCE

Counterforce is not a recent theme in the nuclear arms race. Since at least the start of the 1950s a significant portion of US nuclear weapons were assigned to 'the destruction of known targets affecting the Soviet capability to deliver atomic bombs' – initially known as Bravo (for blunting) targets.[34] With the advent of nuclear-armed ballistic missiles, despite their initially poor accuracy, the theme continued. In 1957 such targets were only considered able to withstand 100 pounds per square inch overpressure. Comparing the prospective US missile force, the Pentagon's Weapon System Evaluation Group concluded that: 'The numbers of successful missiles required to achieve 50 per cent probability of destruction of such a target are 80 ICBMs, 26 POLARISs, 13 THORs, and 2 JUPITERs.'[35] The study seemed intended to show that ballistic missiles were not suitable for counterforce missions (thus supporting continued reliance on bombers), and did not consider Polaris 'suited for employment against 100 psi targets'. But it was not to be long before the Air Force would come to emphasize counterforce in its ICBMs (starting with Titan II and Minuteman II), and pressure would develop for the Navy to compete over the role.

This pressure for a counterforce FBM remained localized until the 1970s. Although initially drawn to counterforce for damage limitation,

Secretary of Defense MacNamara soon switched his public, declaratory stance towards 'assured destruction'. Although the targeting plan, the SIOP, remained based on the earlier counterforce doctrine,[36] nuclear policy came to be publicly justified, and 'sold' to Congress, on the basis of retaliation against urban-industrial targets. Early attempts to fund accuracy enhancements explicitly to provide hard-target kill capability were not then well received.

But as the Soviet Union achieved rough numerical parity in strategic forces with the US, a parity enshrined in the 1972 SALT Treaty, attention shifted increasingly to the quality of the two arsenals. Although defence liberals continued to argue that US counterforce capability reduced *US* security (by potentially placing the Soviet Union in a 'use 'em or lose 'em' situation), hawks pointed to the daunting counterforce capability possessed by the Soviet Union's 'heavy' ICBMs. True, the Soviet Union could not hope completely to disarm the United States, but what would happen if it could successfully destroy the only US counterforce-capable missiles, the ICBMs? Would a US President not then be forced to surrender, given no option other than a suicidal attack on Soviet cities?[37]

This 'second-strike counterforce' argument undercut opposition to counterforce without violating the liberal sentiment that the US should never be, and should never even threaten to be, the nuclear aggressor. To the right of it, however, was to be found a more explicitly hawkish analysis, that suggested that numerical parity should not dissuade the US from the pursuit of 'nuclear superiority' and the political leverage that might follow from it.[38]

All this added up to a climate gradually pushing US official nuclear strategy ('stated posture') towards counterforce. Schlesinger's NSDM 242 of 1974 stopped short of clearly calling for enhanced counterforce capability, but it started a trend. President Carter's 1980 Presidential Directive 59 demonstrated how far the domestic and international political climate – especially the presidential challenge from Reagan – could push towards counterforce a president whose original inclinations were strongly towards a minimum deterrent 'assured destruction' strategy.[39] Both Carter's Secretary of Defense, Harold Brown, and his Under Secretary for Strategic Systems, William Perry, were sympathetic to advocates of increased accuracy in the FBM force.[40] Under Reagan, of course, executive sympathies turned entirely against assured destruction, and towards both counterforce and active anti-missile defences.

This shift in public position certainly had its consequences, for example undercutting the possibilities for Congressional opponents of counterforce to argue – as they had been able to before 1974 – that hard-target kill capability was incompatible with US national strategy. Yet the significance of this shift should not be overstated. 'Stated posture' is only one 'level' of nuclear policy: targeting practice, and acquisitions policy, by no means always follow stated posture. During the heyday of 'assured destruction' there was always a strong lobby, especially in the the Air Force, for counterforce. Counterforce capability was an important determinant of the design of the second two of the three generations of the Minuteman ICBM force, and counterforce targets received high priority in the targeting plan for nuclear war, the SIOP (Single Integrated Operational Plan).[41]

THE MX RELATIONSHIP

Here, however, the second aspect of the 'environment' of Trident D5 development becomes important, its relationship to the proposed new Air Force ICBM, MX. MX's Air Force proponents saw its main virtue as being its dramatic enhancement of US counterforce capability. But – in part at least because of Congressional sentiments – the MX programme was not put forward primarily on these grounds. Instead the main public argument for MX was what became known as the 'window of vulnerability' argument: that growing Soviet counterforce capability threatened the Minuteman force in its fixed silos.

This argument proved to be a double-edged sword. While it increased the acceptability of MX in a climate only gradually moving towards approval of the overt pursuit of hard-target kill capability, it gave high salience to finding a basing mode for MX that would be seen as invulnerable. This proved the Achilles heel of the MX programme. Successive proposals ran into both 'political' and 'technical' difficulties, and the repeated failure to find an acceptable basing mode began to threaten the MX programme as a whole.[42] Paradoxically, this built support for a 'hard-target' Trident on both the 'right' and the 'left'. Advocates of increasing US hard-target kill capability realized the importance of Trident II as a hedge against non-deployment of MX. Dr Seymour Zeiberg, Deputy Undersecretary of Defense for Strategic and Space Systems in the Carter administration, and a proponent of MX, noted the relationship:

> If we move out with a vigorous MPS [Multiple Protective Shelter basing mode for MX] program and we buy a new strategic capability which has high accuracy and has the potential to cope with counterforce missions, certainly the urgency to move out with the Trident II for that reason diminishes ... If we don't have an accelerated MX program of that sort, we would endorse the very accelerated Trident II program.[43]

For this reason, Zeiberg pushed SSPO to see if they could achieve accuracy in Trident II that was comparable with that forecast for the MX.[44]

Congressional 'doves', on the other hand, saw MX as the main enemy. Although many opposed it because of its increased counterforce capability, they made a tactical decision to fight it on the basing issue, where opposition was greatest. This then undercut opposition to Trident II which was 'sold' on its invulnerability. Because of this, and the FBM's enduring image as a retaliatory deterrent, many defence liberals saw Trident as the lesser of two evils at a time when it was politically difficult to oppose both outright.

So as the design decisions for the D5 were being made in the late 1970s and early 1980s, the programme's wider environment was such as to make any internal opposition to counterforce difficult. Indeed, by then, the improved accuracy programme had not only laid the technical basis for providing enhanced accuracy, but had also changed the culture of SSPO. Furthermore, Admiral Levering Smith, seen by many as a formidable opponent of counterforce, retired as SSPO director in November 1977.[45] After years of considering many different options – including improved accuracy C4s, stretched C4s, and a D5 built to have various degrees of commonality with MX – a decision was made by the Reagan administration in October 1981. The planned C4 inventory was to be reduced from 969 to 630 missiles, and a high accuracy D5 was to be developed with IOC of December 1989.[46]

With MX in trouble, the need for careful 'differentiation' of the FBM's nature and mission from those of ICBMs diminished. The 'bureaucratic' logic for opposition to counterforce disappeared. It was still seen as prudent not to present Trident II as a complete alternative to MX – if only because the slowness of communications with submerged submarines limited the credibility of using Trident in a 'first strike' or sophisticated 'war fighting' mode – but direct comparisons between the two appeared for the first time. In 1983, for example, Chief of Naval Operations, Admiral James Watkins, testified that: 'By 1991, we believe you could have four to five D-5 equipped Trident submarines, which is more than the equivalent of an MX field in terms of hard target kill capability.'[47]

DESIGN FOR COUNTERFORCE

Counterforce capability thus became an overt requirement in the design process of Trident D5. And this time round, the pressure from above for counterforce meshed with the interests and capabilities of those who could provide it (even in SSPO). Nowhere was this shift, and the changed relationship to Air Force programmes, more marked than in warhead design. SSPO's original plan to stay with the W-76 warhead was an unpalatable option to the nuclear weapons laboratories, where much work had already been carried out on developing larger yield options for both Trident and MX. The options available for warhead designs over 150 kilotons had been constrained since 1976 by the Threshold Test Ban Treaty. However, given several years' warning of this limitation the weapons laboratories carried out extensive testing in the early 1970s to provide a range of designs for future use. Pressure from the nuclear weapons laboratories to make use of one of these designs also, of course, found favour with those who sought a hard target capable FBM force, and, in December 1982, Deputy Secretary of Defence Carlucci advised the Navy to include funding for a new warhead/reentry body combination.[48]

The warhead options considered for use on Trident II (and on MX) were based on a secondary device[49] that was tested prior to the effect of the Threshold Test Ban Treaty in 1976.[50] The use of normal high explosive by Los Alamos in their primary design (as opposed to the safer insensitive high explosive which the Livermore design was based on) allowed weight savings which the Navy strongly desired, and so swung the decision in favour of that laboratory in 1982.[51] During 1982 and 1983 studies based on the explicit demand for hard-target capability were carried out both in SSPO and in the Strategic and Theatre Nuclear Warfare Division (Op-65) of the Office of the Chief of Naval Operations. These studies reached roughly the same conclusion – that a large warhead, of the order of half a megaton, would maximize Trident II's capability to meet their planning objectives.[52] By this time there was little dispute over these objectives. Trident II was to be designed to provide high confidence of destroying hardened targets, and the studies involved trade-offs which assessed the warhead choice in terms of the numbers that could be carried (both in terms of weight and packaging in the available space) per booster to the desired ranges. In fact, the chosen yield was about as large as possible without drastically reducing the number that could be carried. However, the extra weight of these large warheads meant that a two stage 'cleardeck' missile would no longer provide sufficient range, and so the system was redesigned to include a third stage, as in C4.[53]

After years of avoiding competition with the Air Force, the Navy was now challenging their dominance of the hard-target mission. This competition centered in particular on warhead design. The Air Force too wanted a similar yield warhead for its MX, but with the demands

152

being placed on available nuclear material by the Reagan build-up there was simply not enough to go around. The warhead secondary design under consideration for both Trident II and MX could be boosted to the desired half megaton range by increasing the amount of oralloy (enriched uranium, U-235), but there was not enough available to do this for both systems. The Air Force had intended to use a 500 kiloton warhead for MX, but 'lack of oralloy . . . forced the Pentagon to opt for a warhead that uses less oralloy but which only had a yield of 300 kilotons'.[54] Not surprisingly the Air Force was annoyed when the Department of Defense decided that the Navy Trident II should have a larger warhead to give it greater hard-target kill capability and 'added $88 million to the Navy's Fiscal 1984 budget request to develop a new ballistic reentry vehicle' for the D5.[55] Known as the W-88, the D5 warhead is boosted to 475 kilotons by adding more oralloy. For the first time, a Navy missile was to carry larger yield warheads than its Air Force counterpart: 'Questions are being raised by the [Air Force] over why the Navy will be allowed to deploy the higher yield device requiring more oralloy in short supply in the inventory.'[56]

In addition, the new Mk. 5 reentry body – like the Mk. 4 an ablative design – incorporates a shape stable nosetip intended to reduce dispersion caused by uneven erosion. The carbon-carbon weave is supplemented by metal filaments running along the axis of symmetry which make the shape caused by ablation more predictable, and thus more amenable to compensation.[57] This provides more assurance that unfavourable local weather conditions, such as rain or snow, will not greatly reduce accuracy. The Mk. 5 reentry body heatshield is being manufactured by General Electric Company, making it the first FBM reentry body not to be manufactured by Lockheed.[58]

Both the design of the reentry body and the yield of the warhead reflect the emphasis placed on hard-target kill capability in Trident II. However, in the belief that only a part of the Navy's warheads would be allocated to hard targets, along with concern for the UK's commitment to buy Trident II (but not to carry such blatant 'silo buster' warheads), and perhaps most importantly because of their own concern that the Mk. 5/W-88 combination might be cancelled by Congress because of its 'first strike' implications, SSPO also has retained the 'flexibility' to carry the C4's 100 kiloton Mk. 4 reentry body, and so D5 is designed to accommodate an adapter to take Mk. 4s. Trident II design specifications also required the 'bus' to be compatible with a future Large Accurate Evader reentry body. Both Lockheed and General Electric (the Mk. 500 contractor) have been funded by SSPO to study such a system.[59] Its main function, like the Mk. 500 in the Trident

I programme, seems to be to allow design considerations to be otherwise uncompromised by ABM considerations.

The 'bus' from which the reentry bodies are released is similar in design to that used in C4, but has one new feature that stems from the high accuracy requirement. After separation of the third stage, the bus positions itself to take the stellar sighting and the guidance system is updated as in C4. However, deployment of the reentry bodies differs because in C4 the gas plumes from the vernier thrusters used to reverse the bus away from the reentry body were interfering with its ballistic flight path and causing some inaccuracy. In D5 any vernier rocket which will interfere is not used until the reentry body is out of range of its gas plume.[60]

GUIDANCE AND FIRE CONTROL

The Mk. 6 guidance system designed for the Trident D5 took advantage of the lessons learned from the improved accuracy programme to provide an accuracy comparable to that sought by the Air Force's land-based MX ICBM. For the first time, a particular level of accuracy was not simply a 'goal' (which could implicitly be 'traded-off' against other goals) but a 'requirement' that had to be met. And it was a demanding requirement. The accuracy requirement was considered by those involved to be close to the limits of the possible using an 'evolutionary' development of the C4 system:

> In our case, case of D5, I'd say we have . . . an objective, a requirement in this case . . . such that I'm doing just about everything I know how to do with that technology. Cost hasn't been a major consideration. . . . With the basic technology right now I'm not sure I'd know what else to do . . .[61]

The improved accuracy programme had given SSPO's leadership the confidence to take on an explicit and demanding accuracy requirement. The programme had led to a sophisticated and largely, though not entirely, consensual understanding of the sources of FBM inaccuracy.

It was, for example, agreed that absolute accuracy in the gyroscopes was not *per se* crucial. Sophisticated computer programs along with the star-sighting could compensate for gyro drift. One possible challenger to the existing Mk. 5 system's two degree-of-freedom dry tuned-rotor gyro was the laser gyroscope. However, these looked to be larger than the dry tuned-rotor design, more difficult to integrate with the stellar sensor and difficult to operate in a radiation environment. So it was decided to go for a two degree-of-freedom dry tuned-rotor instru-

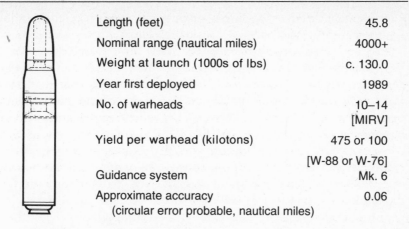

Length (feet)	45.8
Nominal range (nautical miles)	4000+
Weight at launch (1000s of lbs)	c. 130.0
Year first deployed	1989
No. of warheads	10–14 [MIRV]
Yield per warhead (kilotons)	475 or 100 [W-88 or W-76]
Guidance system	Mk. 6
Approximate accuracy (circular error probable, nautical miles)	0.06

Figure 8.1 Trident D-5

ment, built either by Kearfott or Litton. Kearfott (then part of Singer Corporation) was again successful: 'we had a "fly-off" on the ground between Litton and Singer and plain simple Singer won. Their gyro worked, Litton's did not . . . did not meet the performance specs.'[62]

With the accelerometers, on the other hand, the improved accuracy programme was understood to have shown that acceleration sensing errors were important contributors to inaccuracy. Two candidates appeared to offer the required high performance. One was the vibrating beam accelerometer whose simplicity promised small size, easy manufacture, and cheapness. However, it was considered difficult to harden against the effects of radiation and had a slow response time if inverted, and so SSPO reverted to the type of accelerometer used in the original Polaris, the PIGA, believed at the Draper Laboratory to be the most highly accurate accelerometer design.[63] 'They went from 3 PIGAs to 1 PIGA to 0 PIGAs as they went through the early generations, and then of course, now they decided, "Hey, we're going to go for broke", and now they're back talking PIGAs again.'[64] Although not used in the Mk. 3 and Mk. 5 FBM guidance systems, the Draper Laboratory had continued to develop PIGAs, culminating in the 16-PIGA used in MX. For the Mk. 6 a smaller version of this, the 10-PIGA, was used.[65]

The other main area of change in guidance components was the stellar sensor, and here 'trade-offs' continued longest into Trident II development.[66] Some argued that the vidicon technology was obsolete and that better performance could be achieved by moving to a solid state sensor, either a charge coupled device (CCD) or charge injection device (CID). Others felt these new technologies too premature for incorporation into the baseline system, and it was even felt by some that the reason for shifting away from the vidicon, where Kearfott had formidable expertise, was that it would allow the Draper Laboratory to regain design authority lost with the decision to move from inertial to stellar-inertial.[67] However, CCD was selected, and after a further reappraisal, the choice was reaffirmed. Doubts about the choice would, nevertheless, linger on because the CCD production process set up for D5 gave very low yields initially.[68]

Perhaps most thorough-going was the change in the guidance computer and electronics. In the chosen 'all-digital architecture' the output of the inertial components is converted to digital format. 'The digital data format together with the increased capacity of the digital computer permits use of more sophisticated compensation algorithms during missile flight.'[69] Computer capacity has risen to 1 megabyte of PROM and 200 kilobyte plated wire RAM, with widespread use of VLSI (very large scale integration) components and microprocessors.[70] Again, as in Poseidon and Trident I, the earth model used was based on a spherical simplification with gravity variation presets calculated by fire control.[71]

Another guidance innovation involved technology designed not for tactical use (i.e. on operational patrols) but simply for test flights. This was a small strapdown guidance system, known as the three axis instrumentation (TAI), that can be bolted onto the missile guidance inertial measurement unit to provide extra information from some flight tests. The TAI was pushed hard by the Draper Laboratory and accepted with reservations at SSPO. Some, at least, felt that in this instance the Draper Laboratory's technical exuberance had led to a development that was not needed, and which potentially could be damaging. Not only did it involve changing the guidance system case design and complicate interfaces, but it also introduced a difference between test and tactical missiles. The concern is that unnecessary differences should be avoided because they undermine the confidence with which test results can be extrapolated to operational perform-ance.[72] However, in practice no accuracy problems ensued that would have required data from the TAI and it was not flown on enough flights to undermine this confidence.[73] Another innovation, strongly pushed by the guidance community, but not incorporated, was a technique for self-calibration of guidance systems at sea.[74]

A new generation of fire control, the Mk. 98, was also developed for the D5. One major change made for accuracy improvement was in the approach to the development of the stellar correction matrix. Instead of relying on a general model developed from the navigation performance throughout the FBM fleet, each ship has its own particular navigation system errors modelled in an attempt more closely to match the stellar correction feedback.

TRIDENT NAVIGATION

All this, however, was understood as not enough to meet the accuracy requirement without improvements in navigation. With a stellar sensor believed capable of correcting for initial position and azimuth errors, two other aspects of launch condition were identified in the Improved Accuracy Program as prominent error contributors. First, errors in knowledge of initial velocity were understood as not correctable by star sighting and so measuring the submarine's velocity was seen as critical. Various approaches to this problem were considered and a Doppler sonar system was chosen to measure velocity from ocean bottom reflections.

The other concern was initial misalignment in the verticality of the missile guidance platform due to local gravity anomalies. Since an inertial component cannot distinguish inertial from gravitational acceleration, the accuracy of inertial navigation depends on the accuracy of the gravity model used. For the level of accuracy desired in D5, local gravity variation could introduce significant errors into the inertial measurements. One way to reduce this error source was to develop an on-board gravity sensor system (GSS) for the submarine. This consisted of 'a stabilized platform containing a gravity gradiometer and a gravimeter. The gradiometer measures the spatial rate of change of the gravity vector, and the gravimeter measures its magnitude.'[75] By constantly monitoring local gravity anomalies the GSS could help to reduce many errors which would otherwise accumulate in the navigation system and be transferred to the missile guidance system. But although technologically 'sweet' the GSS proved dispensable in practice. SSPO cancelled it in July 1988 due to poor performance and because 'other weapon system equipment was performing above specification and the accuracy of their gravity maps had exceeded expectations'.[76]

This pointed up the importance of the other approach to the gravity problem: more accurate geodetic mapping, both by satellite and by survey ship. Gravitational data provided by previous satellites, initially Transit and then the more sophisticated GEOS III and Seasat systems was judged insufficient for Trident II and a new Geosat satellite was developed for 1983 launching:

The Navy believes the improved Earth gravity models expected from the Geosat spacecraft will provide up to a 10 per cent improvement in circular error target accuracy for certain Trident 2 launch areas. The Geosat data will be most useful for Trident submarine patrol areas in the southern hemisphere and parts of the Northern Pacific where gravitational survey data are limited.[77]

A new ship surveying programme was also initiated, similar to that carried out for Polaris navigation, but mapping not only sea-bed terrain features, but also local gravity. Where available these surveys provide the most accurate method of updating the navigation system whilst avoiding the need to approach the surface. However, such surveying is very expensive and time-consuming, and so it was seen as impossible to survey all the potential patrol areas for a missile with the physical range of D5. SSPO thus accepted the accuracy requirement for the D5 only for a restricted range. Although D5 is capable of considerably longer range than C4 its accuracy specification was thus set for the same nominal range of 4000 nautical miles.[78]

The other main change in navigation for submarines carrying Trident II missiles is the replacement of the traditional SINS with electrostatically-suspended gyroscope systems, no longer merely as 'monitors,' but as the full navigators. The electrostatic gyroscope system is much less susceptible to unpredictable gyro drift than the SINS and so reduces the need for external resets. With sufficient experience to be confident of its reliability SSPO could now rely solely on the electrostatic gyroscope and thus eliminate the need to support two types of gyroscope hardware. Each Trident submarine will then carry two electrostatically supported gyroscope navigators. However, receivers for the traditional external navigation updates, Loran-C and Transit, will be retained. Although offering potentially greater accuracy than Transit, global positioning system receivers will only be 'incorporated into the Trident II weapon system after GPS has demonstrated continuous, worldwide capability equal to or better than Transit'.[79]

MISSILE AND LAUNCHER TECHNOLOGY

Lockheed initially awarded subcontracts for the D5 motors on the basis of the 'cleardeck' two-stage design. Again the 'joint venture' of Hercules and Morton-Thiokol won the competition to do both first and second stages. However, a third stage became 'necessary' to carry the heavier payload of Mk. 5 reentry bodies. This subcontract went to United Technologies Corporation who had unsuccessfully competed for the same work for C4. After their lack of success in the competition for C3 and C4 work, Aerojet – the propellant subcontractor for the first Polaris – did not even bother to tender for D5.

Given the large volume available in the Trident submarine launch tube and diminishing returns of range above about 4000 miles, there was not as much pressure to improve propulsion technology in D5 as there had been in C4. Instead, D5 missile design was considered 'conservative' with the emphasis on dependability and improving 'producibility' to 'reduce repetitive production cost'.[80] The propellant used is nitrate ester plasticized polyethylene glycol which took advantage of work done in the back-up investigation studies initiated because of the Trident I detonations.

Those problems also stimulated a change in the missile case material, from Kevlar to graphite epoxy: 'The decision to go graphite case ... was strongly influenced by our Trident I experience and the knowledge that graphite cases at the same specific strength level degrade more gracefully than Kevlar cases.'[81] Other aspects of missile construction, such as the use of the generalized energy management system (GEMS) to avoid thrust termination, were based on C4 technology. The same type of nozzle technology was used, but with a change in material to all carbon-carbon as this was seen as more reliable.[82] Changes in missile electronics in D5 also drew on the C4 experience, as well as utilizing the latest generation of large scale integrated (LSI) chips. Without the strict space and weight constraints of C4 it was decided to abandon some of the more specialized electronics developed for C4 so as to reduce potential supply difficulties.[83]

Launcher technology is also largely based on that used in previous systems, but obviously on a larger scale. The particular combination of D5's large size and its blunt nose design has, however, resulted in one significant change. All previous launcher systems have used fixed energy ejection systems, based on either compressed air or solid propellant gas generators, which were considered satisfactory for the desired launch depth band. At the shallow end of this band the missile emerged from the water surface faster than at the deep end, but both extremes were within the tolerances set. With Trident II the missile characteristics were considered such that a fixed energy eject system would not allow the same launch depth band as previously without overly stressing the missile during launch. In particular, if there was to be sufficient energy to launch at the deep end of the launch band then the missile would come out too quickly at the shallow end.[84]

The solution was to devise a variable energy eject system in which the energy imparted to the missile was adjusted according to the depth of launch by correspondingly varying the amount of water added to create the steam. Thus by adjusting the amount of energy used in vaporizing water it is possible to impart different amounts of energy to the missile from a fixed energy solid propellant gas generator. This means some variation in the temperature of the steam/gas mixture, but this is kept within the tolerance of the missile. It also means that the Trident II launch system is the first to require a sophisticated computer, in order to adjust the amount of water used.

A 'NON-CONTROVERSIAL' PROGRAMME?

Trident II's accuracy requirement was set to be almost as good as MX and 'at least twice as accurate as the Trident I'.[85] Although with the flexibility to cover a 'full target spectrum', D5 is a system optimized at considerable expense to provide the capability to destroy hardened military targets, such as missile silos.

Because of the shift in the political climate in the US, the peculiar relationship of Trident to MX, and of the FBM system's traditional reputation as a 'good' deterrent, this shift in the nature of the FBM programme has been achieved remarkably smoothly. With MX still bogged down – by a 'scandal' surrounding guidance system production as well as by its other handicaps – and the other Air Force ballistic missile programme, the Small ICBM, threatened with cancellation, Trident II was selected by Congress in November 1987 as a 'non-controversial' programme that could receive, instead of the usual annual funding, a five-year authorization.[86] The 4000 protesters who demonstrated at Cape Canaveral in Florida in January 1987 against the first flight-test of the D5, or the 700 still demonstrating in October 1987 would not have agreed.[87] But unlike the case of MX – where relatively local 'environmental' protest in Utah and Nevada became a major cause of the programme's troubles – Trident's opponents have so far had little impact. Even the December 1987 summit meeting caused only a one day delay in the D5's test programme, as a scheduled flight-test was postponed to avoid the period when Gorbachev was in the US.

Opposition to Trident II – though limited and belated in nature – stemmed especially from its central characteristic as a system designed to provide a high probability of destroying hardened targets. Although most opposition to hard-target counterforce systems focused on the more vulnerable MX (land-basing making it more vulnerable to both Soviet warheads and domestic opposition), Trident II also provoked similar concerns.[88] Opposition to Trident II became more focused in

160

the early 1980s as the implications of the system became more widely understood.[89]

Opposition to Trident II in the formal political system centred on Representative Thomas Markey – initially opposing Trident II outright, and then, when it became clear that the programme would go ahead, opposing the larger W-88 warhead. The underlying rationale of this opposition was that Trident II was a 'first strike' weapon, which, irrespective of US intentions, would engender Soviet fear of pre-emption and so increase the risk of nuclear war starting in times of extreme international tension. Thus in proposing an amendment of the defence authorization bill that would delete W-88 funding, Markey argued:

> do we really want to deploy this missile with a highly destabilizing first-strike capability, or do we basically want it to be a retaliatory weapon?
>
> If we were to deploy the D-5 with the lower yield warhead, it would still be able to destroy a wide range of Soviet military and industrial targets, but it would not be able to threaten a disarming first strike.
>
> Since we all know that there is no point in destroying empty Soviet silos, acquiring such a capability is useless unless we intend to strike first.
>
> And it is against U.S. policy to strike first.
>
> I say that if we are going to go ahead with the D-5, we should return the missile to its original purpose – increasing the range, and therefore the survivability, of the U.S. sea-based missile force.
>
> We should not deploy it as a silobuster.[90]

Despite the endorsement of efforts to enhance 'strategic stability' in the 1983 Report of the Scowcroft Commission on Strategic Forces, such opposition to Trident II was ineffectual. Deep in the conservative Reagan years, and with Soviet–American relations at a low ebb, it proved impossible to rally opposition to both MX and Trident II. Not only did the MX suffer from 'basing mode' vulnerability, but it also seemed more directly orientated to 'first strike'.

It could be argued, for example, that Trident II is much less destabilizing than the land-based MX because it is much less vulnerable.[91] In addition there is a marked contrast between the rapidity of communications of land-based and submarine-based missiles. Many associated with the FBM programme dispute the notion that Trident II can be characterized as 'first strike', not only because they deny that that is its intended purpose, but also because they claim that the communications systems are inadequate for such a purpose. ELF might provide greater assurance than higher frequency systems that all submarines would receive their intended emergency action messages (EAMs), but it is still doubtful that preemptive strikes could be contemplated without effective, prompt, *two-way* communications.

At present, however, the mission of the FBM force appears ambivalent. Trident II is designed to provide hard-target kill capability and has provoked concerns about its destabilizing, first strike potential. Indeed there were people working in the FBM programme who said they would never work on a hard-target FBM, and of those, some left because of Trident II.[92] But if the communications are as slow and patchy as some say, then for all its accuracy and explosive yield, Trident II may not provide the capability it was intended to. Dr Seymour Zeiberg, a key advocate of Trident II in the Carter administration, argued the case for a hard-target FBM in the warfighting language which was codified as national policy in PD-59: 'There are many targets in the Soviet Union that need to be attacked on a short time scale because they represent critical Soviet assets ... We need to stress ... our ability to take out time-urgent Soviet targets.'[93] But whether FBM communications are responsive and flexible enough to enable Trident II to be used in such a warfighting role during a nuclear conflict would seem to be open to question.

This change in mission created potential vulnerabilities for the FBM programme. The FBM's traditional role, that of a survivable, last-resort retaliatory deterrent, was easy to understand, plausible in implementation, and widely and bipartisanly supported. In contrast the hard-target, time-urgent 'warfighting' role that some envisaged for Trident II is both difficult to understand and to implement. Even those who fully comprehend the rationale behind recent US nuclear strategy would admit it is esoteric; though others find it misguided and dangerous. Moreover, the ability to implement such a doctrine is not easily obtained, requiring more than simply high accuracy and yield.

However, the relevance of the debate over nuclear war-fighting has faded with the break up of the Soviet Union and the prospect of very deep cuts in nuclear forces. In this context the FBM programme may easily resume its traditional mantle as the invulnerable 'assured destruction' deterrent. The debate now seems likely to revolve more around which nations will be targeted rather than the pros and cons of hard-target capability.[94]

It was in this rapidly changing strategic environment that the first Trident II missiles were deployed in March 1990 on the ninth Trident submarine. The test flight programme had not gone completely without hitches. The Cape Canaveral launch pad test flights were considered sufficiently successful to allow the cancellation of the final, twentieth one planned.[95] However, the spectacular failure of the first submerged test launch on 21 March 1989, repeated in the next test but one, led to an urgent search for a solution to the problem. In the event the first Trident II missiles were deployed three months later than their originally scheduled date of December 1989.

It was originally planned that the first eight Trident submarines – initially equipped with C4 missiles – would be converted eventually to D5. A total of at least twenty Trident submarines seemed likely as the final force size. However, with the disintegration of the Soviet Union undermining a major part of the rationale for such extensive nuclear forces, a commitment to build only eighteen Trident submarines has been made.[96] Moreover, the eight original Trident submarines deployed in the Pacific with C4 missiles look likely not to be refitted with D5. Of the ten submarines deployed with D5 in the Atlantic only four will carry the large yield Mk. 5 reentry bodies due to problems at the Rocky Flats Plant in Colorado where the fissile 'pits' for the warheads are manufactured.[97] The remaining six Atlantic Trident submarines will carry D5 missiles loaded with the Mk. 4 reentry body, and although potentially able to carry twelve of this smaller, lighter reentry body, are restricted to eight by START commitments.[98] In essence, then, it turns out that the very expensive Trident II programme has resulted in only four submarines with a significant performance advantage over the previous missile.

9 UNDERSTANDING TECHNICAL CHANGE IN WEAPONRY

Understanding the processes of technical change may have general utility in aiding our ability to shape technology to maximize human well-being. In most cases, of course, such a formulation is naïve – all too often one person's well-being is at the expense of another's[1] – but with nuclear weapons the issue seems quite clear-cut. Preventing nuclear war is an all-important goal for the human race, and one towards which studies of nuclear weapons technology should be able to contribute.

The threat of nuclear war deserves this central focus because of the expected enormity and widespread nature of its consequences. But understanding nuclear weapons technology also has everyday importance, though of a less unique nature. The opportunity costs of developing and building nuclear weapon systems are considerable, whatever the possible alternative uses of resources. Understanding how weapons technology 'decisions' come about, and how resources come to be allocated is thus of interest, both to those who wish to improve defence procurement efficiency and to those who would rather devote the resources elsewhere.

As outlined in chapter 2, the relationship between 'technology' and 'society' can be characterized in various ways. A simple dichotomy exists between explanations which see technology as an autonomous influence on society (technological determinism) and those which see society as shaping technology. In turn the latter view can be grouped into two different kinds of explanation, one based on the domestic processes within a state, and the other on the interaction between states.

TECHNOLOGICAL DETERMINISM

Technology-out-of-control

Many authors have claimed, as Ralph Lapp argues, that there is a 'technological imperative – when technology beckons, men are help-

164

less'.[2] Thus, according to the UN *Comprehensive Study on Nuclear Weapons*:

> It is widely believed ... that new weapon systems emerge not because of any military or security considerations but because *technology by its own impetus* often takes the lead over policy, creating weapons for which needs have to be invented and deployment theories have to be readjusted.[3]

In its most extreme form such technological determinism portrays the development of technology as though it were simply the inevitable application of science, which itself can be seen unproblematically as the 'real world' revealed. Scientific discoveries are seen as being applied in technology which then has 'effects'. Such an interpretation of technical change seems, however, to rest on two false premises – that the content of scientific knowledge is simply and 'naturally' determined by the physical world, and that the science–technology relationship is one-way and causal.

For example, John Garnett states that: 'The genesis of a weapon system ... begins with a piece of theoretical science.'[4] In practical terms this would seem to imply that technical application should always trail scientific understanding, but throughout the FBM programme there are many examples, in major areas of technology, where this has not been the case. The widely perceived advances in technology – in, for example, inertial guidance and navigation, reentry vehicle design, and solid propellants – have come about sometimes because of advances in scientific understanding, but, just as often, in spite of the lack of them. In each of these fields advances have relied on the various 'rules-of-thumb' and the 'black art' that go to make up the eclectic craft of technologists. Technological change has not been driven by scientific advances, but rather 'technology' and 'science' have coevolved. In warhead design it still the case that 'you certainly can't do the calculations from first principles, basic physics principles'.[5] According to a veteran of SSPO's navigation branch, 'all the gyro stuff is an art form. They may be engineers, but if you ask somebody ... "is there something written down that says exactly all those things?", and the answer is, maybe five or ten years after it is, but not during the process.'[6]

The craft or 'black art' required to produce, say, inertial components, solid propellants, and reentry vehicle nose-tips cannot be adequately documented in algorithms and formulae. Wise programme managers appreciate this – that the 'tacit knowledge' involved in many technical skills is a key factor in success and that people transfer such skill much more fully than even the most exhaustive documentation.[7] Indeed, it has long been recognized in the FBM programme that the difficulty in exactly specifying a technology makes it critical that nothing is changed from development to production, especially in items where testing is necessarily destructive, such as rocket motors.[8] As we have seen, for example, in the case of Poseidon reentry body graphite nose tips, even barely discernible changes between development and production can have disastrous effects.

Technology cannot, then, be seen as simply applied science, following a 'natural' pathway determined by the 'discovery' of the real world. Even if the production of scientific knowledge were itself such an unproblematic process (which it is not), it still could not be considered the sole, or probably even the most important, factor in technological change.[9] The creation of technology and of scientific knowledge are related processes, but the relationship is by no means one-way or deterministic.[10]

But, setting aside the relationship with science, could technological developments still be seen as the inevitable consequences of 'manipulating' the physical world? Even if technical developments do not directly arise out of the 'laws of physics' does a physical reality still determine the pathways taken by technology? Can technological development be explained in terms of 'natural trajectories'?[11] For example, is the progression from Polaris to Trident II the inevitable result of technological change in which advances in technology provided better accuracy, which in turn led to a change in targeting strategy? In 1973 it was predicted that: 'Just as MIRV was inevitable from the point of view of being a natural accumulating of technical knowledge, hard-target MIRVs also will be irresistible, policy statements to the contrary notwithstanding.'[12] A prediction which has been proven correct, even in the traditionally 'assured destruction' orientated FBM system.

However, this cannot be explained as due to the inevitable push of guidance technology. The physical world does not 'naturally' facilitate the development of high quality inertial components. On the contrary, this is achieved only with great difficulty and at great expense. Where high accuracy was not seen as required, such as in civilian and most military aircraft applications, inertial technology has followed a different course – emphasizing lowering life time costs, developing 'sweet' technologies, but of a different kind to those found in missile guidance.[13]

Similarly, even if improving yield-to-weight ratios was seen as a 'technological trajectory' in nuclear warhead design, it is clear that the practical implications of such a trajectory are ambiguous. Initially, this 'trend' in warhead technology, as noted by Edward Teller, proved a key breakthrough in the development of Polaris. The predicted low weight warhead made a smaller, solid-fuel, submarine-launched missile appear feasible, while the actual yield achieved was not considered especially critical. As yield-to-weight ratios increased (a self-fulfilling trajectory created as much by 'human nature' – the scientific and technological ethos, competition between Los Alamos and Lawrence Livermore, and high funding sustained by the Cold War – as by 'nature') its application in FBM warhead design could have taken a number of different paths. Increasingly larger warheads could have been developed in an attempt to compete with the Air Force for counterforce missions, as indeed some people desired for the Polaris A3 and Poseidon. Instead, of course, what happened was that testing limitations imposed by the nuclear test moratorium (and to some extent Navy reluctance to use Air Force designed warheads) along with concern over Soviet ABM developments and SPO's general commitment to 'assured destruction' led to the development of a MRV system carrying *smaller* warheads. A pattern which continued (and was indeed taken to an extreme) in Poseidon's 40 kiloton warhead. Only then did FBM warhead yield begin to increase – to 100 kiloton in Trident I and 475 kiloton in Trident II – as advocates of a hard target FBM became increasingly influential. Clearly no simple technological determinism was at work. Technology may be limited by the physical world, but it is shaped by the social world.

Trident II's apparent high counterforce capability is not the un-intended result of technical change. Such a capability (relative to the target hardness of the time) has always interested some people. As is clear from the Pentagon's Weapon System Evaluation Group Report of 1957, counterforce capability was even then considered an important criterion by which to judge the performance of ballistic missiles.[14] But, whilst counterforce was enthusiastically taken up by the Air Force in the early 1960s, the pressure for a counterforce FBM remained local-ized until the 1970s.[15] This is not because it was self-evident that mobile FBMs were inevitably bound to be less accurate due to 'technical' difficulties in knowing where the launch point was. This was to some extent compensated for by a much shorter range than US-based ICBMs (as big a difference as 1000 miles compared to 6000), and could be greatly ameliorated, if not removed, by schemes such as contour mapping of the sea-bed for certain launch areas.[16] This would have been especially true if the Navy had really wanted to stress counter-force capability rather than invulnerability.[17] What really made the distinction between accurate ICBMs and inaccurate FBMs that endured until the 1970s was 'social' not 'technical'. The distinction was created by the Navy and the Air Force, and, indeed, it has been suggested that an explicit deal was struck between the two to keep off each other's 'turf'.[18] Thus SPO's interest in projecting the image of the FBM as a counter-city deterrent held at bay the strategists who desired hard-target kill and the technologists who felt they could provide it.

'Technology' typically does not provide a single compelling line of development, but rather offers a number of possibilities. Quite aside from other considerations, budgetary and schedule constraints do not allow all possible technological avenues to be pursued. Even project managers wholly infatuated with technology cannot do everything that seems technically possible, or even everything that seems technically 'sweet'. Typically, there are choices to be made between different technical pathways.

Thus there was a choice in the FBM programme between staying with pure inertial guidance or moving to stellar-inertial. Here the wider political context played a role in augmenting technical doubts which delayed the introduction of stellar-inertial guidance till Trident I. In another case technological developments (especially in computer capabilities) could have led to a switch from a stable platform guidance system to a strapdown one, but did not. Similarly there were choices over the type of accelerometer used – the larger, more expensive, and more accurate PIGAs (pendulous integrating gyro accelerometers) or the more economical PIPAs (pulsed integrating pendulous accelerometers), the size and numbers of warheads carried, and so on.

For example, the choice of warhead size and configuration in the Poseidon missile was heavily influenced by both strategic and bureaucratic factors, and was directly related to issues of system accuracy. Technical choices were thus influenced by the 'macropolitics' of US defence policy, by the organizational politics of the Navy and its relationship with the Air Force, and also by the 'micropolitics' of the technical community. Whether a star-tracker was needed to supplement pure inertial guidance was doubted by dominant opinion at MIT's Instrumentation Laboratory, where there was a strong commitment to the achievement of ultimate accuracy by refinement of unsupplemented inertial sensors. Instead the stellar-inertial option was pushed by outside industry – the Kearfott Division of Singer.

There are many instances of technical choices made in the Fleet Ballistic Missile programme, and good evidence of a range of political and institutional factors shaping these choices. But 'the social' does not simply operate at the level of preferences between pre-defined technical options. It also shapes the options that are available, and may on occasion actually eliminate the possibility of explicit choice.[19]

One example of this concerns homing reentry vehicles, a possibility ruled out in the late 1970s in part because adequate testing of the technology was deemed infeasible. To date, US strategic ballistic missiles have been tested over water, usually impacting either in broad ocean areas or in the Marshall Islands, where indigenous islanders have so far been unable to bring significant legal or political pressure to bear. So the political power of citizens of the mainland US in comparison with Pacific Islanders has made it not feasible to adequately test homing reentry vehicles, as this would require overland testing.

'Soft' determinism – enablement and constraint

Clearly, then, a 'hard' form of technological determinism – in which artefacts are seen as the result of 'applied science' or as following inevitably from their predecessors due to natural trajectories – cannot be sustained. At the same time technology is not simply a dependent variable either; it can be important as an enabling capability or a limiting constraint. Technology as enablement amounts to a very weak form of determinism, if it can be so termed at all. Basic technologies and sciences may feed back into specific developments, both allowing and perhaps stimulating technological advances. Thus work in computing, inertial instruments, geophysics and geodesy has enabled missile accuracy to be greatly improved. Schroeer's claim that computing capabilities have driven missile accuracy might seem a case in point.[20] However, increased computer capabilities could just as reasonably have led to strap-down guidance systems (had cost and ease of maintenance been more important than accuracy) rather than better performance of stable platform designs. Enabling technologies merely provide possibilities, they do not determine the course actually followed. Rather than Schroeer's technological imperative a more suitable term might be Shapley's 'technology creep'.[21]

Furthermore, these advances in inertial instruments, geophysics and geodesy were to a large extent deliberately driven by military requirements for more accurate guidance systems. Even where technological and scientific advances on a broader front feed back into specific military technology, as computers seem to have in this case, it is important not to forget how those advances come about, and are themselves socially shaped. Widely applicable developments need not be unstoppable if no-one has a particular interest in pursuing them because, paradoxically, everyone may leave it to some one else to pick up the costs. Thus the development of the US Global Positioning System of navigation satellites may have been slowed down because all of the armed forces expected to get access to it, but none especially wanted to pay for it.

The development of specific enabling technologies also may be slowed, or stopped, if social conditions are not right. The very high quality inertial components used in strategic missile guidance have few other perceived uses. During the 1980s even advocates of counter-force accuracy in strategic missiles began to doubt whether further improvements in inertial sensors would provide much gain in overall system accuracy. Funds for development of this enabling technology have thus been proving hard to find, and the Draper Laboratory's efforts to develop 'fourth generation' inertial instruments significantly more accurate than the 'third generation' instruments of MX and D5 have not found sources of external support.[22] The 'technical trajectory' of further refining Draper inertial instruments may no longer be socially viable.

And, of course, 'technology creep' not only increases the availability of tempting new technologies, it can also lead to the non-availability of satisfactory old ones. In some areas of the FBM programme, such as the launcher subsystem, the latest technology has been often only grudg-ingly introduced – for example, the launch system initiator, which remained the same design up until Trident II:

> One other new element that's just been introduced for Trident II, we're just introducing it now, we haven't finished developing it, is what we call EBWTBI, electronic bridge wire through bulkhead initia-tor. It's a new device to initiate the burn in the gas generator. The device that we have used up until now is an initiator that was designed for use in Polaris missiles . . . We used it for our purposes but it is now a very ancient design, the manufacturer is no longer making it and it did not seem feasible to go back and start that up again . . . often times we are forced into changes not because in and of itself our program dictates the changes, but rather the market place dictates the changes, something is no longer available because no-one else uses it. For whatever reason other usages have disappeared, they've gone to other technologies, so that although we may not need ourselves to go to another technology, if everyone else has and no longer do we have a suitable source of supply, then we may have to look at this new technology too in order to widen our source of supply. That's what's happened in this initiator, the old initiator is simply out-of-date as far as the rest of the world is concerned so that although I'd be happy to continue to use it, I can't.[23]

Thus to some extent the 'market' not only enables, but also con-strains by determining the technology that is available, at least at a reasonable price.[24] The importance of this was recognized at the start of the Trident I programme when SSPO went to special lengths to stockpile critical items that either had long leadtimes or – in the case of rayon – were considered likely to become scarce because of reduced demand.[25]

'Technology' may also prove a limiting constraint in other ways. Most obviously, in a complex weapons system such as the Navy ballistic missiles, design interfaces need to be fixed and adhered to. From that point on, subsystem technology is constrained by the need to 'fit'. Design decisions may thus have an enduring physical legacy restricting future technology. For example, the physical size of submarine missile mount tubes (which is of course itself limited by the size of the submarine) limits the size of missile possible. All the US Polaris class submarines built in the 1960s had the same size mount tubes. Once some initial extra space had been accounted for, when Poseidon missiles were installed, there remained no space for further expansion. When the Trident I missiles were designed to fit the same submarines, but also to provide about a third more range, this proved a severe constraint, which required much ingenuity to overcome.[26] At the same time, the decision to make the missile compatible with existing FBM submarines led to a series of technical choices which limited the size and yield of warheads that could be carried, and thus provided a physical constraint on those who were pushing for larger yield warheads. Moreover, had it not been decided many years earlier to enhance crew comfort by enlarging the Polaris submarine design after the first ten, then sufficient buoyancy would not have been available to allow the back-fitting of the heavier Poseidon and Trident I missiles.

Such technical constraints may also be understood as social or political. In the debate over Trident, the 'technical' argument for a larger missile was deployed by those in the Navy who favoured building a new, much larger class of submarine. In particular, Admiral Rickover, the 'father' of nuclear propulsion, argued strongly in favour of a large submarine because it would require a new nuclear propulsion system. SPO, on the other hand, were sceptical of the idea of putting more, larger missiles into a bigger submarine. A particular concern was that this meant fewer targets for Soviet anti-submarine warfare, but the question of size was also connected to disputes over the division of responsibility between Special Projects and Admiral Rickover. SPO would have preferred to live with the 'technical constraint' of missile tube size – at least for a few more years – if this had at the same time constrained Rickover's influence on the FBM programme.

171

Technologists-out-of-control?

Technological development thus has the potential to follow a number of different courses, rather than one single predetermined pathway. It provides capabilities and sets some constraints, but is profoundly shaped by the social world. Most immediately, of course, it is shaped by the technologists who develop it, and who have a considerable interest in promoting it. Personal preferences and institutional interests mean that many technologists like to push technologies as far as they can in particular directions.

What evidence is there that technologists are, as Lord Zuckerman amongst others has suggested, manipulating the strategic and political environment so as to create a market for their favoured technology?[27] Certainly in the Navy ballistic missile programme crucial technological advances were developed externally and before any 'requirement' had been formulated for them. However, none found automatic acceptance without careful scrutiny as to how they would affect the goals and interests of the programme. Only if technologists could transform these goals and interests so that they then fitted their preferred technology would the technologists-out-of-control thesis have significance.

Undoubtedly they have tried. For example, Charles Stark Draper clearly perceived that he was trying to engineer people's attitudes as well as guidance systems: 'I had always been interested in people that I had to deal with and their mental attitudes and why they had these mental attitudes and choosing something that the people in charge had to have.'[28] Not 'wanted', but 'had to have'. There are indeed several instances in the history of the Navy ballistic missile programme where technologists sought to persuade 'the people in charge' that they had to have something they had not originally wanted. But these are generally cases where the technologists convinced 'the people in charge' that their existing goals could be better fulfilled by a new device, not where they changed these goals to further a preferred technology.

One candidate case of this is Draper's attempt to persuade the Navy to rival ICBM accuracy.[29] But this was a failed attempt. Another case was the attempt to 'sell' stellar-inertial guidance by reorientating the FBM from assured destruction to counterforce. The attempt failed in the case of Poseidon, exactly because counterforce was seen as politically unacceptible. It succeeded with Trident C4, but only as part of a 'repackaging' that emphasized stellar-inertial guidance's compatibility with assured destruction.

A stronger case is perhaps that of the nuclear weapons laboratories, which, for example, meant that potential warhead designs for Trident II were tested prior to 17 March 1976 even though system development was not given the official go-ahead until the early 1980s. Indeed it seems that key figures in the nuclear weapons laboratories were advocates of the larger yield warhead used in Trident II and of developing a new warhead for Trident I. Or to take an earlier example, the basic idea of the Poseidon MIRV was proposed to the Navy by key advocates – Carl Haussman and Lloyd Wilson – at Lawrence Livermore and Lockheed. This active 'selling', and 'preemptive' development of warhead designs, seems to have been a key part of Livermore's success in strategic warhead development, and thus became the norm for the competition between the two laboratories.[30]

Such behaviour is important, and in the United States technical innovation seems typically to be generated 'from the bottom up'.[31] However, such innovation and the advocacy of technical proponents, either in weapons laboratories or industry, is by no means decisive in determining the technological outcome, though it clearly may limit the range of possible outcomes. To be successful promising technical innovations must be more than simply 'sweet', they must also be compatible with the interests of key actors in the organizational and political world of weapons procurement. Many innovations are generated, but only a few reach deployment. Thus, for example, various proponents have argued the feasibility of manoeuvring reentry vehicles, with or without terminal guidance, for over twenty years. SPO, however, could meet its goals, both in terms of accuracy and ABM evasion, without the need to complicate their task. Only the Mk. 500 Evader was developed, without enthusiasm, and with no serious intent to deploy.

To gain acceptance for their innovations, technologists must convince people that they are needed. Success therefore depends not only on engineering the physical world, but also on manipulating the social world – on what has been called *heterogeneous engineering*.[32] Support must be gained from laboratory chiefs, key members of the armed services, career civil servants and political appointees in the Pentagon, and ultimately perhaps from the administration and Congress. Success depends not just on how 'sweet' a technology is (although depicting a technology as 'sweet' can be persuasive), nor on how well it matches a military 'need' (which is, of course, something of a movable feast, especially in the largely hypothetical world of nuclear warfare), but also on how skilfully it is 'sold', on how effectively support is enrolled and opposition minimized. Thus, although the nuclear weapons laboratories have been strong advocates for certain warhead designs, those which were successful were so because they matched the interests of either SPO (in the case of Poseidon) or the Office of the Secretary of Defense (in the case of Trident I and II), while at the same time not engendering significant opposition from other key actors.

So, although technological enthusiasts (from, say, the nuclear weapons laboratories, the Charles Stark Draper Laboratory, or Kearfott) have been key influences on the development of FBM technology, they have not been able to manipulate at will the goals and interests of SPO. Indeed FBM programme managers have been actively aware of the threat that over-zealous technologists can pose to their programme's success. A former Director of SSPO recalled that:

> there's always going to be a technologist somewhere who doesn't feel comfortable until you've applied all the technology you could possibly apply. And the problem of the program manager, of course, is to try to take all this and balance it and make a prudent choice of what he thinks can be done and can be done within a program cost and schedule that he can predict and is good enough to meet the need.... You simply can't afford to put all the technologies into a system that the technologists can promise.[33]

POLITICS-IN-COMMAND: RATIONAL ACTORS AND REALISM

If technology is not out of control, then can it be seen simply as a tool, created to fill a specific use, such as deterrence? Can nuclear weapons be seen as the product of political decision-making aimed at fulfilling national security requirements based on the state of international relations?

The balance-of-power or realist school holds the anarchic structure of the international system to be a dominant factor in international relations. Systemic constraints inherent in this self-help environment are seen as explaining continuity in state behaviour. Realism's leading proponent, Kenneth Waltz, has little to say, however, on the theory's implications for weapons technology. His single observation is that: 'Contending states imitate the military innovations contrived by the country of greatest capability and ingenuity. And so the weapons of major contenders, and even their strategies, begin to look much the same all over the world.'[34]

Evangelista's comparative study of tactical nuclear weapon development in the United States and USSR suggests that this proposition is only partially valid.[35] Similarly, Soviet submarine launched ballistic missile technology emulated many, but not all, aspects of the US FBM programme. It would have been misleading to see the Soviet submarine missile force as simply a mirror image of the US FBM force. For a variety of reasons – including geography and the historical development of military organizations and of political control – the land-based ICBM force had much greater prominence in the Soviet Union.

Thus, although the superpower nuclear arms race would seem to be explained in gross terms by 'balancing' behaviour, this does not provide a very powerful way of understanding the detail of weapons development. Apart from anything else it explains only reactive behaviour and provides little insight into the way that weapons technology develops. Realists, it seems, simply assume an unending stream of technical innovation 'contrived by the country of greatest capability and ingenuity'.

One explanation of technical innovation is, of course, that it is directed through the decisions of governmental 'rational actors' in response to external events, such as the Soviet 'threat'. What has been termed the action–reaction phenomenon focuses on external determinants of weapons technology. The technology is said to be a response to what the other side – the Soviets (or even the Chinese) – is doing. Thus, for example, Poseidon's MIRV design is said to have been a response to the appearance of the Galosh ABM.

The problem with the action-reaction phenomenon in practice is that the reaction has often been premature, excessive, or even completely inappropriate (as in the case of the Polaris A3 PX-2 penetration aids). The reasons for this would seem, at root, to be 'internal' in two ways.

Firstly, what the 'external' world consists of is not unambiguous, and what it will look like in, say, five years must be speculative. No matter how 'technically' proficient intelligence collecting methods are, the data collected still need to be analysed and interpreted. In this process they are inevitably mediated by the expectations and biases of domestic actors (which may be organizations or key individuals). Secondly, even when a consensus is reached about what the external world looks like, it still remains to be decided what is to be done about it. So although external actions are an important input, by no means would they seem to determine what the output – the reactions – will be. And even once such 'decisions' as to the most appropriate reaction are reached there remains the question of whether technical change is something that simply can be directed by political elites.

Just how powerful are the President, the Secretary of Defense, and Congress (to name the major actors) in directing technical change in weaponry? Even if they were capable of analysing the state of the external world, and deciding which technologies would maximize the interests of the USA, would they then be able to implement those decisions unproblematically? The same question arises even if they make decisions on weapons procurement for quite different reasons, such as the state of domestic politics.[36] On the face of it, there is much evidence which suggests that political elites can be very important in 'deciding' important attributes of weapons technology. For example, Posen argues that British innovation in air defense prior to World War II (including the critical construction of radars and fighter aircraft) came about largely because of the pressures exerted by civilian leaders as a result of their perception of the German bomber threat.[37] This outcome, Posen argues, could be explained only by the rational actor model: 'If there were such a thing as technological determinism, or if organization theory had the explanatory power claimed by some of its proponents, then this innovation should not have occurred.'[38]

The evidence from the FBM programme is less clearcut. Certainly, pressure for improved counterforce capability in the FBM system was exerted downwards from the Office of the Secretary of Defense (and also less effectively from the Office of the Chief of Naval Operations) during most of the 1960s and 1970s. Most obviously Secretary Schlesinger's 1974 review of nuclear strategy towards more flexible limited nuclear options and his pressure for the improved accuracy programme were especially significant. However, it is clear from this example that this was not a question of command in the archetypal military sense. For two reasons it was simply not possible to command the technology into being.

First of all there is a general limitation to command. Technological change simply does not possess either the transparency or the predictability that would be required for straightforward command to be possible. Dominant social groups, whether these be political, business or military elites, are typically in no position to shape technological change in the conscious, literal sense that we can imagine an artist moulding clay. If they choose between given technological options, then those who present the options to them have an opportunity both to set the agenda (deciding which options to present) and to influence the decision in the way they portray the advantages and disadvantages of different options. If they seek to create a new technology, then they may well need advice as to feasibility – for what they desire may be physically impossible, or hopelessly expensive, or whatever. Thus SPO was able to avoid committing itself to overly ambitious technical developments. As a former technical director recalled, 'SP[O] has never had a requirement in its life, they've had thresholds that usually were not very ambitious because SP[O] helped define them.'[39]

Secondly, and more specifically, politics-in-command fails to provide an adequate explanation in the US political context. Here the nature of the democratic political system with complex and over-lapping jurisdictions creates a situation where political leaders such as a president or secretary of defense have to engage in a process more akin to bargaining than to giving orders.

Clearly, however, there are certain positions in the formal political system which can exert very important influence on weapons technology. Depending on their personal interests, the president, secretary of defense, secretary of state, national security advisor, director of the CIA, and chairs of key Congressional committees can all wield considerable influence. A presidential decision (such as that by President Reagan to advocate strategic defenses) can be a powerful event. But no matter how persuasive an advocate the president is, and regardless of his formal position as commander-in-chief, his power can be formally limited by Congress, informally limited by obdurate bureaucracies, and ultimately limited by a maximum tenure of eight years.

Typically the administration and Congress have played a mainly passive role in managing the development of weaponry. Within funding limits and a general post-war consensus on national security the fine detail of weapons characteristics, numbers, and operational strategy have been largely left to the services. An exception, of course, was during McNamara's term as Secretary of Defense when many such issues came under close scrutiny by OSD. Since then, though not to its former extent, defence 'decision-making' has become decentralized again. Increasingly Congress has concentrated on the fiscal aspects of weapons procurement – so much so that many feel that such legislation now greatly hinders programme managers. Much of the time, however, Congress and the Secretary of Defense have 'rubber stamped' the services' recommendations – at least on issues considered to be 'technical'. General congruence with stated defence policy helps, but is by no means always necessary to gain Congressional approval, when in some cases parochial constituency issues can dominate. On the occasions when Congress does take an active role in shaping weapons technology decisions, such concerns, rather than the national response to an external 'threat' may be most influential.[40]

Even when a president takes an active interest in the details of nuclear weapons policy there are limits to his power. President Carter's initial interest in changing US nuclear posture to dependence on only a few FBM submarines so as to provide assured destruction

177

retaliation provides an illustrative example.[41] Such a proposal, naïve as it no doubt appeared to insiders, was not inconsistent with the bulk of US declaratory statements about strategic deterrence made over the previous decade. These seemed to indicate that the potential for assured destruction of a substantial part of Soviet urban-industrial areas (that is, cities) was the central plank of deterrence. So why not simply rely on a few of the apparently invulnerable Poseidon-carrying submarines? The answer was, of course, that assured destruction was only the declaratory rationale for nuclear weapons, it was not the 'real' reason why most defence insiders supported a large, diversified triad of nuclear weapons with varying capabilities, including some (such as high accuracy ICBMs) which made little sense simply for assured destruction.

As President Carter would come to learn, these reasons included not only rational (if somewhat esoteric) arguments about the political utility of counterforce and the symbolic need to match (or exceed) Soviet capabilities, but also domestic factors such as interservice rivalry and electoral politics. Carter was persuaded to drop his radical proposals as he came to view the world through the eyes of the defence establishment, attuned not only to the Soviet threat, but also to the political need to pander to various domestic constituencies.

DOMESTIC EXPLANATIONS

Domestic explanations of weapons technology focus on the effect that the internal organization of a state has on weapons development. Three variants of this approach are considered here. 'Bureaucratic politics' theory has its origins in dissatisfaction with realist explanations, seeing foreign policy or weapons technology as the product not of rational decisions, but rather of organizational conflict and compromise. The 'military-industrial complex' approach sees a particular sector of society as able to exert undue influence on the weapons procurement process, often placing this in a Marxist analysis of the nature of a capitalist society. Finally, some authors have focussed on the way in which military R&D is organized within the USA.

Bureaucratic Politics

The limitations on the power of top political authorities have been thoroughly documented by the bureaucratic politics approach. This emphasizes that states are not unitary actors, but are complex ensembles of often sharply divided organizations. Policy is not 'decision', with that term's connotation of the formulation of goals and then rational choice of the means to fulfil those goals, but 'outcome', the often internally contradictory result of multiple and repeated contest.[42]

A bureaucratic politics explanation accords well with much of the history of FBM technology. Throughout there has been the pervasive significance for the FBM programme of conflict between the Navy and the Air Force (or, to be more exact, of the studious avoidance of such conflict).

One example from the history of FBM technology is the October 1971 'decision' by President Nixon to accelerate FBM submarine construction as a 'bargaining chip' for SALT. What at first sight might seem a rational decision based on international politics was in fact the outcome of interactions between various parts of 'the bureaucracy'. Initially the idea came from Paul Nitze, the Secretary of Defense's representative at the SALT negotiations. Nitze – always of a somewhat 'hawkish' disposition – was becoming increasingly annoyed at the way Kissinger manipulated presidential access, and worried about what he saw as Kissinger's tendency to make concessions in order to get a deal.[43] On noting that the Soviet delegates at SALT seemed especially concerned about US plans to replace Polaris submarines, Nitze reported back to Secretary of Defense Laird and his deputy Packard that a decision to proceed with FBM submarine construction 'would give the United States considerable leverage at the talks'.[44] Nixon, it seems, was persuaded of this bargaining chip rationale, but White House staff generally favoured building more of the existing FBM submarine design rather than accelerating the development of the proposed ULMS submarine. To Kissinger, however, the bargaining chip was something to be used straightaway, not against the Soviet Union, but against Admiral Moorer, Chairman of the Joint Chiefs of Staff. The SALT talks were stalemated on the issue of limits for FBM submarines, which Kissinger was willing to concede the Soviet Union should be allowed more of because of their lesser capability (particularly compared to the MIRVed Poseidon). To make this palatable to Admiral Moorer and gain service support Kissinger agreed to accelerate US submarine construction at the same time.[45]

But then Packard worked with factions within the Navy (such as Admiral Rickover's office) to exclude Kissinger from the final choice. To avoid the possibility of simply constructing more submarines of the existing type (which some White House staff were known to favour), OSD carried out studies which were prepared to show that ULMS

179

acceleration was the best choice.[46] The White House was not consulted and when Secretary of Defense Laird announced the decision to accelerate ULMS it was, it seems, *without* President Nixon's explicit agreement. This was a satisfactory result for many parts of the Navy (but not SPO, of course) and for people in OSD who were sick of the interference of the Kissinger instigated Defense Program Review Committee. The outcome, however, was felt by many to be of dubious value as a bargaining chip, and also to be questionable as the best choice for the future of the FBM force. Moreover the decision to agree to the accelerated schedule (in order to make the ULMS option appear competitive with building more Poseidon type FBM submarines or converting existing attack submarines) was to cause the programme great embarrassment in the future.

It would be hard to explain this episode without reference to the organizational wranglings of bureaucratic politics. However, particular formulations of the bureaucratic politics approach have been rightly criticized.[47] It is clearly inconsistent to treat organizations as unitary. If 'America' must be disaggregated, so must 'the Navy'. It is clear that 'the Navy' itself is not unitary, and that conflicts within it (e.g. between SPO and Rickover, or SPO and the Great Circle Group) have influenced FBM programmes. Furthermore, subunits such as SPO can themselves be disaggregated, and found to contain technologically important tensions, for example those between SP-23 (guidance and fire control) and SP-24 (navigation).

Nor are particular individuals necessarily the predictable products of their organizational location. The formal hierarchical authority of the Secretary of Defense or President is not unimportant, even though it is only one political resource amongst several. Private corporations, as well as state bureaucracies, are important – for example, the important role in FBM guidance decisions played by the activities of Kearfott. Nor has the external world – in particular, Soviet behaviour – been irrelevant, however important are the bureaucratic processes by which crucial data, such as in this case about Soviet anti-submarine warfare and anti-ballistic missile capabilities, are processed.

Graham Allison's classic study of the Cuban Missile Crisis – in attempting to demonstrate the model for a very 'hard' case – has come in for particular criticism.[48] These critiques argue that organizational process and bureaucratic politics[49] are often of only peripheral interest, and that *real* decision-making happens at a higher level. Thus in the case studies of Allison (Cuban Missile Crisis) or Halperin[50] (ABM decision) it is clear that the President was a very important figure, and that the behaviour of many key actors could not be explained in terms of their organizational affiliations. Allison's popular aphorism – 'Where you stand depends on where you sit' – seemed frequently to be wrong.[51]

Nonetheless, the essential insights of the bureaucratic politics approach – that policy and weapons procurement should be viewed as the *outcome* of social interactions in which rational argument is only one factor – are confirmed by this study. Moreover, a distinction should also be made between the development of policy and that of technology. An important policy decision *can* be made overnight, and is thus much more susceptible to 'top-down' command. A group of individual leaders – such as the members of the US Executive Committee in the Cuban Missile Crisis – can reach decisions which go against their organizational affiliations (if indeed they have any). When it comes to implementation, however, the policy must (except in very exceptional cases) pass through the relevant bureaucracies, and then organizational interests and preferences may take effect. If the policy demands instant action then there will be limited scope for alteration, but if it sets in motion a long-term process bureaucratic politics inevitably becomes more influential. Modern weapons technology, of course, may take a decade or more to develop and during this time will be subjected repeatedly to the influence of bureaucratic interactions.

And, of course, the weapons procurement process is to a large extent the realm of military organizations, in which the uniformed military provide an unusual degree of consistency. Here doctrinal uniformity and organizational loyalty do tend to produce predictable allegiances. Whilst politicians and civilian appointees may be less the product of their bureaucratic affiliation, they are also likely to be less important in shaping a weapons technology over the full term of its development. They are not, as this study shows, unimportant, but they must operate in an environment shaped by the exigencies of bureaucratic interactions.

The military-industrial complex and capitalist interests

Another domestic explanation of weapons procurement is that which has come to be known as the military-industrial complex.[52] Briefly characterized, this viewpoint explains high levels of military spending in the USA as the result of the 'vested interests' of the military, defence corporations, governmental and legislative elites, defence-related scientists and technologists, and other pressure groups (such as right-wing 'think-tanks' and veterans' associations).

Weapons procurement and defence R&D provide the links by

which corporate, scientific-technical and military interests mutually benefit. As a corollary of this it would not be surprising to find that these groups are mutually supportive, nor that they would be actively encouraged by regional legislators who would appear likely to gain political benefit from any creation (or retention) of jobs in their locality.[53] Given the levels of funding which go to defence R&D and procurement in the United States this 'network' of interests is likely to form a powerful force pushing weapons technology.[54] Thus in his farewell address in 1961 President Eisenhower delivered his famous warning that 'we must guard against the acquisition of unwarranted influence, whether sought or unsought, by the military-industrial complex'.[55]

Explanations for what might underpin such a complex vary, however. Three types of analysis have been put forward, though two are analytically very similar.[56] Both see weapons procurement under the sway of a powerful elite, but differ as to where this power is located. In one version it is the military who are seen as perpetuating excessive weapons development, whereas in the other it is the administrative bureaucracy. An example of the former is the view of Heilbroner 'that the military establishment constitutes itself as a self-contained entity, capable of impressing its views and imposing its will not only on the civil establishment to which it pays ritual obeisance, but over a section of the economy in which the language of private enterprise is merely a fiction to hide its absolute authority'.[57] The administrative bureaucracy view is most typically expressed in the work of Seymour Melman.[58] The third type of analysis of the military-industrial complex draws on a Marxist perspective. Narrowly viewed, defence corporations are seen as sustaining the arms race and thus weapons procurement in order to keep themselves in business. More broadly, big business in general is seen as imposing its capitalist interests on US foreign policy.

To take the idea of dominant military elites first, it is clear that the interests of the military are important, but any theory which takes a monolithic view of these interests is unsatisfactory. Interservice rivalry has been one of the most powerful shaping influences in US nuclear weapons systems development. There is not one unitary military actor, but rather many, often competing ones. While all parts of the military may act in unison in order to advocate large defence budgets, sometimes the different services will fail even to present a coherent front on this uncontentious issue. When it comes to deciding how the budgetary pie should be sliced up, agreement is even more difficult to achieve. Interservice cooperation in presenting a united front no longer allows the Secretary of Defence so easily to divide and rule, as happened prior to about 1965.[59] But disagreement and bargaining between (and within) the services, as well as with the Secretary of Defence, remain pervasive factors in the weapons development process.

What, then, of the idea of an administrative elite sustaining a 'permament war economy'? Seymour Melman identifies the 'McNamara revolution' as institutionalizing a militarization of US society. Although not articulated with any great clarity, Melman's 'Pentagon Capitalism' seems to be based on the symbiotic relationship between a centralized, expansionistic bureaucracy and a non-competitive defence industry. More and newer weapons are thus produced in order to satisfy the bureaucracy's self-perpetuating interests, and are produced inefficiently and expensively because of the non-competitive relationship that industry has with the Pentagon.

Setting aside the fact that the Pentagon comprises many factions with differing interests, the idea of an administrative elite, like that of a military elite, also ignores the real, if sometimes limited, power that can be exerted through the political process by Congress and the President. Also in the FBM programme – admittedly perhaps an exceptional case – it is clear that SPO was able to operate relatively free of interference from such bureaucracies. What pushed succeeding FBM generations seems to have been a combination of SPO's organizational need to stay in business along with widely held perceptions of plausible and 'necessary' new missions for nuclear weapons, not bureaucratic momentum from within the Pentagon.

What of the Marxist interpretation of the military-industrial complex – that it stems at root from the capitalist system? Two aspects of this can be distinguished. One analysis focuses specifically on the profit motive of defence corporations in particular rather than American capitalism as a whole. For example, can the apparent phenomenon of the 'follow-on imperative'[60] – whereby defence corporations are kept in business through the awarding of contracts for successor weapons systems – be explained as the result of the machinations of the military-industrial complex? The history of FBM technology, with each succeeding generation non-competitively awarded to Lockheed, would appear to be a classic case of such a 'follow-on imperative'. However, what has been called the 'weapons succession process' cannot be explained simply in terms of corporate profit (or survival).

Such economic arguments for weapons succession fail to explain technical change. If the sole factor was maintaining corporate profitability or survival then this might be achieved by continued pro-

183

duction of the same technology, with technical innovation restricted to improving the *process* not the *product*. But, in fact, the opposite is typically the case – technical innovation in weaponry usually focuses on product, not process. The weapons succession process is characterized by its emphasis on product innovation, often producing 'gold-plated', 'baroque' technology.

Indeed it would seem a general failing of military-industrial complex theories that whilst they may account for the scale of resources allocated to military technology, they provide little explanation for the nature of technical change. A variety of 'vested interests' may share a common interest in, and gain mutual benefit from, high levels of spending on the development and production of weapons technology, but they are unlikely to exhibit such unanimity on exactly which projects should benefit or how they should take shape. The military-industrial complex may be an identifiable and powerful alliance of interests, but it is not without internal divisions.

Although subject to the same criticism, another Marxist-type approach is more encompassing in its analysis. Rather than focusing just on defence corporation profits it viewed the Cold War between the superpowers as really an economic rather than military competition.[61] The main function of the US military apparatus was to maintain, and if possible extend, foreign markets for US goods. That, above all else, was why they had to be protected from communism. Thus, it is argued, US military policy since World War II has been guided by economic imperialism. Historical evidence for such a view is not difficult to find in the record of US military intervention, undercover operations, arms supplies, and foreign aid. Many undemocratic regimes have thus been installed or maintained because they promised 'stability' and kept the world 'free for capitalism'.

A similar economic imperialism analysis can be applied to the development of nuclear weaponry. In this the shift towards counterforce and the proliferation of hard-target weapons developments (Trident II, MX, Pershing II, and cruise missiles) in the late 1970s is seen as an attempt to regain US nuclear superiority, and in particular to sustain 'extended deterrence'.[62] Competition in the Third World and the coercive potential of nuclear superiority can be seen as decisive elements in the thinking of key counterforce advocates in the Carter administration, such as Zbigniew Brzezinski. Thus the decision to chose the biggest MX missile option was explained later by Director of Defence Research and Engineering, William Perry: 'The geopolitical arguments outweighed the technical arguments.'[63] In this formulation, however, the extended deterrence issue is not just a product of US capitalism, but also of its superpower status in the world system of states. Whether this competition over resources and the Third World can be seen as a purely capitalist phenomenon is questionable. If seen simply as *realpolitik* then the influence of such factors on weapons development, although clearly not irrelevant, is subject to the limitations already discussed above.

R&D organization and 'internal arms races'

As argued earlier, neither 'technology' itself nor the technologists that develop it would seem to have determining roles in technological developments. That is not to say, of course, that previous technology and the preferences of technologists are not very important. They are – in both setting historical constraints on technology which builds on that of the past (both literally, as in the physical constraints of, say, a submarine missile mount tube, and culturally, in the ideas and paradigms that provide the intellectual basis that technologists draw on) and in shaping the interests of the technical community.[64]

It is possible, however, to have a wider analysis which goes beyond such a narrow definition of the interests of the technical community, but which still argues that a kind of 'technological imperative' exists, albeit one based on the institutionalized nature of military research and development in the USA. Thus, for example, Mary Kaldor has argued that the nature of military R&D organizations, particularly in the USA, determines the type of technology developed.[65] In the USA this technology is typically 'baroque' – produced through the continuing 'improvement' of several performance parameters, such as speed, accuracy, range, but in which the '"improvements" become less and less relevant to modern warfare, while cost and complexity become military handicaps'.[66] Baroque technology, Kaldor argues, is produced by sovereign R&D establishments which are nevertheless heavily dependent on government contracts – that is, defence orientated corporations such as Lockheed. Preoccupied with maintaining full capacity employment they emphasize the continual 'improvement' of weapons along conservative, already established lines – 'normal' rather than radical technology:

> These large firms emphasize risk minimization and thus tend not to push new ideas or applications. Research is more likely to be done on increasing the performance of a device, rather than developing some totally new device. This 'evolutionary' R&D tends to match the forms and objectives of the firms and the DoD and even to address the questions these firms are willing to ask. (More far-reaching questions

185

would pose a threat to existing organizations – an airplane manufac-
turer would not want the usefulness of airplanes questioned, nor
would a military pilot.)[67]

The succession of FBM generations would at first sight seem a classic
instance of baroque improvement. Once established as the missile
contractor for Polaris, Lockheed Missiles & Space Co. has received
non-competitive contracts for succeeding generations of ever more
elaborate missiles. However, a more detailed look at the FBM history
suggests that the 'baroque' explanation of weapons succession has
only general utility.

Certainly, organizational interests will generally tend to exclude
radical new technologies (especially if 'not-invented-here'). Everyone,
whether private corporation, government-sponsored non-profit
organization (such as the Draper Laboratory and Johns Hopkins
Applied Physics Laboratory), or military (such as SSPO), prefers continuity. Radical technological developments can threaten such continuity, whereas 'evolutionary' technical change reinforces and sustains
it. But that alone does not explain *which* parameters should be chosen
for incremental 'improvement', why in the FBM programme first range
should be considered critical (from Polaris A1 to A2 to A3), then ABM
penetration (in Poseidon), then range again (in Trident I), and finally
accuracy (in Trident II). Nor does it explain how radical innovations
were introduced, such as MRV in Polaris A3, MIRV in Poseidon, or
stellar-inertial guidance in Trident I. These are not just more of the
same, incremental changes. Moreover, throughout the FBM development, reliability has remained an attribute which increasing cost and
complexity do not appear to have compromised. (It was never as good
as publicly portrayed in the early FBM systems and it has probably
improved since then.) In some areas of the system much of the
technology remained unchanged whilst the Polaris submarines were
updated to carry first the Poseidon and then the Trident I missiles.
Often indeed such technology would only be replaced by a new one
because the original was too 'obsolescent' for replacements to be
obtained at a reasonable price.

Nor does the Trident submarine development – which in many
ways appears to be a classic example of 'baroque' technology – exactly
fit an explanation based on corporate determination to maintain (and
if possible expand) its operations. Although Electric Boat's corporate
interests played a role, the Trident design was mainly driven by the
technical preferences of Admiral Rickover of the Navy's Nuclear Propulsion Directorate. But as a state-financed, government-dependent
organization this should, in Kaldor's classification, be a source of
'conservative' technical change.[68]

What this suggests is that although Kaldor's distinctions between the differing styles of different R&D organizations may be useful, they cannot alone explain the nature of technical change. 'Baroque' technology is a symptom of recent US weapons developments because continuity is in the interest of most of the organizations involved. But it is not just the nature of the organizations that matters, but also their interaction with others. The Draper Laboratory has been continually improving its paradigmatic floated gyroscope since the 1940s.[69] But under pressure from the Navy they did eventually agree to incorporate a stellar sensor into their FBM guidance systems, knowing, of course, that this would tend to undercut future arguments for further gyroscope improvement.

Corporate or institutional continuity must sometimes yield to the organizational interests of the services. Occasionally the administration and/or Congress may be able to exert sufficient pressure to overcome the inertia preventing the development and adoption of 'radical' technology. An explanation of technical change in weaponry must take into account such organizational interactions.

Such interactions are considered important in one view which sees technical change in weapons as the product of an 'internal' arms race. Ernest Yanarella suggests that a 'technological imperative' was institutionalized in the United States at the end of the 1950s and the beginning of the 1960s.[70] Organizations set up to help the Office of the Secretary of Defense manage advances in military technology – most notably the Office of the Director of Defense Research and Engineering (DDR&E) and the Advanced Projects Research Agency (ARPA) – provided a focus for the assessment and encouragement of change in military technology, and, Yanarella argues, 'institutionalized new sources of dynamism into defense planning at the pinnacle of the administration'.[71] This was followed by the further centralization of weapons technology decision-making – at an unprecedented level of technical detail – into OSD during McNamara's tenure as Secretary of Defense, and by doctrinal reassessments of nuclear strategy:[72]

> Centralized in the executive agency of the Defense Department and guided by the most advanced techniques of administration and analysis, military R&D in strategic weaponry was institutionalized and pursued during the McNamara years in an organizational framework characterized by the mutual interaction of military R&D in offensive technology with military R&D in defensive technology. . . the 'technological imperative' took on nearly all the features of an 'internal arms race' pitting, within the same agencies, American scientists and technicians in offensive R&D against their counterparts in defensive R&D.[73]

187

A classic example of the 'mirror imaging' consequent of such an 'internal arms race' can be found in the FBM programme. The configuration of the Polaris A3 payload was designed to defeat the then proposed US ABM system, the Nike Zeus, and turned out to have little capability against the Soviet Galosh:

> The penetration aid designs done originally for the Polaris A2 and also for the Polaris A3 were built around the notion of an antiballistic missile which looked very like America's Nike Zeus which was our design for an ABM system. Since we didn't know what the Soviets were doing we assumed that they were being smart people, were doing exactly what we were doing.[74]

That such 'mirror imaging' happens is not in doubt, but to what extent does it constitute a technological imperative, and to what extent did the period in question mark a distinctive change? Was it really the case that 'this technological planning process . . . increasingly adopted the features of a closed system where interest in the character of the Soviet threat, Soviet perceptions of specific weapons programs, and other "external" data were of secondary importance to "internal" requirements of the system'?[75]

In fact, of course, 'mirror imaging' was not a new phenomenon in military planning – as can be seen by looking back at the previous decade. McNamara's OSD may have brought a more analytical emphasis to assessing and justifying weapons requirements – and made explicit, for example, how much 'assured destruction' was enough – but the basic processes remained the same. But previously each service would produce its own distinctive analysis of the threat and of *their* requirements to counter it. Indeed in a 1961 briefing to the Secretary of Defense the Navy was still justifying a figure of forty-five FBM submarines without mentioning the nuclear forces of the other services:

> The briefing began with a list of targets to be destroyed, a calculation as to how many missiles should be programmed per target, how many were needed on station, how many were needed in the total force to maintain that number on station, and thus why a force of 45 Polaris submarines was required. In the entire briefing, there was not one reference to the existence of the Air Force or its weapons systems, despite the fact that most of our nuclear firepower was then in Air Force bombers.[76]

What each service 'required' depended primarily on their dominant technological and organizational traditions, and on what looked likely to enhance their portion of the defence budget. Radically new technologies, such as ballistic missiles, were thus not 'required' as much as the more traditional weapons, such as bombers and aircraft carriers.

188

Moreover, throughout the 1950s the size and nature of forces remained largely up to the services to decide within the constraint of their budget allocation. In so much as weapons acquisition required justi-fication each service constructed its own rationales based on its own interpretation of intelligence data. Thus during the 1950s the Air Force acquired huge numbers of nuclear bombs – and a large bomber force to carry them – by 'finding' ever more Soviet targets to attack.[77]

Lacking any coherent, consensual, systematic way of analysing the utility of nuclear forces, the main focus of the 'internal arms race' during the 1950s was interservice rivalry. Technological developments were no less sought than in the 1960s, they were simply less chan-nelled towards specific, explicitly defined *national* missions. Indeed weapon systems development proliferated so much during the 1950s that by the end of the decade the Air Force alone was engaged in programmes for three ICBMs (Titan, Atlas, and Minuteman), an IRBM (Thor), an air-launched ballistic missile (Skybolt), several cruise miss-iles (Snark, Matador, Mace, and Hound Dog), three conventional bombers (B52, B58, and B70) and a nuclear-powered bomber. This last programme, known as the ANP (for aircraft nuclear propulsion), involved a curious example of 'rhetorical' mirror-imaging. Under development since just after World War II, the ANP programme came under particularly critical examination in the late 1950s as its feasibility and utility were questioned.[78] Proponents of the ANP were then conveniently able to 'reveal' that the Soviet Union was flight testing a similar aircraft and the journal *Aviation Week* even published sketches of it.[79] The ANP was eventually cancelled by the Kennedy administration, and with it, its Soviet mirror-image coincidently van-ished too.

It was as a response to the uncoordinated technological proliferation of the 1950s that the offices of DDR&E and ARPA were formed, and McNamara's more centralized managerial methods, such as the Planning-Programming-Budgeting System, introduced.[80] By explicitly defining the purposes of nuclear forces – using criteria such as 'assured destruction' – these changes certainly did channel technological change in particular directions. At the same time, however, they also provided OSD with the 'tools' that allowed many programmes, includ-ing Skybolt, Snark, the B70, and ANP, to be cancelled. The changes institutionalized in OSD were as much a check on technological devel-opments as a part of their stimulus.

In any case the 'technological imperative' of the 'internal arms race' is neither completely impervious to 'external' events (no matter how much intelligence of Soviet behaviour is mediated by inevitable judge-

189

mental interpretation), nor a strong determinant of the nature of technical change. An 'internal arms race' between offence and defence would be expected to stimulate the development of ABM technologies to destroy incoming missiles, on the one hand, and penetration aids to maintain 'assured destruction', on the other. This might appear to have been the case in Poseidon where large numbers of small warheads were chosen to enhance penetration against the possibility of widespread deployment of Galosh-type ABMs (which, of course, drew at least partly on knowledge of what the Soviets were doing). It would not explain, however, why *at the same time* the Air Force Minuteman MIRV placed so much more emphasis on the ability to attack hard targets rather than penetration, or why subsequent developments in Trident I and II would increasingly emphasize counterforce capability with no significant penetration aids produced (except the undeployed Mk. 500 Evader).

In fact, the notion of an 'internal arms race', important though it might be as a stimulus for R&D, cannot account for the importance of the growing mutual disillusionment with ABM defences during the 1960s that eventually led the United States and USSR to sign the ABM Treaty in 1972, nor for the interest in counterforce (and its differing attraction for the Air Force and the Navy). The closed system of an 'internal arms race' fails to account for the importance of these broader influences in shaping technological change.

TECHNOLOGICAL NETWORKS AND THE NUCLEAR ARMS RACE

All these models of the nature of technical change in weaponry have limitations. As expected, the bureaucratic politics approach captures much of the essence of day-to-day shaping of the FBM system. However, technology is not just a product of human endeavour, but also an integral part of it; not something separate from, or in a simple sense caused by, say, politics or economics, but rather political and social through and through. To say, then, that technology is shaped by bureaucratic politics would be misleading because it implies an artificial separation. Technology is not just a result of bureaucratic politicking, it is also a cause of it, and indeed a means by which it is pursued. Just as bureaucratic politics shapes technology, so technological change shapes bureaucratic politics. Thus, it was only with the advent of the FBM that the Navy came to embrace assured destruction, a counter-city strategy that it had earlier found immoral when employed by the Air Force.[81] Assured destruction would thereafter for many years be central in differentiating SPO's missiles from those of the Air Force.

In the sense used here, the 'pulling and hauling' of bureaucratic politics is an inevitable consequence of any social system where issues of jurisidiction and hierarchy are not totally clearcut. Technological developments will then necessarily be shaped by conflict and compromise between (and within) organizations. Successful technological developments depend on skilful handling of this kind of politics.

As Langdon Winner argues in general, modern technology tends to be out of control (of most of us) exactly because of the need *for control* of the organizations that develop it.[82] Nuclear weapons comprise a technological system which requires many parts of the physical and the social world to be held in place (under control) if they are to 'work'. Ensuring success leads organizations to strive for as much autonomy as possible, while at the same time enrolling the support of others, as indeed Sapolsky has well documented in the case of Polaris and the Special Projects Office.[83] It is these *social networks*, not just the artefacts themselves, that constitute a technology.

As Posen's study of French, British, and German military doctrine in the interwar period suggests, bureaucratic politics will tend to dominate during peacetime.[84] So long as the civilian leadership does not perceive any immediate threat, the military will to a great extent be left alone. The irony of the nuclear era is that a greater threat to national survival than ever before has become accepted as normal, as 'peace', and has only occasionally received critical attention from political leaders. Lacking the potentially catastrophic, though of course by no means unambiguous, evidence of warfare, the plausibility of a weapons technology is likely to be sustained for organizational reasons.

Technological systems, such as those comprising US nuclear weapons in the Cold War era, are not just laboratory developments then, but rather necessarily extensive networks of interests. A nuclear weapons 'military-industrial complex' has indeed been created and perpetuated. Those enrolled to support this complex – whether it be for patriotic or self-seeking reasons – constitute a powerful, though non-uniform, constituency of vested interests. This very network of interests that comprises the technology also gives it a powerful momentum.

Bureaucratic politics have dominated the day-to-day shaping of US nuclear weapons systems, but that is not to say that it is the 'correct' model for explaining such developments. The social 'network' that must be created and maintained for a technology to work is more

191

extensive than that. Maintaining such a network requires that the technology is plausibly seen to 'work' both in the technical sense of its physical functioning and in the political sense of carrying out a desirable mission.

Whether or not nuclear weapons systems actually 'work' in the technical sense has always been a contentious issue which thankfully has been generally settled through testing, not use. While scope exists for negotiating the criteria by which performance is judged – what it means to 'work' is of course not unproblematically obvious – the possibility of failure exists and can be disastrous for the maintenance of a technological network. This network includes both gyroscopes and Senators, and if one is seen not to work as intended, the other may not either. Indeed both parts of the network can be obdurate, requiring skill in their engineering.

This heterogeneous engineering must operate not only on Senators and the President, and on other potentially disruptive or uncooperative organizations, but also on non-human components of the network. Several of the components of missiles – notably solid rocket motors, reentry vehicle casings and inertial sensors – are amongst the most difficult of human products, involving highly skilled 'art-like' production processes with ineliminable elements of 'tacit knowledge'.[85] 'Producibility' – which, of course, as shown in the case of Honeywell and the electrostatic gyroscope includes 'social' as well as 'physical' elements – has been a major factor in decisions on items such as inertial components for the FBM programmes.

Problems with 'technical' details can be very important in undermining the plausibility of claims as to whether a technology works, and so of course can changes in the world outside the control of the system builders. There can be no doubt that the 'realist' interests of a superpower, particularly the rivalry with the Soviet Union, have been a major factor in the development of US nuclear weapons systems. The Soviet 'threat' provided not only motivation for many, but also a powerful resource that they could bring to bear in support of a technology. The very uncertainties involved in analysing the behaviour of a secretive state, and emotive ideological differences, heightened rather than weakened the power of this resource. But, while powerful, the effect of realism on technological developments is also crude. It may set the agenda, but it is unlikely to shape the detail.

Purely 'realist' explanations of nuclear weapons force structures are possible, of course; indeed they constitute the 'official line' taken by governments.[86] These are in large part, however, *post hoc* rationalizations of weapons systems and force structures whose development is an historical legacy firmly rooted not just in military hardware, but also in organizational interests.

The FBM programme is a 'hard' case in this context because it is probably the most consensually supported and uncontroversial nuclear weapons system developed by the United States. This is, of course, partly due to the effort expended exactly to gain support for the FBM and to avoid controversy or over-ambitious missions. The 'assured destruction' image cultivated from Polaris to Trident I was not only relatively less demanding than 'silo-busting', but also less likely to generate domestic political opposition. Broadly speaking, over a thirty-year span the FBM programme can be argued to have matched a realist analysis of the deterrence needs of the United States. However, the nature of this deterrence has been in dispute for much of this time, and the 'need' for greater hard-target capability in the FBM pro-gramme was perceived by many at the 'rational actor' level almost right from the start of the programme, but not implemented in a whole-hearted manner until the 1980s.

Changes in the world situation are clearly having an effect on developments in US nuclear weapons systems. It could be argued that US nuclear weapons, such as the FBM system, played a significant role in shaping the events that led to the disintegration of the Soviet Union. That is unprovable, but there is little doubt that the disappearance of the Soviet threat has greatly undermined the rationale for such a large and diverse stockpile of nuclear weapons. An important part of the network sustaining nuclear weapons development has been disrupted, although some of the system builders continue to argue for 'business as usual' and raise the spectre of different threats.

CONCLUSIONS

Technology is not completely out of control (in the technological determinist sense), but neither is it very much under control (at least by most of us). There are powerful vested interests involved in the development of weapons technology, and their power in part stems from their ability to delineate the boundaries of what is 'technical', and therefore not a legitimate question of 'political' interest.[87] Institutional and economic interests push very strongly towards 'follow-on' weapons systems, as does explicit governmental policy aimed at main-taining specialized research teams. All this, however, is a social process involving many actors – the 'military-industrial complex' is not mono-lithic. Scrutiny of its workings reveals a complex of often contradictory tensions, not a conspiracy. Ignorance of the processes involved does little to contradict the appearance of the inevitable 'follow-on' system, but tends instead to be self-fulfilling.

Those interested in continuing weapons succession are so for various reasons. Corporate managers are, of course, primarily concerned with the financial well-being of their company. Those in the Department of Defense and in the armed services are focused on the military means of international relations, as well as on their own particular organizational loyalties. In the administration and Congress too, questions of weapons technology are largely, and not surprisingly, left to those most imbued with that particular culture. If the weapons succession process goes on unchecked, it is not because of an internal technological imperative, but because those involved are too often unrestrained by those (the rest of us) who are not.

The US Navy's FBM programme has been a very successful technological development. Originally formed only for the Polaris development, the Special Projects Office has survived (with slight name changes) for over thirty years since the completion of that mission. Whether it can continue to prosper in a world without a Soviet threat will be a demanding test for the network builders.

APPENDIX: LIST OF
INTERVIEWEES

Vice Admiral Levering Smith (US Navy, Retired). San Diego, 31 March, 1, 2 April 1987, 9 March 1989.

Captain Louis Shock (US Navy, Retired). San Diego, 1 April 1987.

Rear Admiral N. G. Ward (US Navy, Retired). San Diego, 1 April 1987.

Herbert York. San Diego, 2 April 1987.

Rear Admiral Robert Wertheim. (US Navy, Retired). Calabasas, Los Angeles, 3 April 1987 and San Diego, 9 March 1989.

Robert Aldridge. Santa Clara, 4 April 1987.

Willy Fiedler. Los Altos Hill, 4 April 1987.

George Mechlin. Pittsburgh, 8 April 1987.

Rear Admiral Harvey Lyon (US Navy, Retired). Arlington, Virginia, 21 April 1987.

Eliott Mitchell. Washington, DC, 27 April 1987.

Captain Grayson Merrill (US Navy, Retired). San Diego, 4 May 1987.

Robert Fuhrman. Calabasas, Los Angeles, 5 May 1987.

Werner Kirchner. San Dimas, Los Angeles, 5 May 1987.

Carl Haussman. Cupertino, California, 5 May 1987.

Derald Stuart. Sunnyvale, California, 6, 8 May 1987.

Chet Zimmerman. Sunnyvale, 6 May 1987.

Ted Postol. Stanford University, 7 May 1987, 7 November 1988.

Dave Montague. Sunnyvale, 8 May 1987.

David Nixon. Sunnyvale, 8 May 1987.

William Whitmore. Los Altos Hills, California, 9 May 1987.

Ben Olson. Cambridge, MA, 11 May 1987.

Graydon Wheaton. Cambridge, MA, 11 May 1987.

Robert Duffy. Cambridge, MA, 11 May 1987.

David Hoag. Cambridge, MA, 11 May 1987.

Larry Smith. Cambridge, MA, 14 May 1987.

Sam Forter. Cambridge, MA, 15 May 1987.

Sanford Cohen. Cambridge, MA, 15 May 1987.

Paul Dow. Cambridge, MA, 15 May 1987.

Sam Claypoole and Hyman Strell. Long Island, New York, 18 May 1987.

Vice Admiral Glenwood Clark. Arlington, Virginia, 21 May 1987.

John Brett. Washington, DC, 28 May 1987.

James Martin. McLean, Virginia, 9 June 1987.

David Gold. Washington DC, 19 June 1987.

Phil Faurot and Ron Kranz. Arlington, Virginia, 12 June 1987.

John Coyle. Washington, DC, 17 June 1987.

Joe Cestone. Arlington, Virginia, 22 June 1987.

Seymour Zeiberg. Washington, DC, 27 June 1987.

Richard DeLauer. Arlington, Virginia, 30 June 1987.

Rear Admiral Ross Williams (US Navy, Retired). Arlington, Virginia, 7 July 1987.

Captain Steven Cohen (US Navy, Retired). Falls Church, Virginia, 9 July 1987.

Vice Admiral Robert Y. Kaufman (US Navy, Retired). Potomac, MD, 10 July 1987.

Alexander Kossiakoff. Silver Spring, MD, 13 July 1987.

Sam Sugg and Andy Andrews. Silver Spring, MD, 13 July 1987.

Bob Jenkins. Silver Spring, MD, 13 July 1987.

Marvin Stern. Washington, DC, 13 July 1987.

Jack Fagin. Arlington, VA, 14 July 1987

Bob Dietz. Stanford University, 8 February 1989, 14 June 1989.

Tom Dowler. Los Alamos National Laboratory, New Mexico, 12 April 1989.

Thurman Talley. Los Alamos National Laboratory, 12 April 1989.

Edward Teller. Stanford University, 24 March 1990.

John Harvey. Stanford University, 3 April 1990.

Don Westervelt. Los Alamos National Laboratory, 18 December 1990.

J. Carson Mark. Los Alamos National Laboratory, 10 December 1991.

INTERVIEWS CONDUCTED BY DONALD MACKENZIE

Ralph Ragan. Cambridge, MA, 4 October 1984.

Edward J. Hall. Cambridge, MA, 4 October 1984.

Paul Dow and Ben Olson. Cambridge, MA, 5 October 1984.

David Hoag. Cambridge, MA, 5 November 1984.

Vice Admiral Levering Smith (US Navy, Retired). San Diego, 23 February 1985.

Rear Admiral Robert Wertheim. (US Navy, Retired). Burbank, Los Angeles, 4 March 1985.

Morris Kuritsky, Murray Goldstein and Ed Solov. Wayne, NJ, 18 March 1985.

Andrew DePrete. Arlington, VA, 28 March 1985.

Vice Admiral Glenwood Clark. Arlington, GA, 28 March 1985.

Robert Mitchell and Clifton Chappel. Arlington, VG, 29 March 1985.

Captain Steven Cohen. Arlington, VA, 29 March 1985.

Thomas A. J. King. Arlington, VA, 2 April 1985.

Larry Smith. Cambridge, MA, 10 April 1985.

NOTES

1 The US Fleet Ballistic Missile system: technology and nuclear war

1 The UK Trident submarines will carry sixteen Trident II missiles.
2 The W-88 warhead has a yield of approximately half a megaton, about thirty times the Hiroshima bomb; the W-76, which now looks likely to comprise most of the Trident payload, is about 100 kilotons, or roughly seven times the Hiroshima bomb.
3 I use this term, rather than reentry vehicle (an Air Force term), to remain consistent with the US Navy's own usage. It is a characteristic example of terminological differentiation between the two services.
4 Interview with Bob Dietz, 8 February 1989.
5 Stated Navy policy is that the absence of any communications, and thus the presumption that perhaps they had been destroyed in a nuclear attack, is not enough to allow submarine commanders to fire their missiles: 'Our commanding officers have got to have positive direction. . . . They must have positive direction to launch, regardless of the scenario.' Lawrence Meyer, 'AF Locks System Urged for Navy's Nuclear Missiles', *The Los Angeles Times* (14 October 1984), p. 28 quoted in Desmond Ball, 'Nuclear War at Sea', *International Security*, vol. 10, no. 3 (Winter 1985–86) reprinted in Steven E. Miller and Stephen Van Evera (eds.), *Naval Strategy and National Security* (Princeton: Princeton University Press, 1988), 310.
6 PALs were introduced in the 1960s to prevent unauthorized use of nuclear weapons, say, by terrorists. For a defence of the Navy position – which stresses that ships and submarines are secure areas, unlikely to be infiltrated by terrorists, and that communications problems could make reception of a PAL code uncertain – see Vice Admiral G.E. Miller, US Navy (Retired), 'Who Needs PALs?' *United States Naval Institute Proceedings* (July 1988), 50–56.
7 An account of the procedures for launch on a Poseidon carrying submarine is given in Phil Stanford, 'Nuclear Missile Submarines and Nuclear Strategy', in David T. Johnson and Barry R. Schneider (eds.), *Current Issues in US Defense Policy* (New York: Praeger, 1976). The EAM must be checked by two officers, two other officers then must open a double safe which only they (and two backups) have the combinations to and which requires each of them to open one door (neither has the combination for the other) and take the key from the safe to the captain. This key is required to activate the

firing sequence, which also requires the weapons officer to remove a 'trigger' from another safe which he has the combination to in order to fire the missile. See also John M. Weinstein, 'Command and Control of Strategic Submarines', *National Defense* (March 1989), 19–21.

8 For a summary of some of the likely effects, see Owen Green, Ian Percival and Irene Ridge, *Nuclear Winter* (Cambridge: Polity Press, 1985).

9 It should be noted, however, that the perceived utility of nuclear weapons is the exception rather than the rule. Many nations quite able to develop a nuclear capability (such as, for example, Canada and Sweden) have foresworn the option, and one (India), having exploded a nuclear device, has chosen not to develop and deploy nuclear weapons.

10 The best discussion of the concept of 'arms race' in this context is Colin Gray, *The Soviet–American Arms Race* (Westmead: Saxon House, 1976).

11 Though much political capital can be made out of small numerical differences.

12 Another concern is that technological advances may also spur on superpower rivalry, thus undermining *arms race stability*.

13 Of course, not all technical innovation is necessarily destabilizing. The development of effective early warning radars, for example, or indeed of the FBM system itself, could be argued to have reduced the risk of surprise attack.

14 Desmond Ball, *Targeting for Strategic Deterrence* (London: International Institute for Strategic Studies, 1983), 14.

15 Ibid.

16 Ibid., 11–12. In practice the 'no cities' counterforce strategy of 1961 retained the ultimate threat of counter-city retaliation while the later 'assured destruction' rhetoric left the counterforce elements in the actual warplan unchanged.

17 If restricted to single warhead missiles, neither of two sides possessing roughly equivalent missiles forces could expect a first strike to achieve high success. With reliability inevitably something short of 100 per cent, the side firing first would need to expend all its missile force in order to destroy only a portion of the other's.

18 To obtain the same increase in a missile's destructive effectiveness against a hardened target as that achieved by a doubling of accuracy would require an eightfold increase in explosive yield.

19 For a single warhead exploding in the vicinity of a hardened target this is expressed as a single shot kill probability which depends on warhead yield, warhead accuracy, and target hardness. For an example of the mathematics involved, see Donald MacKenzie, *Inventing Accuracy: A Historical Sociology of Nuclear Missile Guidance* (Cambridge, MA: MIT Press, 1990), 436–39.

20 The difficulties involved in locating and destroying missile-carrying submarines (SSBNs) make a complete first strike capability apparently unobtainable in the near-future, although the Soviet Union's large emphasis on ICBMs, low SSBN alert rate, and its geographic encirclement made it seem most vulnerable in this respect. Two recent surveys of strategic anti-submarine warfare are Tom Stefanik, *Strategic Antisubmarine Warfare and Naval Strategy* (Lexington, MA: Lexington Books, 1987) and Donald C.

Daniel, *Anti-submarine Warfare and Superpower Strategic Stability* (London: Macmillan/International Institute for Strategic Studies, 1986).

21 See, in particular, A. Roberts, 'Preparing to Fight a Nuclear War', *Arena*, no. 57 (1981), 45–93; reprinted in D. MacKenzie and J. Wajcman (eds.), *The Social Shaping of Technology* (Milton Keynes: Open University Press, 1985), 279–94; also Robert C. Aldridge, *First Strike: The Pentagon's Strategy for Nuclear War* (London: Pluto Press, 1984).

22 F. Halliday, *The Making of the Second Cold War* (London: Verso, 1983), 225, emphasis added.

23 H. M. Sapolsky, *The Polaris System Development: Bureaucratic and Programmatic Success in Government* (Cambridge, MA: Harvard University Press, 1972).

24 T. Greenwood, *Making the MIRV: A Study of Defense Decision Making* (Cambridge, MA: Ballinger, 1975).

25 D. Douglas Dalgleish and Larry Schweikart, *Trident* (Carbondale, IL: Southern Illinois University Press, 1984). For a review, see G. Spinardi, 'Trident: Tracing the Course of Nuclear Weapons Technology', *Social Studies of Science*, vol. 17 (1987), 371–81.

26 These are abbreviated to *SASC* in the references.

2 Theoretical models of weapons development

1 For various versions in the nuclear weapons context, see Deborah Shapley, 'Technology Creep and the Arms Race: ICBM Problem a Sleeper', *Science*, vol. 201 (22 September 1978), 1102–5; Marek Thee, *Military Technology, Military Strategy and the Arms Race* (London: Croom Helm, 1986); Dietrich Schroeer, 'Quantifying Technological Imperatives in the Arms Race', in D. Carlton and C. Schaerf (eds.), *Reassessing Arms Control* (London: Macmillan, 1985), 60–71; Ralph E. Lapp, *Arms Beyond Doubt: The Tyranny of Weapons Technology* (New York: Cowles Book Co., 1970).

2 See R.R. Nelson and S.G. Winter, 'In Search of a Useful Theory of Innovation', *Research Policy*, vol. 6 (1977), 36–76.

3 Schroeer, 'Quantifying Technological Imperatives', 60–71.

4 Dietrich Schroeer, *Science, Technology and the Nuclear Arms Race* (New York: Wiley, 1984), 299.

5 Herbert F. York, *The Advisors: Oppenheimer, Teller, and the Superbomb* (San Francisco: W. H. Freeman, 1976), 11.

6 Shapley, 'Technology Creep', 1102.

7 Lord Zuckerman, 'Science Advisers and Scientific Advisers', *Proceedings of the American Philosophical Society*, vol. 124 (1980), 241–55, at 250–51.

8 Robert O. Keohane, 'Theory of World Politics: Structural Realism and Beyond', in Ada W. Finifter (ed.), *Political Science: The State of the Discipline* Washington, DC: American Political Science Association, 1983) 507–8.

9 Kenneth Waltz, *Theory of International Politics* (Reading, MA: Addison-Wesley, 1979).

10 For a summary of this literature, see Bruce Russett, 'International Interactions and Processes: The Internal vs External Debate Revisited', in Ada W. Finifter (ed.), *Political Science: The State of the Discipline* (Washington, DC:

American Political Science Association, 1983). One of his conclusions (p. 553) is that 'internal processes do matter, and matter a great deal'.

11 Quoted in Thee, *Military Technology*. For an historical analysis supporting the action-reaction phenomenon, see George W. Rathjens, 'The Dynamics of the Arms Race', *Scientific American* (April 1969).

12 Desmond Ball, *Politics and Force Levels: The Strategic Missile Program of the Kennedy Administration* (Berkeley: University of California Press, 1980).

13 See Alan Wolfe, *The Rise and Fall of the Soviet Threat: Domestic Sources of the Cold War Consensus* (Boston: South End Press, 1984) for an analysis of US national security policy based on electoral considerations.

14 See Fred Kaplan, *Wizards of Armageddon* (New York: Simon and Schuster, 1983), 347.

15 A classic account of the bureaucratic politics approach is Graham T. Allison, *Essence of Decision: Explaining the Cuban Missile Crisis* (Boston: Little, Brown and Company, 1971).

16 Major works adopting this approach are Harvey Sapolsky, *The Polaris System Development: Bureaucratic and Programmatic Success in Government* (Cambridge, MA: Harvard University Press, 1972) and E. Beard, *Developing the ICBM: A Study in Bureaucratic Politics* (New York: Columbia University Press, 1976).

17 Graham Allison and Morton Halperin, 'Bureaucratic Politics: A Paradigm and Some Policy Implications', *World Politics*, vol. 24 (1971), 42.

18 For one formulation of this see Paul Baran and Paul Sweezy, *Monopoly Capital* (London: Penguin Books, 1966). Another Marxist-type analysis could attempt to explain specific technological developments in term of class conflict, as in David Noble, *Forces of Production: A Social History of Industrial Automation* (New York: Knopf, 1984).

19 Mary Kaldor, 'Military R&D: Cause or Consequence of the Arms Race?', *International Social Science Journal*, vol. 35, no. 1 (1983), 25–45, at 26.

20 Ibid., 42.

21 Kosta Tsipis, 'Science and the Military', *Bulletin of the Atomic Scientists*, vol. 33, no. 1 (January 1977), 10.

22 Ibid.

23 Ted Greenwood, *Making the MIRV: A Study of Defense Decision Making* (Cambridge, MA: Ballinger, 1975), 141–43.

24 Matthew Evangelista, *Innovation and the Arms Race: How the United States and the Soviet Union Develop New Military Technologies* (Ithaca: Cornell University Press, 1988), 20.

25 For a good introduction to this field, see Wiebe E. Bijker, Thomas P. Hughes, and Trevor Pinch, *The Social Construction of Technological Systems* (Cambridge, MA: MIT Press, 1987).

26 Which need not be taken to imply philosophical or moral relativism.

27 T. J. Pinch and W. E. Bijker, 'The Social Construction of Facts and Artefacts: or How the Sociology of Science and the Sociology of Technology Might Benefit Each Other', *Social Studies of Science*, vol. 14 (1984), 399–441.

28 Ibid., 406.

29 Ibid., 409.

30 T. P. Hughes, *Networks of Power: Electrification in Western Society* (London and Baltimore, MD: The Johns Hopkins University Press, 1983).

31 John Law, 'On the Social Explanation of Technical Change: The Case of the Portuguese Maritime Expansion', *Technology and Culture*, vol. 28, no. 2 (1987), 227–52, at 231, emphasis in original.

32 John Law, 'Technology and Heterogeneous Engineering: The Case of Portuguese Expansion', in W. Bijker, T. P. Hughes, and T. Pinch (eds.), *The Social Construction of Technological Systems* (Cambridge, MA: MIT Press, 1987), 113.

33 B. Latour, '*The Prince* for Machines as well as for Machinations', in Brian Elliott (ed.), *Technology and Social Process* (Edinburgh: Edinburgh University Press, 1988), 20–43, at 29.

34 See, in particular, B. Latour, *Science in Action* (Milton Keynes: Open University Press, 1987), 108–32.

35 See Langdon Winner, 'Do Artefacts Have Politics?', *Daedalus*, vol. 109 (1980), 121–36.

36 Latour, *Science in Action*, 132–44.

3 Heterogenous engineering and the origins of the Fleet Ballistic Missile

1 Quoted in James Baar and William E. Howard, *Polaris!* (New York: Harcourt, Brace and World, 1960), 52.

2 The reasons for this in the US Air Force are considered in R. Perry, *The Interaction of Technology and Doctrine in the USAF* (Santa Monica, CA: The RAND Corporation, January 1979, P-6281), esp. 8–15.

3 See Clayton R. Koppers, *JPL and the American Space Program* (New Haven: Yale University Press, 1982).

4 W. Lucas, 'Political Bugs' in 'Rocketry in the 50s', *Astronautics and Aeronautics*, vol. 10, no. 10 (October 1972), 44.

5 Robert Perry, *The Ballistic Missile Decisions* (Santa Monica, CA: The RAND Corporation, 1967; P-3686), 4n.

6 W. D. Miles, 'The Polaris', in E. M. Emme (ed.), *The History of Rocket Technology: Essays on Research, Development and Utility* (Detroit, Wayne State University Press, 1964), 163.

7 Vincent Davis, *The Politics of Innovation: Patterns in Navy Cases*, the Social Science Foundation and Graduate School of International Studies Monograph Series in World Affairs, IV, 3 (Denver, CO: University of Denver Press, 1967), 33.

8 Baar and Howard, *Polaris!*, 14. This is described in more detail in B. D. Bruins, 'US Naval Bombardment Missiles, 1940–1958: A Study of the Weapons Innovations Process' (Columbia University PhD Thesis, 1981), 233–34: 'BuShips examined the problems of controlling shipboard damage which might result from accidents involving SLBMs. In cooperation with the Army Ordnance's HERMES project, a series of damage control experiments were conducted at White Sands, New Mexico, using captured V-2 missiles. When a fuelled and burning V-2 was tipped over on a mock-up of a ship's deck, the resulting damage abruptly ended any ideas which the

Army and General Electric, the Army's contractor, may have had in regard to building ballistic missiles for shipboard use. Naval officers noted that, after an initial tremendous blast, main structural members had been cracked, probably by thermal shock; that the deck plating had been ruptured, whether by blast or thermal shock; and that fuel and liquid oxygen poured through the rupture, ignited, and, had the accident occurred aboard a real ship, threatened to repeat the cycle until it blew a hole through the vessel's bottom.'

9 Captain Dominic A. Paolucci (US Navy, Retired), 'The Development of Navy Strategic Offensive and Defensive Systems', *United States Naval Institute Proceedings*, vol. 96 (May 1970), 204–23, at 210. By far the best source on Regulus and other Navy bombardment missiles in this period is Bruins, 'US Naval Bombardment Missiles'.

10 Ibid.

11 For extensive documentation of this, see, in addition to Perry, *Ballistic Missile Decisions*, E. Beard, *Developing the ICBM: A Study in Bureaucratic Politics* (New York: Columbia University Press, 1976).

12 In 1955 the operational requirement for the Triton Navy cruise missile was a circular error probable of 600 yards, whilst that of the proposed Fleet Ballistic Missile was 4000 yards. Bruins, 'US Naval Bombardment Missiles', 285.

13 Bruins, 'US Naval Bombardment Missiles', 280.

14 Interview with Ellliot Mitchell, 27 April 1987.

15 Interview by Donald MacKenzie with Vice Admiral Levering Smith, 23 February 1985.

16 According to Herbert York: 'the term fleet ballistic missile was used for political reasons. If they'd called it an IRBM, an intermediate range missile, it would then have been seen as competing with Thor and Jupiter.' Interview, 2 April 1987.

17 Davis, *Politics of Innovation*, 34.

18 Beard, *Developing the ICBM*, 197.

19 Technological Capabilities Panel of the Scientific Advisory Committee, 'Meeting the Threat of Surprise Attack' (Washington, DC: 14 February 1955), 38.

20 According to Bruins, 'US Naval Bombardment Missiles,' p. 279: 'OPNAV [the Office of the Chief of Naval Operations] was resistant to the February 1955 recommendation of the Technological Capabilities Panel (TCP) that a sea-based intermediate-range ballistic missile (IRBM) be developed. Recommended by the TCP, more popularly known as the "Killian Committee", promoted by technical personnel in both the Naval Research Laboratory (NRL) and BuAer, and backed by Assistant Secretary Smith, the naval IRBM was strongly opposed within OP-51.'

21 Davis, *Politics of Innovation*, 37.

22 Ibid.

23 Ibid., 38.

24 Harvey M. Sapolsky, *The Polaris System Development: Bureaucratic and Programmatic Success in Government* (Cambridge, MA: Harvard University Press, 1972), 21.

25 D. A. Rosenberg, 'Arleigh Albert Burke' in R. W. Love, Jr, *The Chiefs of Naval Operations* (Annapolis, MD: Naval Institute Press, 1980), 263–319, at 278.
26 Davis, *Politics of Innovation*, 38.
27 Rosenberg, 'Arleigh Albert Burke', 278.
28 A November 1955 memo from Secretary of Defense Wilson said that: 'The dollar requirements for the IRBM program are separate from the dollar requirements or limitations applicable to any other Army and Navy program, and will be justified separately.' Quoted in Bruins, 'US Naval Bombardment Missiles', 287.
29 M. H. Armacost, *The Politics of Weapons Innovation: The Thor–Jupiter Controversy* (New York: Columbia University Press, 1969), 71.
30 Interview with Vice Admiral W. F. Raborn by J. T. Mason, Jr, 15 September 1978, 17.
31 Rosenberg, 'Arleigh Albert Burke', 278.
32 BuOrd and BuAer were combined in a Bureau of Naval Weapons (BuWeps) in 1958.
33 Sapolsky, *Polaris System Development*, 63.
34 Quoted in Lockheed Missiles and Space Company, Inc., *Fleet Ballistic Missiles – 25 Years* (Sunnyvale, CA: Lockheed Missiles and Space Company, Inc., n.d.), 1.
35 The memorandum is reprinted in Lockheed Missiles and Space Company, Inc., *The Fleet Ballistic Missile System: Polaris, Poseidon, Trident* (Sunnyvale, CA: Lockheed Missiles and Space Company, Inc., n.d.), 6–7. The Civil Service Commission was persuaded to rate SPO positions at relatively high rates. Sapolsky, *Polaris System Development*, 36.
36 Ibid.
37 Baar and Howard, *Polaris!*, 43; see also Robert E. Hunter, 'Politics and Polaris: The Special Projects Office of the Navy as a Political Phenomenon' (unpublished Senior Honours Thesis, Wesleyan University, June 1962), 61.
38 Hunter, 'Politics and Polaris', 61, paraphrased from Raborn's regular 'peptalk'.
39 Ibid., 56.
40 Sapolsky, *Polaris System Development*, 187–88, refutes beliefs that the management fund greatly enhanced SPO's ability for flexible accounting.
41 Hunter, 'Politics and Polaris', 100.
42 Ibid., 104; Sapolsky, *Polaris System Development*, 35.
43 E. Rees, *The Seas and the Subs* (New York: Duell, Sloan and Pearce, 1961), 139.
44 Robert A. Fuhrman, 'The Fleet Ballistic Missile System; Polaris to Trident', *Journal of Spacecraft*, vol. 5, no. 5 (September–October 1978), 265–86, at 267.
45 Ibid., 266.
46 Ibid., 267; see also N. L. Baker, 'Polaris Pioneers Future Ballistic Missile Design', *Missiles and Rockets* (February 1958), 137, which stresses the advantage of the higher acceleration of solid fuel.
47 Raborn's first encounter with General Medaris, the head of the Army's missile office at Huntsville, Alabama, was reportedly not a success, with Medaris keeping Raborn waiting in his outer office for about three hours. Interview with Jack Fagin, 14 July 1987.
48 See Sapolsky, *Polaris System Development*, 25–26.

49 Ibid., 26. Lockheed Missile and Space Division's first involvement with the FBM program seems to have been a request of 11 July 1955 from the Chief of Naval Operations for comment on such a missile. The response was 'A Preliminary Study – Fleet Ballistic Missile (MSD/1399)', dated 1 November 1955. J. P. McManus, *A History of the FBM System* (Lockheed Missiles and Space Company, 1988), A-7.

50 Fuhrman, 'Fleet Ballistic Missile System', 267.

51 Sapolsky, *Polaris System Development*, 27.

52 Baar and Howard, *Polaris!*, 15. Big Stoop was tested three times in 1951 to a range of about 20 miles.

53 Sapolsky, *Polaris System Development*, 28.

54 Ibid.

55 Baar and Howard, *Polaris!*, 31–33.

56 See Herbert York, *Race to Oblivion: A Participant's View of the Arms Race* (New York: Simon and Schuster, 1970), 90.

57 William F. Whitmore, 'Military Operations Research – A Personal Retrospective', *Operations Research*, vol. 9 (March–April 1961), 263.

58 Rear Admiral Robert Wertheim, who headed the Polaris warhead development for SPO, recalls that Livermore had already at this point tested a lightweight device in Nevada. Interview, 9 March 1989. This must have been during the Operation Teapot series when Livermore carried out three successful tests, Tesla, Turk, and Post with respective yields of 7, 43, and 2 kiloton, according to T. B. Cochran, William M. Arkin, Robert S. Norris and Milton M. Hoenig, *Nuclear Weapons Databook, vol. II: US Nuclear Warhead Production* (Cambridge, MA: Ballinger, 1987), 154–55.

59 Interview with Edward Teller, 24 March 1990. Mark does not recall this particular incident. Interview with J. Carson Mark, 10 December 1991. However, the story certainly accurately reflects the different approaches of the two nuclear weapons design laboratories at this time. Mark recalls 'giving the opinion to von Neumann [John von Neumann, chair of the influential Strategic Missiles Evaluation Committee which compiled its report between November 1953 and February 1954] that we could do a megaton in a ton'.

60 Fuhrman, 'Fleet Ballistic Missile System', 267–68

61 Ibid., 268.

62 Baar and Howard, *Polaris!*, 73.

63 James C. Freund, 'The "Revolt of the Admirals"', *The Airpower Historian*, vol. 10, no. 1 (January 1963), 1–10.

64 Quoted in D. A. Rosenberg, 'The Origins of Overkill: Nuclear Weapons and American Strategy, 1945–1960', *International Security*, vol. 7, no. 4 (1983), 3–71, at 15.

65 D. A. Rosenberg, 'American Atomic Strategy and the Hydrogen Bomb Decision', *Journal of American History*, vol. 66, no. 1 (1979), 62–87, at 69.

66 Quoted in ibid., 70.

67 Rosenberg, 'Origins of Overkill', 16.

68 Rosenberg, 'American Atomic Strategy', 73.

69 Quoted in ibid., 72.

70 Ibid., 74.

71 Rosenberg, 'Origins of Overkill', 51.
72 Ibid.
73 Paolucci, 'The Development of Navy Strategic Offensive and Defensive Systems', 211. Regulus I was finally retired from active service ten years later in mid-1964.
74 Rosenberg, 'Arleigh Albert Burke', at 282.
75 See D. A. Rosenberg, '"A Smoking Radiating Ruin at the End of Two Hours": Documents on American Plans for Nuclear War with the Soviet Union, 1945–1955', *International Security*, vol. 6, no. 3 (Winter 1981–82), 3–38.
76 Rosenberg, 'Origins of Overkill', 53.
77 Sapolsky, *Polaris System Development*, 44; see also Baar and Howard, *Polaris!*, 26.
78 'Navy Views Polaris as Support Weapon', *Aviation Week*, vol. 66 (17 June 1957), 31.
79 Vice Admiral R.E. Libby quoted in Rosenberg, 'Origins of Overkill', 52.
80 Naval Warfare Analysis Group Study no. 1, 'Introduction of the Fleet Ballistic Missile into Service' (January 1957), Serial 007P93. I am grateful to the author John Coyle for supplying me with a copy of this report which was declassified in March 1980 by the Office of the Chief of Naval Operations.
81 Rosenberg, 'Origins of Overkill', 56–57.
82 A classic statement of this case for Polaris is P. H. Backus, 'Finite Deterrence, Controlled Retaliation', *United States Naval Institute Proceedings*, vol. 85, no. 3 (March 1959), 23–29.

4   Building Polaris

1 Harvey M. Sapolsky, *The Polaris System Development: Bureaucratic and Programmatic Success in Government* (Cambridge, MA: Harvard University Press, 1972), 158.
2 Interview with Vice Admiral Raborn by John T. Mason, 15 September 1978 22.
3 Sapolsky, *Polaris System Development*, 55.
4 Rear Admiral William F. Raborn, 'Navy within a Navy' in 'Rocketry in the 50's', *Astronautics and Aeronautics*, vol. 10, no. 10 (October 1972), 63–65, at 64.
5 Sapolsky, *Polaris System Development*, 41–60.
6 The differentiation of nuclear strategy is discussed in detail in chapter 3 above, pp. 33–34.
7 Sapolsky, *Polaris System Development*, 45–47.
8 Ibid., 48–50.
9 Robert E. Hunter, 'Politics and Polaris: The Special Projects Office of the Navy as a Political Phenomenon' (unpublished Senior Honours Thesis, Wesleyan University, June 1962), 102–4.
10 PERT is discussed in great detail in Sapolsky, *Polaris System Development*, 94–130. His view is that SPO's much vaunted management 'techniques either were not applied on a significant scale in the operations of the Special Projects Office until after the test and deployment of the initial FMB

[sic] submarines, or they were applied, but did not work, or they were applied and worked, but had a totally different purpose than that officially described', ibid., 106.

11 Quoted in ibid., 124

12 Ibid., 129.

13 Ibid., 64–68.

14 William F. Whitmore, 'The Origins of Polaris', *United States Naval Institute Proceedings* (March 1980), 56–59, at 57.

15 Ibid.

16 Robert A. Fuhrman, 'The Fleet Ballistic Missile System: Polaris to Trident', *Journal of Spacecraft*, vol. 5, no. 5 (September–October 1978), 268.

17 Ibid.

18 D. A. Rosenberg, 'Arleigh Albert Burke' in R. W. Love, Jr, *The Chiefs of Naval Operations* (Annapolis, MD: Naval Institute Press, 1980), 284–85. The Gaither Report was officially known as the report of the Security Resources Panel of the Science Advisory Committee.

19 Fuhrman, 'Polaris to Trident', 268.

20 Whitmore, 'The Origins of Polaris', 58.

21 Sapolsky, *Polaris System Development*, 54.

22 Ibid., 79–80.

23 Ibid., 81.

24 Interview with Levering Smith, 1 April 1987.

25 Interview with Dr George Mechlin, 8 April 1987.

26 James Baar and William E. Howard, *Polaris!* (New York: Harcourt, Brace and World, 1960), 66.

27 Ibid.

28 Mechlin interview.

29 Ibid.

30 Baar and Howard, *Polaris!*, 111.

31 Mechlin interview.

32 Westinghouse, 'To the End of the Rainbow – Evolution of the Marine Division', typescript, 49. I am grateful to David Nixon of Westinghouse for providing me with this.

33 Mechlin interview.

34 See 'Polaris Launcher Production Hits Four a Week', *Missiles and Rockets*, vol. 10 (12 February 1962), 32–33.

35 See '"Pop-Up" Site Saves Millions in Polaris R&D', *Missiles and Rockets* (25 July 1960), 28–30.

36 Letter from Levering Smith, 27 August 1988.

37 Interview with Sam Forter, 15 May 1987.

38 See D. MacKenzie, 'Missile Accuracy: A Case Study in the Social Processes of Technological Change', in W. E. Bijker, T. P. Hughes, and T. Pinch, *The Social Construction of Technological Systems* (Cambridge, MA: MIT Press, 1987), 195–222.

39 See quote from Ragan interview in Donald MacKenzie, *Inventing Accuracy: A Historical Sociology of Nuclear Missile Guidance* (Cambridge, MA: MIT Press, 1990), 146.

40 See W. F. Raborn and J. P. Craven, 'The Significance of Draper's Work in the

Development of Naval Weapons', in S. Lees (ed.), *Air, Space and Instruments: Draper Anniversary Volume* (New York: McGraw-Hill, 1963), 23.

41 Forter interview.

42 Ibid. This contract was one of three issued by SPO in 1956. One was to Lockheed and Aerojet to investigate the Jupiter S concept, one was to General Electric to explore the use of radio-inertial guidance (which they were developing for the Air Force ATLAS missile) for Navy use, and the third was to the Instrumentation Laboratory to look at antenna stabilization at sea for radio-inertial guidance. It was under this third contract that the laboratory was able to investigate other guidance options.

43 See R. H. Battin, 'Space Guidance Evolution – A Personal Narrative', *Journal of Guidance and Control*, vol. 5 (1982), 97–110. Q-guidance was the first manifestation of one of SPO's long-standing rules of thumb, said to have originated from Dave Gold, SP-23's branch engineer: 'Do nothing in flight that you can do in fire control, do nothing in fire control that you can do ashore, and do nothing ashore that you do not have to do at all.' Interview with Steven R. Cohen, 9 July 1987.

44 Forter interview.

45 Letter from Vice Admiral Levering Smith to Donald MacKenzie, 13 October 1986.

46 Interview and letter from Vice Admiral Levering Smith, 27 August 1988.

47 Raborn and Craven, 'Significance of Draper's Work', 27.

48 As recalled by Sam Forter (letter to author, 12 December 1991): 'there was considerable opposition from the Air Force for the Instrumentation Lab to take on the guidance development task because of the possible interference with their THOR guidance work at the Lab. This opposition was finessed by convincing General Schriever that Doctor Draper was completely sincere in this promise not to let it interfere and further and most important, he really wanted to take on the work. In addition the Navy agreed to accept the cost and responsibility for a significant part of the inertial components which were common to both THOR and POLARIS.'

49 Letter from Ben Olson, 7 December 1991. For the first year General Electric was subcontracted through Lockheed, but thereafter was contracted directly by SPO.

50 The origin and functioning of the Draper 'floated gyro' are described in MacKenzie, *Inventing Accuracy*, 80–85.

51 B. O. Olson, 'History of FBM Guidance at CSDL' (10 March 1975), typescript, 2.

52 Interview with Sanford Cohen, 15 May 1987.

53 Olson, 'FBM Guidance', 2.

54 Forter interview.

55 Ibid.

56 Interview by Donald MacKenzie with Ralph Ragan, see MacKenzie, *Inventing Accuracy*, 147–48.

57 My thanks to Ben Olson for clarifying this, letter, 7 December 1991.

58 Fuhrman, 'Polaris to Trident', 272.

59 M. Getler, 'Improved Polaris Fire-Control System Going to Sea Duty Shortly', *Missiles and Rockets*, vol. 13 (4 November 1963), 32–33, at 32.

60 Interview with SPO personnel by Donald MacKenzie, see MacKenzie *Inventing Accuracy*, 148.
61 Interview with Captain L. L. Schock, Jr, 1 April 1987.
62 Raborn and Craven, 'Significance of Draper's Work', 25.
63 Schock interview and letter to author, 7 January 1992.
64 This is recorded in an 18 July 1958 memorandum from the Ballistic Missile Panel: 'The all-inertial navigational system for the submerged subs was making so little progress that the Navy has entered this winter into a contract with the North American Aviation Co. for an alternate all-inertial navigational system and plans to install it in at least the first two subs. The developmental schedule of the new system is exceedingly tight but the contractor is confident of his ability to meet the required delivery dates (first unit in July '59).' Memorandum for: Dr J. R. Killian, Jr. From: Ballistic Missile Panel. Subject: Status of Ballistic Missile Programs. (Declassified Documents Reference Collection, Carrollton Press, 1988, no. 1141.)
65 Schock interview.
66 Interview by Donald MacKenzie with Vice Admiral Levering Smith, 23 February 1985.
67 See B. McKelvie and H. Galt, Jr. 'The Evolution of the Ship's Inertial Navigation System for the Fleet Ballistic Missile Program', *Navigation: Journal of the Institute of Navigation*, vol. 25 (Fall 1978), 310–22, at 312.
68 Interview by Donald MacKenzie with Vice Admiral (US Navy, Retd.) Levering Smith, 23 February 1985.
69 Schock letter.
70 Ibid.
71 Interview by Donald MacKenzie with Thomas A. J. King, quoted in MacKenzie, *Inventing Accuracy*, 142.
72 S. A. Conigliaro, 'From Polaris to Trident Navigation' (Mimeo of speech given to National Marine Meeting, Institute of Navigation, US Merchant Marine Academy, Kings Point, Long Island, New York, 23 October 1973), 6; 'marginal accuracy' had been added to the text by hand in the copy provided to me at Unisys.
73 Interestingly, however, periscopes of this general kind remain in use in the French submarine-launched ballistic missile fleet, whose dependence on other, American dominated, navigation aids would be unacceptable.
74 See B. Miller, 'Radio Sextant Developed for Submarines', *Aviation Week* (29 February 1960), 81–83. Sapolsky suggests that work on the radiometric sextant was funded as part of SPO's public relations with scientists rather than because it was thought likely to contribute to the FBM's navigation needs. *Polaris System Development*, 145.
75 A useful summary of navigation resets can be found in Owen Wilkes and Nils Petter Gleditsch, *Loran-C and Omega: A Study of the Military Importance of Radio Navigation Aids* (Oslo: Norwegian University Press, 1987).
76 See ibid., 81.
77 See P. J. Klass, 'Computer Simplifies Loran-C Navigation', *Aviation Week and Space Technology* (15 June 1964), 95–97.
78 Schock interview.

79 D. A. Anderton, 'Loran-C Extension Proposed for Tracking', *Aviation Week and Space Technology* (1 October 1962), 41–47.

80 Conigliaro, 'From Polaris to Trident Navigation', 6.

81 Wilkes and Gleditsch, *Loran-C and Omega*, especially Chapter 11.

82 See *The First Forty Years* (Silver Spring, MD: Johns Hopkins University Applied Physics Laboratory, 1983), 109–17.

83 The Transit programme is discussed in more detail in chapter 5.

84 Leon H. Dulberger, 'Computer Helps Polaris Subs Navigate', *Electronics* (6 January 1961), 40–41.

85 Smith interview, 1 April 1987.

86 SPO Technical Directive 3–56 gave this authorization. J. P. McManus, *A History of the FBM System* (Sunnyvale, CA: Lockheed Missiles and Space Company, 1988), A-8.

87 Sapolsky, *Polaris System Development*, 81, n. 36.

88 The X-17 was the launch vehicle used to explode nuclear warheads at an altitude of 300 miles in PROJECT ARGUS.

89 'A History of Lockheed', *Lockheed Horizons*, no. 12 (Burbank, CA: Lockheed Corporation, 1983), 81.

90 Letter from Vice Admiral Levering Smith, 27 August 1988.

91 Interview with Elliot Mitchell, 27 April 1987.

92 Letter from Elliot Mitchell, 2 December 1991.

93 See Baar and Howard, *Polaris!*, 32–3.

94 E. H. Kolcum, 'First Polaris Launched From Submarine', *Aviation Week*, vol. 73 (25 July 1960), 32

95 G.G. Whipple, 'Power for Polaris', *Ordnance* (January–February 1962), 583–85 at 584.

96 Fuhrman, 'Polaris to Trident', 275.

97 McManus, *History of the FBM System*, A-12.

98 Interview with Derald Stuart, 6, 8 May 1987.

99 As recalled by Rear Admiral Robert Wertheim: 'the improvement that we were able to achieve was not so much that the nuclear device was improved, but because of the way we went about designing the reentry vehicle and warhead combination we were able to save enough weight to be able to allocate more to the warhead and therefore get a higher yield than we had before'. Interview with Rear Admiral Robert Wertheim, 9 March 1989.

100 Fuhrman, 'Polaris to Trident', 270.

101 It seems that the W-47 warhead took integration further than any other design, then or since, in that the beryllium heatshield also functioned as part of the tamper for the warhead.

102 See M. A. Armacost, *The Politics of Weapons Innovation* (New York: Columbia University Press, 1969), 144–46.

103 Interview with Vice Admiral Levering Smith, 1 April 1987.

104 *Aviation Week*, vol. 68 (17 March 1958), 24.

105 Heating is reduced because the blunt reentry vehicle creates a detached shock wave in advance of it which dissipates most of the energy of reentry.

106 Herbert F. York, *Making Weapons, Talking Peace: A Physicist's Odyssey from Hiroshima to Geneva* (New York: Basic Books, 1987), 76.

107 Interview with Carl Haussmann, 10 December 1990. One area where Los Alamos is now acknowledged to have been 'slightly in a rut' was in the design of the fission triggers or primaries, and this may have been one aspect of the Polaris design which saved weight. Interview with Don Westervelt, 18 December 1990.

108 Fuhrman, 'Polaris to Trident', 275.

109 Various sources give the yield of the first version of the Polaris warhead, the W47-Y1, as between 450 and 600 kilotons. It is given as 500 kiloton in a presentation before the Department of Defense Subcommittee of the House Committee on Appropriations by General N. F. Twining (13 January 1960), Dwight D. Eisenhower Library, White House Office, Staff Secretary Subject Series, Defense Dept. Subseries, Box 11.

110 Interview with Rear Admiral Robert Wertheim, 3 April 1987.

111 Fuhrman, 'Polaris to Trident', 270.

112 Wertheim interview.

113 Fuhrman, 'Polaris to Trident', 272.

114 Jack W. Rosengren, *Some Little-Publicized Difficulties with A Nuclear Freeze* (Marina del Ray, CA: R&D Associates, October 1983), 15; Statement of Roy D. Woodruff, Before the Subcommittee on Arms Control and Disarmament, Armed Services Committee, US House of Representatives (20 September 1985), mimeo, 11. See also Chuck Hansen, *US Nuclear Weapons: The Secret History* (Arlington, TX: Aerofax, 1988), 204; T. B. Cochran, W. M. Arkin, R. S. Norris and M.M. Hoenig, *Nuclear Weapons Databook Volume II: US Nuclear Warhead Production* (Cambridge, MA: Ballinger, 1987), 48, who define one-point safety as requiring 'that the probability of achieving a nuclear yield greater than four pounds of TNT equivalent shall not exceed one in one million in the event of a detonation initiated at the single most sensitive point in the high explosive system'.

115 Interview with J. Carson Mark, 10 December 1991.

116 Rosengren, *Some Little-Publicized Difficulties with A Nuclear Freeze*, 15.

117 Ibid., 16.

118 Interview with J. Carson Mark, 10 December 1991.

119 The replacement *Scorpion*, SSN-589, was lost at sea in May 1968.

120 Except perhaps for Sperry, which was also a navigation integrator in 1958 and was a traditional Navy contractor.

121 See chapter 5.

122 McManus, *History of the FBM System*, A-6.

123 Baar and Howard, *Polaris!*, 139.

124 Interview with Jack Fagin, 14 July 1987.

125 Fuhrman, 'Polaris to Trident', 275. McManus, *History of the FBM System*, A-11–A-18, gives a detailed account of the FTV, AX and A1X flight tests. See also 'Longer Range Promised Through Improved Motors', *Missiles and Rockets*, vol. 7 (25 July 1960), 20–23.

126 Fuhrman, 'Polaris to Trident', 276.

127 Ibid.

128 Ibid., 277.

129 See 'Polaris A3 Reaches Advanced Test Phase', *Aviation Week and Space Technology* (4 May 1964), 16.
130 McManus, *History of the FBM System*, A-13.
131 Fuhrman, 'Polaris to Trident', 277.
132 Ibid.
133 McManus, *History of the FBM System*, A-14–A-15.
134 Ibid., A-16–A-18.

5   Success and successors

1 Quoted in Robert E. Hunter, 'Politics and Polaris: The Special Projects Office of the Navy as a Political Phenomenon' (unpublished Senior Honours Thesis, Wesleyan University, June 1962), 272.
2 Interviews with Vice Admiral Levering Smith, 1 April 1987 and Rear Admiral Robert Wertheim, 3 April 1987.
3 Interviews with Vice Admiral Levering Smith, 1 April 1987 and 23 February 1985 (by Donald MacKenzie).
4 Wertheim interview.
5 Richard B. Kershner, 'Technical Innovations in the APL Space Department', *Johns Hopkins APL Technical Digest*, vol. 2 (January–March 1981), 264–78, at 269.
6 Naval Warfare Analysis Group Study no. 1, 'Introduction of the Fleet Ballistic into Service' (January 1957), Serial 007P93, 7.
7 Harvey M. Sapolsky, *The Polaris System Development: Bureaucratic and Programmatic Success in Government* (Cambridge, MA: Harvard University Press, 1972), 141.
8 Interview with Captain L. L. Schock, Jr, 1 April 1987.
9 James Baar and William E. Howard, *Polaris!* (New York: Harcourt, Brace, and World, 1960), 198.
10 C. E. Selberman and S. S. Parker, 'The Economic Impact of Defense', *Fortune*, vol. 57 (June 1958), 215, cited in Hunter, 'Politics and Polaris', 145. See also Baar and Howard, *Polaris!* 215–16; D. A. Rosenberg, 'Arleigh Albert Burke', in R. W. Love, Jr, *The Chiefs of Naval Operations* (Annapolis, MD: Naval Institute Press, 1980), 310–12.
11 Quoted in D. A. Rosenberg, 'The Origins of Overkill: Nuclear Weapons and American Strategy, 1945–1960', *International Security* (1983), 57.
12 Sapolsky, *Polaris System Development*, 39.
13 Ibid., 58–60.
14 Quoted in ibid., 61.
15 Ibid., 5. The JSTPS comprised 219 SAC personnel, 29 Navy, 10 Army, 3 Marine, and 8 additional non-SAC Air Force. Admiral Burke did, however, obtain agreement that the SAC commander's deputy for SIOP development would be a senior naval officer.
16 A good account of McNamara's new management philosophy and methods can be found in Alain C. Enthoven and K. Wayne Smith, *How Much Is Enough? Shaping the Defense Program, 1961–1969* (New York: Harper and Row, 1971).

17 See testimony of Admiral Burke quoted in Hunter, "Politics and Polaris', 149.
18 Quoted in Hunter, 'Politics and Polaris', 155.
19 Ibid., 146.
20 Ibid., 147.
21 Fred Kaplan, *The Wizards of Armageddon* (New York: Simon and Schuster, 1983), 254–45.
22 Interview with Herbert York, 2 April 1987.
23 See Desmond Ball, *Politics and Force Levels: The Strategic Missile Program of the Kennedy Administration* (Berkeley: University of California Press, 1980).
24 'Live Polaris Launch,' *Aviation Week* (14 May 1962), 35; also Robert A. Fuhrman, 'The Fleet Ballistic Missile System: Polaris to Trident', *Journal of Spacecraft*, vol. 5, no. 5 (September–October 1978), 277.
25 Anon., 'Fixes planned for Minuteman deficiencies', *Aviation Week and Space Technology* (3 February 1964), 26–27.
26 A recent manifestation of this issue was the debate over missile accuracy in the early 1980s. See Donald MacKenzie, *Inventing Accuracy: A Historical Sociology of Nuclear Missile Guidance* (Cambridge, MA: MIT Press, 1990), Chaper 7.
27 R. Lindsey, 'B–3 Polaris Expected To Be Operational in '70', *Missiles and Rockets*, vol. 15 (24 August 1964), 28, quotes Lockheed Missiles and Space Corporation general manager Stanley Burris as saying that Polaris A3 was 'at least 25 to 30%' more reliable than A2, which was a similar advance over A1. Some of the efforts to improve component reliability in A2 and A3 are detailed in Robert Lindsey, 'Polaris A2 Parts Rejection Slashed', *Missiles and Rockets* (8 April 1963), 33–34.
28 Interview with Derald Stuart, 6, 8 May 1987.
29 Interview with Vice Admiral Levering Smith, 1 April 1987.
30 Fuhrman, 'Fleet Ballistic Missile System', 278.
31 Lockheed Missiles and Space Company, Inc., *Fleet Ballistic Missiles – 25 Years* (Sunnyvale, CA: Lockheed Missiles and Space Company, Inc., n.d.), 4.
32 Ibid.
33 Fuhrman, 'Fleet Ballistic Missile System', 278.
34 See 'Longer Range Promised Through Improved Motors', *Missiles and Rockets*, 20.
35 Interview with Carl Haussmann, 5 May 1987. The 1 megaton version of W-47 actually drew on the same technology used in the Polaris A3 W-58. When the A3 design was decided the test moratorium meant that Livermore could not test a scaled up version of the 200 kiloton design that became the W-58. After the end of the moratorium they were able to scale it up to a megaton for the W-47.
36 In fact the failure rate for the W47-Y2 when tested during 1966 was three in four. Jack W. Rosengren, *Some Little-Publicized Difficulties with A Nuclear Freeze* (Marina del Rey, CA: R&D Associates, October 1983), 17.
37 Ibid; see also statement of Roy D. Woodruff, Before the Subcommittee on Arms Control and Disarmament, Armed Services Committee, US House of Representatives (20 September 1985), mimeo, 11. The W-47 warhead also suffered from problems with corrosion of its fissile material. See Chuck

Hansen, *US Nuclear Weapons: The Secret History* (Arlington, TX: Aerofax, 1988), 204–5.

38 Interview with Derald Stuart, 6, 8 May 1987.

39 Eight of these also formed part of the test programme for the next Polaris, A3, and involved reconfigured A2X missiles carrying the Mk. 2 guidance and reentry body systems. J. P. McManus, *A History of the FBM System* (Sunnyvale, CA: Lockheed Missiles and Space Company, 1988), B-1.

40 Strategic Systems Program Office, *FBM Facts/chronology – Polaris, Poseidon, Trident* (Washington, DC: Navy Department, 1986), 28.

41 McManus, *A History of the FBM System*, B-4.

42 Interview with Derald Stuart, 6, 8 May 1987.

43 McManus, *A History of the FBM System*, E-23.

44 Interview with Bob Dietz, 8 February 1989.

45 Interview with Rear Admiral Robert Wertheim, 3 April 1987; also Ted Greenwood, *Making the MIRV: A Study of Defense Decision Making* (Cambridge, MA: Ballinger, 1975), 161.

46 Letter from Rear Admiral Robert H. Wertheim, 17 August 1988.

47 Again, as with the W-47, warhead corrosion was to cause some concern. This was discovered during the 1970s in W-58 warheads, but 'the Navy were able to counter these problems by certain minor changes to the warheads at Navy maintenance facilities, without any further nuclear tests being required or any major rebuilding'. Rosengren, *Some Little-Publicized Difficulties with A Nuclear Freeze*, 18.

48 Equivalent megatonnage is a measure of the destructive effect against a large, 'soft' target, such as a city. If y is the yield of a warhead, its equivalent megatonnage is $y^{2/3}$. The blast, etc., from a nuclear explosion is propagated outwards in what is roughly a sphere, so the 'lethal radius' for any immediate effect is approximately proportional to the cube root of the yield. Area damage is therefore roughly proportional to the square of the cube root – i.e. $y^{2/3}$.

49 Interview with Bob Dietz, 8 February 1989.

50 Fuhrman, 'Fleet Ballistic Missile System', 280.

51 Interview with Bob Dietz, 8 February 1989.

52 See M. Yaffee, 'Ablation Wins Missile Performance Gain', *Aviation Week* (18 July 1960), 54–65; and 'Pyrolytic Graphite Studied for Re-Entry', *Aviation Week* (25 July 1960), 26–28.

53 McManus, *A History of the FBM System*, B-13.

54 Since the reentry body motors added velocity the guidance system obviously gave the release command 'early'.

55 Fuhrman, 'Fleet Ballistic Missile System', 280; interview.

56 Letter from Admiral Wertheim, 17 August 1988.

57 Interview with Bob Dietz, 8 February 1989.

58 Ibid.

59 See John Prados, *The Soviet Estimate: U.S. Intelligence Analysis and Soviet Strategic Forces* (Princeton, NJ: Princeton University Press, 1986).

60 The reentry bodies were 'separable to more than double the predicted interceptor lethal radius'. L. Smith, R. H. Wertheim, and R. A. Duffy,

'Innovative Engineering in the Trident Missile Development', *The Bridge (National Academy of Engineering)*, vol. 10, no. 2 (Summer 1980), 11.

61 McManus, *A History of the FBM System*, E-23.

62 Letter from Vice Admiral Levering Smith, 27 August 1988.

63 Fuhrman, 'Fleet Ballistic Missile System', 280.

64 'Problems May Cut Polaris A3 Range Goal', *Aviation Week and Space Technology* (4 September 1961), 31.

65 McManus, *A History of the FBM System*, B-14.

66 Fuhrman, 'Fleet Ballistic Missile System', 280.

67 Ibid.

68 Letter from Sam Forter, 22 November 1991.

69 Interview with Sam Forter, 15 May 1987.

70 B. O. Olson, 'History of FBM Guidance at CSDL' (10 March 1975), typescript), 3.

71 Ibid.

72 According to L. Smith, et al., 'Innovative Engineering in the Trident Missile Development', at 11, SPO set an objective of making the Polaris A3 about four times more accurate than the A2 at the longer range. The recollections of many participants suggest, however, that this is a retrospective rationalization of what actually happened.

73 C. S. Draper, 'Submarine Inertial Navigation – A Review and some Predictions', paper presented to the Polaris Steering Task Group on 22 October 1959 (Draper Laboratory Library, CSD-107), 3.

74 Interview with Derald Stuart, 6, 8 May 1987.

75 Olson, 'History of FBM Guidance at CSDL', 4.

76 J. C. Hung and G. B. Doane, III, 'Progress in Strapdown Technology' in *Inertial Navigation Components and Systems: AGARD Conference Proceedings no. 116* (papers presented at the 15th meeting of the Guidance and Control Panel of the NATO Advisory Group for Aerospace Research and Development, Florence, 2–5 October 1972), 14-1-14-9, at 14-1.

77 Olson, 'History of FBM Guidance at CSDL', 4.

78 McManus, *A History of the FBM System*, A-9.

79 Ibid., A-10.

80 Ibid., B-20.

81 Fuhrman, 'Fleet Ballistic Missile System', 280.

82 Interview with Rear Admiral Robert Wertheim, 3 April 1987.

83 Interview with Rear Admiral Robert Wertheim, 9 March 1989.

84 Ibid.

85 Interview with Bob Dietz, 8 February 1989

86 Interview with Rear Admiral Robert Wertheim, 9 March 1989. Sir Solly (now Lord) Zuckerman was sceptical about whether the UK Polaris A3 missiles needed the Topsy radiation protection, but was persuaded by Levering Smith's argument that it was best to keep the UK and US missiles identical. Interview with Vice Admiral Levering Smith, 9 March 1989.

87 The first test of an 'improved' A3 in November 1966 and the completion of the A3T exchange in July 1970 are noted in SSPO, 'FBM Facts', 33, 36.

88 *SASC FY76, Part 10, Research and Development* (Washington, DC: US GPO,

1975), 5353. The radiation hardening modification had been incorporated by the time Polaris A3 missiles were supplied to the UK.
89 At the point of dispersal each sector would be given a different velocity so that although not spatially separated then they would be by the time of reentry.
90 McManus, *A History of the FBM System*, E-25.
91 Interview with Bob Dietz, 8 February 1989. The Army was unwilling to have the complete Antelope package tested against its Safeguard system and had to be told what to expect because of concern that it would lose out in a 'shoot-out'.
92 Although never deployed, Antelope is considered by some to have been important in undermining opposition to the ABM Treaty because it was seen as demonstrating, both to Soviet leaders and to domestic opponents, that ABM defences could always be overwhelmed.
93 Interview with Rear Admiral Robert Wertheim, 9 March 1989.
94 McManus, *A History of the FBM System*, E-26.
95 Tom Logsdon and Charles W. Helms, 'Comparison Between the Capabilities of the Navstar GPS and other Operational Radionavigation Systems', paper prepared for presentation at EASCON '81, Washington, DC (Rockwell International: 16 November 1981), 5.
96 Captain Robert F. Freitag, 'Project Transit – Navigation Satellite', *United States Naval Institute Proceedings* (May 1961), 77–83, at 83. Transit was briefly shifted to the NavAir Bureau, but concern that the Navy would use it as a way of transgressing on the Air Force's space programme 'turf' led to its return to SPO which was, in any case, the key user. Interview with Rear Admiral Robert Wertheim, 9 March 1989.
97 Richard B. Kershner, 'Technical Innovations in the APL Space Department', *Johns Hopkins APL Technical Digest*, vol. 2 (January–March 1981), 264–78, at 265.
98 Ibid., 268.
99 Richard B. Kershner, 'Transit Program Results', *Astronautics* (May 1961), 113.
100 Kershner, 'Technical Innovations', 269; see also Leon H. Dulberger, 'Geodetic Measurements From Space', *Space/Aeronautics* (June 1965), 34–43.
101 Kershner, 'Technical Innovations', 269.
102 Interview with Bob Jenkins, 13 July 1987.
103 R. J. Anderle, 'Error Model for Geodetic Positions Derived from Doppler Satellite Observations', *Bulletin of Geodesy*, vol. 50 (1976), 43–77, at 43.
104 B. McKelvie and H. Galt, Jr. 'The Evolution of the Ship's Inertial Navigation System for the Fleet Ballistic Missile Program', *Navigation: Journal of the Institute of Navigation*, vol. 25 (Fall 1978), 310–322, at 315; 'Navy Standardizes Polaris SINS System', *Aviation Week and Space Technology* (4 May 1964), 16.
105 C. D. LaFond, 'New SINS Nears Sea Tests', *Missile and Rockets*, vol. 10 (30 April 1962), 33.
106 Interview with Vice Admiral Levering Smith, 1 April 1987.
107 Ibid.
108 SSPO, 'FBM Facts', 30.

109 McKelvie and Galt, 'Evolution of the Ship's Inertial Navigation System', 316.

110 G. B. Kistiakowsky, *A Scientist at the White House* (Cambridge, MA: Harvard University Press, 1976), 162.

111 See D. Ball, *Politics and Force Levels*, 46.

112 Ibid., 63, fn 7. Other accounts attribute the number of forty-one submarines to a more deliberate appraisal of what was needed to cover the target set. See Sapolsky, *Polaris System Development*, 160–61.

113 D. Ball, 'The Counterforce Potential of American SLBM Systems', *Journal of Peace Research*, vol. 14 (1977), 23–40, at 25.

114 Ball, *Politics and Force Levels*, 63.

115 Ibid., 64.

116 Quoted in ibid., 275.

117 Sapolsky, *Polaris System Development*, 69.

118 Vincent Davis, *The Politics of Innovation: Patterns in Navy Cases*, the Social Science Foundation and Graduate School of International Studies Monograph Series in World Affairs, IV, 3 (Denver, CO: University of Denver Press, 1967), 36.

119 Quoted in N. Polmar and T. Allen, *Rickover* (New York: Simon and Schuster, 1982), 540.

120 R. Hewlett and F. Duncan, *Nuclear Navy* (Chicago: University of Chicago Press, 1974), 308.

121 Polmar and Allen, *Rickover*, 543.

122 Ibid., 548–49.

123 Quoted in Sapolsky, *Polaris System Development*, 238.

124 Ibid., 238–9.

125 E. Rees, *The Seas and the Subs* (New York: Duell, Sloan and Pearce, 1961), 169.

126 Ibid.

127 W. M. Arkin and R. Fieldhouse, 'Nuclear Weapon Command, Control and Communication', in *SIPRI Yearbook 1984*, 512, fn 156. Following Annapolis, the first to be completed was at Cutler which went on air on 1 January 1961, SSPO, 'FBM Facts', 28.

128 See testimony of Vice Admiral R. Y. Kaufman, *SASC Hearings FY1978* (Washington, DC.: US GPO, 1977), 6706.

129 Ibid.

130 Malcom Spaven, 'Communicating with submarines', *Jane's Defence Weekly*, vol. 4 (23 November 1985), 1152–56, at 1153.

131 Ibid.

132 *Los Angeles Times* (26 May 1972), cited in Desmond Ball, *Can Nuclear War Be Controlled* (London: International Institute for Strategic Studies, 1981; Adelphi Paper no. 169), 24.

133 See B. G. Blair, *Strategic Command and Control: Redefining the Nuclear Threat* (Washington, DC: Brookings Institution, 1985), 98, n. 35; Malcolm Spaven, *Extremely Low Frequency Communications for Submarines: A Background Briefing on British Plans* (Brighton: Armament and Disarmament Unit, University of Sussex, January 1986), 4.

134 Spaven, 'Communicating with submarines', 1152.

135 Malcolm Spaven, 'ELF: Surviving the traumas – part 2', *Jane's Defence Weekly*, vol. 4 (November 1985), 1194–97, at 1194.

136 *Bulletin of the Atomic Scientists* (December 1989), 51. Eliot Marshall, 'ELF Resurrected After Drowning by Navy', *Science*, vol. 212 (May 8, 1981), 644–5, at 644 notes that the early 1960s ELF scheme involving a 6000 mile long antenna 'would have embraced 41 percent of the state of Wisconsin'. For the environmental case against ELF, see Lowell L. Klessig and Victor L. Strite, *The ELF Odyssey: National Security Versus Environmental Protection* (Boulder, CO: Westview Press, 1980); for Navy rebuttals see *SASC FY 1978*, 6677–756.

137 Sapolsky, *Polaris System Development*, 238.

138 Ibid., 239.

139 Ibid., 240.

140 Ibid., 239.

141 Ibid., 240; also Blair, *Strategic Command and Control*, 169.

142 Quoted in Blair, *Strategic Command and Control*, 169.

143 See A. B. Carter, 'Communications Technologies and Vulnerabilities' in, A. B. Carter, J. D. Steinbruner, and C. A. Zraket (eds.), *Managing Nuclear Operations* (Washington, DC: Brookings Institution, 1987), 217–81, at 237; also D. A. Boutacoff, 'New Tacamo Aircraft Being Developed to Support Trident Missile Submarines', *Defense Electronics*, vol. 16 (March 1985), 108–11.

144 Quoted in Blair, *Strategic Command and Control*, 170.

145 Ibid., 170–71.

146 Cited in General Accounting Office, *An Unclassified Version of A Classified Report Entitled 'The Navy's Strategic Communications Systems – Need for Management Attention and Decisionmaking'* (Washington, DC: US GAO, 2 May 1979), PSAD-79-48A, 9.

147 'Problems May Cut Polaris A3 Range Goal', *Aviation Week and Space Technology* , vol. 75 (4 September 1961), 31.

148 Interview with Rear Admiral Robert Wertheim, 3 April 1987; also D. C. Breasted, 'Navy Seeks Approval For Polaris Follow-on', *Missiles and Rockets* (4 November 1963), 18.

149 This section from Interview with George Mechlin, 8 April 1987; also see Robert Lindsey, 'Material Refinement Assists Poseidon Launcher Designers', *Technology Week* (13 June 1966), 32–33.

150 Clarke Newlon, 'Polaris Major Factor in Proposed 1000-Missile Force for NATO', *Missiles and Rockets*, vol. 7 (25 July 1960), 12–13.

151 Dr George Mechlin of Westinghouse quoted in Lindsey, 'Material Refinement Assists Poseidon Launcher Designers', 33.

152 Mechlin interview.

153 See R. Lindsey, 'Improved Launch System for Polaris', *Missiles and Rockets*, vol. 13 (2 December 1963), 27–28.

154 Quoted in Robert Lindsey, 'B-3 Polaris Expected To Be Operational In '70', *Missiles and Rockets*, vol. 15 (24 August 1964), 28.

6 Poseidon

1 Interview by Donald MacKenzie, 4 March 1985.
2 'Problems May Cut Polaris A3 Range Goal', *Aviation Week and Space Technology*, vol. 75 (4 September 1961), 31; Robert Lindsey, 'First Polaris A3 Launch Draws Near', *Missiles and Rockets*, vol. 11 (9 July 1962), 17.
3 'Lockheed Polaris A–3 Tests Slated', *Aviation Week and Space Technology*, vol. 76 (2 April 1962), 23.
4 Ted Greenwood, *Making the MIRV: A Study of Defense Decision Making* (Cambridge, MS: Ballinger, 1975), 33.
5 Norman Friedman, *US Naval Weapons* (Conway Maritime Press, 1983), 223.
6 Interview with Rear Admiral Robert Wertheim, 3 April 1987.
7 Interview by Donald MacKenzie with Rear Admiral Robert Wertheim, 4 March 1985.
8 'Draft Presidential Memorandum, Subject: Recommended FY 1964–FY 1968 Strategic Retaliatory Forces', (21 November 1962), 22–23. I am grateful to Lynn Eden for providing me with copies of the now declassified McNamara DPMs.
9 Interview by Donald MacKenzie with Rear Admiral Robert Wertheim, 4 March 1985.
10 D. C. Breasted, 'Navy Seeks Approval For Polaris Follow-on', *Missiles and Rockets*, vol. 13 (4 November 1963), 18.
11 J. P. McManus, *A History of the FBM System* (Sunnydale, CA: Lockheed Missiles and Space Company, 1988), C-1. One of these, B3H, incorporated an aerodynamic manoeuvring warhead KAYAK, a concept that would later be taken up again in the Trident I programme as the Mk. 500. Ibid., E-26.
12 Letter from Bob Dietz, 29 August 1991.
13 Harvey M. Sapolsky, *The Polaris System Development: Bureaucratic and Programmatic Success in Government* (Cambridge, MA: Harvard University Press, 1972), 220.
14 Robert A. Fuhrman, 'The Fleet Ballistic Missile System; Polaris to Trident', *Journal of Spacecraft*, vol. 5, no. 5 (September–October 1978), 281.
15 Apparently this grew out of Air Force concerns over the effect of thrust termination on ICBM accuracy. At the long ranges in question a small error in reentry vehicle velocity at thrust termination could result in a large target miss. (Roughly, a difference of one foot per second leads to a change in down range impact of a foot for every mile of range; so for a 6000 mile ICBM a foot per second error would translate into a miss of 6000 feet.) To reduce this error the idea was devised of a platform to more precisely eject the reentry vehicle. It was then realized that more than one reentry vehicle could be carried by the same 'bus' and so MIRV technology originated.
16 A similar Air Force concept was known as P-Ball. See Greenwood, *Making the MIRV*, 31.
17 Interview with Ben Olson, 11 May 1987. However, it soon became clear that implementing Q-guidance with multiple reentry bodies would be very complex and probably involve using explicit guidance anyway, thus undermining the rationale for staying with Q-guidance. Letter from Ben Olson, 7 December 1991.

18 Greenwood, *Making the MIRV*, 45. This small reentry vehicle, initially known as the Mk. 100, was recommended for Polaris B3 in the June 1964 Scientific Advisory Board Nuclear Panel report called 'Review of Advances in Design of Multiple Warhead Possibilities' and in the August 1965 final report of the Pen-X study. See ibid., 40.

19 Earlier names for the Mk. 3 reentry body were Mk. 100, CRESS, and Pebbles. The recollection of one Lockheed engineer is that the name changes were 'to keep OSD off balance'. Interview with Bob Dietz, 8 February 1989.

20 Greenwood, *Making the MIRV*, 22. The Great Circle Group was set up to study 'Naval Contributions to Damage Limiting' as a response to the damage limitation study – the 'Kent Study' – begun in March 1964 in the office of DDR&E. D. A. Paolucci, 'The Development of Navy Strategic Offensive and Defensive Systems', *United States Naval Institute Proceedings*, vol. 96 (1970), 220.

21 See Sapolsky, *Polaris System Development*, chapter 6.

22 *Navy Magazine* (July 1964), 28.

23 Sapolsky, *Polaris System Development*, 220.

24 'Draft Memorandum for the President, Subject: Recommended FY 1966– 1970 Programs for Strategic Offensive Forces, Continental Air and Missile Defense Forces, and Civil Defense', (3 December 1964), 30.

25 Sapolsky, *Polaris System Development*, 71.

26 Quoted in Greenwood, *Making the MIRV*, 6.

27 Quoted in *Missiles and Rockets* (25 October 1965), 16.

28 The flexibility of using a large number of small reentry bodies appealed to SPO because it reduced the dangers that unexpected developments in Soviet defences would threaten penetration, as Galosh had with Polaris A3.

29 Fuhrman, 'Fleet Ballistic Missile System', 280.

30 Sapolsky, *Polaris System Development*, 198.

31 Interview with Marvin Stern, 13 July 1987. On 3 February 1961 Stern accompanied McNamara on a visit to Omaha where they were briefed on the new targeting plan, SIOP-62, which was due to come into operation on 1 July 1961. 'As a minimum, SIOP-62 called for the launching of the U.S. strategic nuclear alert force in its entirety as quickly as possible. This included 2,164 megatons and was calculated to kill 175 million Russians and Chinese.' This led to Stern, Alain Enthoven, and William Kaufman convincing McNamara 'as to the benefits of a strategy of "controlled response" [in which the] first priority would be to blunt an enemy's capability for strategic nuclear strike against you. There would then be a graded response against his additional military, war-fighting and industrial capability. Finally, and only as a last resort, there would be the destruction of his cities together with the attendant large civilian casualties.' Letter from Marvin Stern, 26 November 1991. In Stern's view, improved accuracy in ballistic missiles was important not just to threaten very hard targets, like ICBM silos, but also to threaten the many intermediate targets while minimizing collateral damage (i.e. fatalities).

32 Greenwood, *Making the MIRV*, 45.

33 Ibid.

220

34 Interview by Donald MacKenzie with Rear Admiral Robert Wertheim, 4 March 1985.
35 Greenwood, *Making the MIRV*, 22–23; also D. A. Paolucci, 'The Development of Navy Strategic Offensive and Defensive Systems', *United States Naval Institute Proceedings*, vol. 96 (1970), 204–23.
36 Greenwood, *Making the MIRV*, 55. A view also expressed by one of my interviewees, Marvin Stern, 13 July 1987.
37 Greenwood, *Making the MIRV*, 45. By this time the original six Mk. 12 Mailman configuration had been reduced to four reentry bodies so that enough propulsion could be carried to give a greater footprint.
38 Ibid.
39 Interview by Donald MacKenzie with Rear Admiral Robert Wertheim, 4 March 1985.
40 Interview with Bob Dietz, 8 February 1989.
41 US Congress, Senate, *Committee on Armed Services, Fiscal Year 1975 Authorization for Military Procurement, Part 6, Research and Development* (Washington, DC: US GPO, 1974), 3297–8.
42 Letter from William W. Kaufmann, 30 July 1987.
43 Greenwood, *Making the MIRV*, 68–69. Another technological embodiment of the interest in damage limitation at this time was support for an inflight reliability reporting system for Polaris. Lockheed were contracted to develop a Polaris A3 version, PY-3, in March 1965 and production began in late 1967. This system was mounted in the equipment section of the missile and a transmitter/antenna would be ejected following successful reentry body deployment, and this information relayed back to the submarine. However, although delivered in 1968 the system was not deployed because of the submariners' concern that the receiving antenna deployment would compromise their concealment. McManus, *A History of the FBM System*, C-5.
44 James McCormack, 'Memorandum to the Files, subject: the Poseidon Contract', 10 November 1968. MIT Archives and Special Collections, Albert Hill papers, 83–40, box 4. Vice Admiral Smith's comment on this in 1986 was that he was sure that he would have said 'that the lesser improvement to the guidance system *could* have been done by an industrial contractor rather than that it *would* have been assigned to an industrial contractor'. Letter from Vice Admiral Levering Smith, emphasis added.
45 Sapolsky, *Polaris System Development*, 221–22.
46 Interview by Donald MacKenzie with Vice Admiral Levering Smith, 23 February 1985.
47 As late as early 1967 press reports were still referring to Poseidon as 'designed primarily to launch the Mk. 17'. Edward H. Kolcum, 'U.S. Stressing New Re-entry Technology', *Aviation Week and Space Technology* (6 February 1967), 26.
48 Levering Smith, Robert H. Wertheim, Robert A. Duffy, 'Innovative Engineering in the Trident Missile Development', *The Bridge* (National Academy of Engineering), vol. 10, no. 2 (Summer 1980), 10–19, at 11.
49 Interview with Sam Forter, 15 May 1987.
50 B. O. Olson, 'History of FBM Guidance at CSDL' (March 1975), typescript, 4.

51 Interview with Graydon Wheaton, 11 May 1987.
52 Interview by Donald MacKenzie with Ben Olson and Paul Dow, 5 October 1984. The move to permanent magnet rather than electromagnets for torquing was actually not a small step in the context of the laboratory, Olson recalled, because Dr Draper 'just didn't like them'.
53 Graydon M. Wheaton, 'Electronics Manufacturing for Inertial Guidance Systems', (9 May 1986), typescript, 8. I am grateful to the author for providing me with this.
54 Interview with Sanford Cohen, 15 May 1987.
55 Wheaton, 'Electronics Manufacturing', 5.
56 Interview by Donald MacKenzie with Andrew DePrete, 28 March 1985.
57 Interview with Dave Montague, 8 May 1987.
58 Interview by Donald MacKenzie with Rear Admiral Robert Wertheim, 4 March 1985.
59 A fuller account of the history of stellar-inertial guidance will be found in D. MacKenzie, 'Stellar-Inertial Guidance: A Study in the Sociology of Military Technology', in *Sociology of the Sciences Yearbook 1988* (Dordrecht: Reidel).
60 Interview with Marvin Stern, 13 July 1987.
61 Interview by Donald MacKenzie with Vice Admiral Levering Smith, 23 February 1985.
62 Interview with Vice Admiral Levering Smith, 1 April 1987.
63 Interview with Sam Forter, 15 May 1987.
64 Ibid. Also letter from Sam Forter, 4 March 1990.
65 Interview by Donald MacKenzie, quoted in *Inventing Accuracy*, 266.
66 Interview by Donald MacKenzie with Ben Olson, 5 October 1984.
67 Interview with Sam Forter, 15 May 1987.
68 Interview by Donald MacKenzie with Rear Admiral Robert Wertheim, 4 March 1985.
69 Interview with Ben Olson, 11 May 1987.
70 Interview with John Brett, 28 May 1987.
71 Letter from Ben Olson, 7 December 1991.
72 US Congress, *Senate, Armed Services Committee FY 1969, Part 3* (Washington, DC: US GPO, 1968), 1052.
73 Interview with John Brett, 28 May 1987.
74 Quoted in Stockholm International Peace Research Institute, *SIPRI Yearbook of World Armaments and Disarmament, 1968/69* (Stockholm: Almqvist and Wiksell, 1970), 109.
75 A. Frye, *A Responsible Congress: The Politics of National Security* (New York: McGraw-Hill, 1975), 55.
76 Ibid., 69–70.
77 Ibid., 70, n 1.
78 Interview with Dave Montague, 8 May 1987.
79 Greenwood, *Making the MIRV*, 136.
80 MacKenzie, *Inventing Accuracy*, 270.
81 Greenwood, *Making the MIRV*, 137.
82 Interview by Donald MacKenzie with Rear Admiral Robert Wertheim, 4 March 1985.

83 Interview with Ben Olson, 11 May 1987. A couple of Mk. 4 systems were built and tested in the laboratory.

84 T. A. King and H. Strell, 'Underwater Navigation' entry in *McGraw-Hill Encyclopedia of Science and Technology* (New York: McGraw-Hill, 1982), 399–402, at 400.

85 *Senate Armed Services Committee FY1975, Part 6* (Washington, DC: US GPO, 1974), 3280.

86 Ibid., 3278.

87 J. Dassoulas, 'The Triad Spacecraft', *APL Technical Digest*, vol. 12, no. 2 (April–June 1973), 2–13, at 2.

88 T. A. Stansell, Jr, 'The Many Faces of Transit', *Navigation: Journal of The Institute of Navigation*, vol. 25, no. 1 (Spring 1978), 55–70, at 62.

89 Owen Wilkes and Nils Petter Gleditsch, *Loran-C and Omega: A Study of the Military Importance of Radio Navigation Aids* (Oslo: Norwegian University Press, 1987), 99.

90 On WGS 72, see T. O. Seppelin, 'The Department of Defense World Geodetic System 1972', *The Canadian Surveyor*, vol. 28, no. 5 (December 1974), 496–506.

91 Stansell, 'Many Faces of Transit', 62.

92 *Senate Armed Services Committee, FY 1975*, 3286.

93 H. W. Knoebel, 'The Electric Vacuum Gyro: Pinpoint for Polaris Launching', *Control Engineering* (February 1964), 70–73.

94 P. J. Klass, 'New Gyro nears Operational Use', *Aviation Week and Space Technology* (19 June 1972), 50–52.

95 P. J. Klass, 'Navy to Test Electrically Suspended Gyro', *Aviation Week and Space Technology* (6 February 1961), 85–91.

96 B. McKelvie and H. Galt, Jr, 'The Evolution of the Ship's Inertial Navigation System for the Fleet Ballistic Missile Program', *Navigation: Journal of the Institute of Navigation*, vol. 25 (Fall 1978), 321.

97 In addition to pushing the ESG, Honeywell also played the key role in the development of the laser gyroscope, a technology that since the late 1970s has brought the corporation a major share of the aircraft inertial navigation market.

98 Klass, 'New Gyro', 50.

99 Klass, 'Navy to Test', 87; P. J. Klass, 'Inertial System uses Electrostatic Gyros', *Aviation Week and Space Technology* (30 September 1963), 87–89, at 88.

100 Klass, 'Navy to Test', 87; Knoebel, 'The Electric Vacuum Gyro', 71.

101 R. C. Langford, 'Unconventional Inertial Sensors', paper presented to Second American Institute of Aeronautics and Astronautics Annual Meeting, San Francisco, 26–29 1965 July 18.

102 The original Mk. 2 Mod. 0 SINS was improved gradually through a series of changes, such as a better 'binacle' to enclose it which reduced errors due to variations in temperature and air flow. After these modifications the Mk. 2 Mod. 0 was renamed the Mk. 2 Mod. 4, providing good enough performance for the 2500-mile Polaris A3. Autonetics new SINS, the Mk. 2 Mod. 2, featured an improved version of the G7A gyro, the G7B, and was installed in submarines twenty to thirty (the 627-class). This was designed

to allow a modification involving the addition of a fourth monitor gyro which provides compensation for the drift rates in the other gyros. Thus modified it was known as the Mk. 2 Mod. 3 and in this form it was retrofitted to the five 608-class submarines (formerly using the Sperry Mk. 3 Mod. 0) and fitted to the final twelve FBM submarines (the 640-class). By the end of the 1960s the forty-one Polaris submarines contained a mixture of Mk. 2 Mod. 4 and Mk. 2 Mod. 3 SINS. A further modification of the Mk. 2 SINS, the Mod. 6, was developed and retrofitted into the thirty-one submarines which were converted to carry Poseidon. See McKelvie and Galt, 'The Evolution of the Ship's Inertial Navigation System'. MIT's Instrumentation Laboratory attempted to get back into SINS design in the early 1960s with a Mk. 4 SINS which was tested by SPO during the summer of 1962 and Sperry developed a Mk. 3 Mod. 3, but neither was chosen for FBM use. See Charles D. LaFond, 'New SINS Near Sea Tests', *Missiles and Rockets* (30 April 1962), 33.

103 Interview by Donald MacKenzie with T. A. J. King, see MacKenzie, *Inventing Accuracy*, 278.

104 *Senate Armed Services Committee FY 1977* (Washington, DC: US GPO, 1976), 6553.

105 Composite modified double base propellant, not surprisingly, is a combination of the double base technology (using a mixture of nitroglycerine and nitrocellulose) and the composite technology (using ammonium perchlorate, aluminium and a binder).

106 Fuhrman, 'Fleet Ballistic Missile System', 281.

107 'Hercules, Thiokol Win Poseidon Work', *Missiles and Rockets* (25 October 1965), 16; also Sapolsky, *Polaris System Development*, 207.

108 Interview with Vice Admiral Glenwood Clark, 21 May 1987.

109 Interview with Bob Dietz, 8 February 1989.

110 Ibid.

111 Ibid. However, a former Lockheed engineer, Robert Aldridge, has claimed that the 'Mark-3 reentry body fell considerably short of the design goal for radiation hardness.' Robert C. Aldridge, 'How Defense Industries Keep the Business Coming', *Bulletin of the Atomic Scientists*, vol. 32, no. 5 (May 1976), 46.

112 For a discussion of the asymmetries which result in reentry vehicle torques, see R.W. Carlson and C.A. Louis III, *Introduction to reentry Flight Dynamics*, LMSC-D050690 (Sunnyvale, CA: Lockheed Missiles & Space Company, 15 March 1968). The Air Force Mk. 12 reentry vehicle apparently had even more serious problems with spin-up and spin-down.

113 Interview with Dave Montague, 8 May 1987.

114 McManus, *A History of the FBM System*, C-18.

115 Interview with Rear Admiral Robert Wertheim, 3 April 1987.

116 See 'The Poseidon Misadventure', *Business Week* (13 October 1973); 'Gradual Poseidon Modification Planned', *Aviation Week & Space Technology* (17 September 17, 1973), 19.

117 Lawrence Livermore identified an ageing problem in the W-68 Poseidon warhead carried by the Mk. 3. Chemical changes in the LX-09 high explosive used to implode the primary produced effluents which interacted

with other components of the warhead raising fears that the detonator might fail. Starting in 1979 the high explosive in all 3200 W-68 warheads was replaced with an alternative, known as LX-10, that had been tested in the original development. See Jack W. Rosengren, *Some Little-Publicized Difficulties with A Nuclear Freeze* (Marina del Rey, CA.: R&D Associates, October 1983), 19–20; also T. B. Cochran, R. S. Norris, W. M. Arkin, and M.M. Hoenig, *Nuclear Weapons Databook Volume II: US Nuclear Warhead Production* (Cambridge, MA: Ballinger, 1987), 50–1.

118 McKelvie and Galt, 'The Evolution of the Ship's Inertial Navigation System', 317.

119 W. N. Dean and D. P. Roth, 'The AN/BRN-5 Loran receiver', *Navigation – Journal of the Institute of Navigation*, vol. 23 (Winter 1976), 287–97.

120 T. A. King and H. Strell, 'Underwater Navigation', 399; also McKelvie and Galt, 'The Evolution of the Ship's Inertial Navigation System', 317–18.

121 See Robert Lindsey, 'Material Refinement Assists Poseidon Launcher Designers', *Technology Week* (13 June 1966), 32–33.

122 See James R. Kurth, 'Aerospace Production Lines and American Defense Spending', in Steven Rosen (ed.), *Testing the Theory of the Military-Industrial Complex* (Lexington, MA: Lexington Books, 1973), 135–56.

123 Sapolsky, *Polaris System Development*, 225.

124 Ibid., 71.

125 Greenwood, *Making the MIRV*, 44.

126 See 'Poseidon Missiles To Get More RVs – But Not 14', *Aerospace Daily* (30 October 1980), 331–32.

127 See D. Ball, 'The Role of Strategic Concepts and Doctrine in US Strategic Nuclear Force Development', in B. Brodie, M. D. Intriligator, and R. Kolkowicz (eds.), *National Security and International Security* (Cambridge, MA: Oelgeschlager, Gunn and Hain, 1983), 37–63, at 55.

128 'The Navy initially used cost-plus fixed fee contracts. The contractor received compensation for all costs, plus a fixed percentage of the initial estimate. The contractor was thus given something of a blank check. Whenever something had to be changed, the government picked up the tab; consequently, contractors didn't balk at changes, but did whatever had to be done to achieve the standards required. 'To the End of the Rainbow: Evolution of the Marine Division' (typescript of Westinghouse history), 47.

129 Sapolsky, *Polaris System Development*, 201.

130 Norman Polmar and Captain D. A. Paolucci, 'Sea-Based "Strategic" Weapons for the 1980s and Beyond', *United States Naval Institute Proceedings/Naval Review 1978* Vol. 104 (May 1978), 108.

131 Sapolsky, *Polaris System Development*, 224.

132 Interview with James Martin, 9 June 1987. Apparently the Poseidon Mk. 3 reentry bodies were targeted to the same Designated Ground Zeros as the Air Force Minuteman Mk. 12 reentry vehicles, whose W-62 warhead had significantly lower yield than had been intended. The Air Force was not happy about this.

7 Strat-X, ULMS, and Trident I

1 Mary Schumacher, *Trident: Setting the Requirements* (Case Study C15-88-802.0, Harvard University John F. Kennedy School of Government, 1987), 10. I am very grateful to Mary Schumacher for supplying me with her work on Trident and with the Rhodes thesis (see next note).
2 F. Leary, 'ULMS: Strategic Emphasis Shifts Seaward', *Space/Aeronautics* (June 1970), 24–33, at 26; also interview with Rear Admiral Robert Wertheim, 3 April 1987; Edward Rhodes, 'Trident: Bureaucratic Politics and Military Procurement' (unpublished thesis, Harvard College, March 1980), 12.
3 *The Strat-X Report* (Arlington, Virginia: Institute for Defense Analysis, August 1967), 1.
4 Leary, 'ULMS', 26; Captain Dominic A. Paolucci (US Navy, Retired), 'The Development of Navy Strategic Offensive and Defensive Systems', *United States Naval Institute Proceedings*, vol. 96 (May 1970), 223, also mentions the SLMS.
5 Norman Polmar, 'The U.S. Navy: Strategic Missile Submarines', *United States Naval Institute Proceedings* (March 1980), 141. According to one Strat-X participant, there was 'some funny accounting in displacements to shift the cost algorithm to favour ULMS'. Letter from Bob Dietz, 29 August 1991.
6 On Strat-X and ULMS, see J. Steinbruner and B. Carter, 'Organizational and Political Dimensions of the Strategic Posture: the Problems of Reform', *Daedalus*, vol. 104 (Summer 1975), 131–54; N. Polmar and T. Allen, *Rickover* (New York: Simon and Schuster, 1982), chapter 26; also *The Strat-X Report*.
7 Interview with Vice Admiral Levering Smith, 1 April 1987.
8 *The Strat-X Report*, 84.
9 Paolucci, 'The Development of Navy Strategic Offensive and Defensive Systems', 223.
10 Schumacher, *Trident: Setting the Requirements*, 5; Rhodes, 'Trident', 26.
11 Schumacher, *Trident: Setting the Requirements*, 5.
12 J. P. McManus, *A History of the FBM System* (Sunnyvale, CA: Lockheed Missiles and Space Company, 1988), D-5.
13 Rhodes, 'Trident', 28.
14 Smith quoted in Schumacher, *Trident: Setting the Requirements*, 8
15 Schumacher, *Trident: Setting the Requirements*; also Rhodes, 'Trident', 31–32.
16 Rhodes, 'Trident', 33.
17 Conversation with David Packard as recalled by R. W. Cousins (Vice Chief of Naval Operations), 'Memorandum for the Chief of Naval Material. Subj: ULMS Studies. Ser 00308P31' (10 November 1970), cited in Rhodes, 'Trident', 128, note 11.
18 Schumacher, *Trident: Setting the Requirements*, 10.
19 In ibid., 10.
20 Known as C3D after Bob Dietz of Lockheed, the inventor (and US patent holder) of the concept of having a third stage up through the reentry bodies in order to gain extra range. The C3D concept had originated during Strat-X but because it undermined the Navy's preference for a big new missile, Lockheed 'very carefully put it in the bottom drawer for about four

years'. It was first made known to SSPO as PECS, Poseidon Extra Capability System, but CNO Zumwalt ordered it stopped because it undermined the new large submarine. SSPO then reintroduced the concept under a new name, EXPO. Interview with Bob Dietz, 8 February 1989.

21 McManus, *A History of the FBM System*, D-6.
22 Rhodes, 'Trident', 41.
23 Ibid., 44.
24 Ibid., 44.
25 Schumacher, *Trident: Setting the Requirements*, 12. Apparently an unintended miscommunication between Zumwalt and Smith also left the former feeling snubbed by the latter. Letter from Captain Steven R. Cohen, 3 December 1991.
26 Steinbruner and Carter, 'Organizational and Political Dimensions of the Strategic Posture', 138.
27 Ibid.
28 Rhodes, 'Trident', 60.
29 Ibid., 62.
30 Schumacher, *Trident: Setting the Requirements*, 13; also see *SASC FY 1973, Part 5, Research and Development* (Washington, DC: US GPO, 1972), 2634–36.
31 Rhodes, 'Trident', 65.
32 Ibid., 66–67.
33 Ibid., 68.
34 Quoted in ibid., 68.
35 *SASC FY 1973*, 2636.
36 Quoted in Schumacher, *Trident: Setting the Requirements*, 15.
37 Ibid., 15, n.
38 This was officially confirmed on 2 December 1971 when National Security Advisor Henry Kissinger 'requested Laird to give favourable consideration to "an expanded strategic submarine program" in a way that was highly visible to the Soviets'. H. Kissinger, *The White House Years* (Boston: Little, Brown and Co., 1979), 1129. Apparently Paul Nitze had relayed Soviet concern over US FBM developments from the SALT negotiations during late 1970 and early 1971. See Elmo R. Zumwalt, Jr, *On Watch* (New York: Quadrangle, 1976), 154.
39 Steinbruner and Carter, 'Organizational and Political Dimensions of the Strategic Posture', 140.
40 Rhodes, 'Trident', 80.
41 A 1 November 1971 memorandum from the Deputy Secretary of Defense to the Secretary of the Navy directed the Navy to: 'Initiate a study immediately of the alternative ways of providing early increases in the deployment level of our sea-based strategic offensive weapons.' See *SASC FY 1973*, 3188.
42 Schumacher, *Trident: Setting the Requirements*, 17.
43 Kissinger, *The White House Years*, 394–97.
44 Rhodes, 'Trident', 85.
45 Quoted in M. Schumacher, *Trident Contracting (A): Drafting the Request for Proposals* (Kennedy School of Government Case Program, Draft, 1988), 12.
46 Schumacher, *Trident Contracting (A)*, 18.
47 Quoted in M. Mintz, 'Depth Charge: Cost Overruns on New Trident Sub

Leave a Muddied Wake', *Washington Post* (4 October 1981), reprinted in Dina Rasor (ed.), *More Bucks, Less Bang: How the Pentagon Buys Ineffective Weapons* (Washington, DC: Fund for Constitutional Government, 1983), 211–23, at 214.

48 Interview with Bob Dietz, 8 February 1989. Also letter from Captain Steven R. Cohen, 3 December 1991. Of course, despite having two sources for this story the possibility remains that both may have heard the same rumour deliberately initiated to discredit Laird.

49 Interview with Vice Admiral Levering Smith, 1 April 1987.

50 See J. W. Canan, *The Superwarriors: The Fantastic World of Pentagon Super-weapons* (New York: Weybright and Talley, 1975), 184–86; Zumwalt, *On Watch*, 158–63.

51 Quoted in Canan, *Superwarriors*, 187.

52 Interview with Captain Steven R. Cohen, 9 July 1987.

53 Polmar and Allen, *Rickover*, 579 and 576.

54 See Schumacher, *Trident Contracting (A)*; Mintz, 'Depth Charge', 215–17.

55 Schumacher, *Trident Contracting (A)*, 7. Typically fixed-price contracts might have a ceiling price (say, about 30 per cent more than the agreed cost) up to which the Government and the contractor would share the extra costs.

56 M. Schumacher, *Trident Contracting (B): Evaluating the Bids* (Kennedy School of Government Case Program, Draft, 1988), 7.

57 Ibid., 5–6.

58 Patrick Tyler, *Running Critical: The Silent War, Rickover, and General Dynamics* (New York: Harper and Row, 1986), 131–33.

59 Ibid., 134–35.

60 M. Schumacher, *Trident Contracting (C): Negotiating the Contract* (Kennedy School of Government Case Program, Draft, 1988), 8.

61 Mintz, 'Depth Charge', 218.

62 See Tyler, *Running Critical*.

63 *SASC FY 1972, Part 3, Research and Development* (Washington, DC: US GPO, 1971), 2233.

64 Interview with John Brett, 28 May 1987.

65 Ibid.

66 Interview with Vice Admiral Glenwood Clark, 21 May 1987.

67 In March 1972 testimony to the Ad Hoc Research and Development Sub-committee of the Senate Armed Services Committee, Admiral Levering Smith noted that: 'The reentry body for the ULMS I missile is based on extension of the Poseidon Mk 3 design. The Mk 3 was limited to a maximum range of [deleted] miles and therefore increased heat protection and structural strengthening will be required for the reentry body to survive the reentry environment at ULMS I ranges.' *SASC FY1973, Part 5* (US GPO, 1972), 3157.

68 Interview with Bob Dietz, 8 February 1989.

69 Mk. 3 reentry bodies had been tested to 6000 miles with a modified heat-shield.

70 Interview with Seymour Zeiberg, 27 June 1987.

71 T. B. Cochran, W. M. Arkin, and M. M. Hoenig, *Nuclear Weapons Databook*,

vol. 1: US Nuclear Forces and Capabilities (Cambridge, MA: Ballinger, 1983), 142.

72 The ballistic coefficient – the weight-to-drag ratio – of the Trident Mk. 4 is said to be 1800 pounds/square foot, almost as high as the Minuteman III Mk. 12A. M. Bunn, *Technology of Ballistic Missile Reentry Vehicles* (Cambridge, MA: MIT Program in Science and Technology for International Security Report no. 11, March 1984), 6–7.

73 L. Smith, R. H. Wertheim, R. A. Duffy, 'Innovative Engineering in the Trident Missile Development', *The Bridge (National Academy of Engineering)* vol. 10, no. 2 (Summer 1980), 10–19, at 19.

74 Ibid., 19.

75 Ibid., 12.

76 Ibid., 14.

77 Letter from Captain Steven Cohen to Donald MacKenzie, 2 December 1986 see Donald MacKenzie, *Inventing Accuracy: A Historical Sociology of Nuclear Missile Guidance* (Cambridge, MA: MIT Press, 1990), 276–77.

78 Smith et al., *Innovative Engineering*, 15.

79 Ibid., 17.

80 Ibid.

81 J. P. Reding and D. M. Jecmen, 'An Advanced Aerospike to Minimize Nose Drag', *Lockheed Horizons,* 15 (1984), 46–54, at 47.

82 'Trident Subsystem Tests in Final Phase', *Aviation Week and Space Technology* (3 November 1975), 34–38, at 37.

83 'Updated Propulsion System Seen Extending Trident Range', *Aviation Week and Space Technology* (18 June 1973), 19.

84 Smith et al., *Innovative Engineering*, 18.

85 Ibid.

86 Ibid.

87 *SASC, FY1977, Part 12, Research and Development* (Washington, DC: US GPO, 1976), 6617.

88 Quoted in 'Trident failures "not hitting readiness"', *Jane's Defence Weekly* (1 September 1984), 308. SSPO insiders point out, however, that Trident I system reliablity remained above its goal. Letter from Captain Steven R. Cohen, 3 December 1991.

89 See '73 Trident I's Withheld from Fleet due to Defects', *Defense Daily*, vol. 135, no. 32 (16 August 1984), 249–50.

90 Smith et al., *Innovative Engineering*, 18.

91 'Trident Subsystem Tests in Final Phase', *Aviation Week and Space Technology* (3 November 1975), 34.

92 'Trident Missile Capabilities Advance', *Aviation Week and Space Technology* (16 June 1980), 99.

93 See 'Specified Range Forecast for Trident', *Aviation Week and Space Technology*, vol. 102 (5 May 1975), 55.

94 In a three-gimbal system an axis of sensitivity can be 'lost' when two of the gimbals become parallel, leading to a potentially disastrous failure of platform stabilization.

95 Interview by Donald MacKenzie with Vice Admiral Glenwood Clark, 28 March 1985.

96 Ibid.
97 A crucial paper is Edwin W. Howe and Paul H. Savet, 'The Dynamically Tuned Free Rotor Gyro', *Control Engineering* (June 1964), 67–72.
98 Interview with Sam Forter, 15 May 1987.
99 Interview with Robert Duffy, 11 May 1987.
100 Interview with Rear Admiral Robert Wertheim, 3 April 1987.
101 Graydon M. Wheaton, 'Electronics Manufacturing for Inertial Guidance Systems' (9 May 1986, typescript), 5.
102 Interview with Rear Admiral Robert Wertheim, 9 March 1989.
103 See D. Shapley, 'Arms Control as a Regulator of Military Technology', *Daedalus*, vol. 109, no. 1 (Winter 1980), 145–57 at 149.
104 DDR&E Memorandum to the Assistant Secretary of the Navy for Research and Development, 8 February 1973 quoted in *SASC FY1976, Part 10*, Research and Development (Washington, DC: US GPO, 1972), 5358.
105 Letter from Admiral Smith, 27 August 1988.
106 Smith et al., *Innovative Engineering*, 12.
107 Because it was intended to demonstrate a capability and not to go into production, SP-23 did not want to waste time with the Mk. 500 guidance system and so all the Mk. 500 work was done out of SP-27.
108 However, weight for weight the Mk. 500 could deliver much less explosive yield than a ballistic reentry body.
109 D. D. Dalgleish and L. Schweikart, *Trident* (Carbondale, IL: Southern Illinois University Press, 1984), 91.
110 McManus, *A History of the FBM System*, D-22.
111 Ibid., D-22.
112 *SASC FY1981, Part 6*, 4099.
113 McManus, *A History of the FBM System*, D-21, 22.
114 Interview by Donald MacKenzie with Captain Steven R. Cohen, see MacKenzie, *Inventing Accuracy*, 267.
115 Interview.
116 B. McKelvie and H. Galt, Jr, 'The Evolution of the Ship's Inertial Navigation System for the Fleet Ballistic Missile Program', *Navigation: Journal of the Institute of Navigation*, vol. 25 (Fall 1978), 320.
117 Interview by Donald MacKenzie with T. A. J. King, see MacKenzie and Spinardi, 'US Fleet Ballistic Missile Guidance and Navigation: "Going for Broke"', 592.
118 Of the eighteen pad launches and seven submarine launches only one (14 February 1978) is not recorded as successful in Strategic Systems Program Office, *FBM Facts/Chronology Polaris – Poseidon, Trident* (Washington, DC: Navy Department, 1986), 47–53.
119 Ibid., 51.
120 Interview with Captain Steven R. Cohen, 9 July 1987.
121 The submarines backfitted at Portsmouth Naval Shipyard during scheduled overhauls were *Simon Bolivar* (SSBN 641), *Benjamin Franklin* (640), *George Bancroft* (643), *Casimir Pulaski* (633), *Von Steuben* (632), and *James Madison* (627). See SSPO, 'FBM Facts/Chronology', 14–15.
122 These were the *Daniel Boone* (629), *John C. Calhoun* (630), *Stonewall Jackson*

(634), *Henry L. Stimson* (655), *Francis Scott Key* (657), and *Mariano G. Vallejo* (658).

123 'Navy Shifts Trident Management Focus', *Aviation Week and Space Technology* (16 June 1980), 111.

124 C. A. Robinson, Jr, 'New Propellant Evaluated for Trident Second Stage', *Aviation Week and Space Technology* (13 October 1975), 17; also *SASC FY 1977*, 6553.

125 Interview by Donald MacKenzie with Robert Mitchell, 29 March 1985.

126 It was a significant improvement over Poseidon not only in having a smaller CEP at the longer range, but also in not having the bias problem that Poseidon had. Apparently over the test flight azimuths used for Poseidon there was a consistent skewing of where the reentry bodies fell which could not be accounted for in accuracy models, and so could not be extrapolated to other azimuths with any confidence.

127 W. M. Arkin, 'Sleight of Hand with Trident II', *Bulletin of the Atomic Scientists*, vol. 40 (December 1984), 5–6. Many interviewees also confirmed that C4's accuracy performance had exceeded that requested, though not to the extent of doubling it.

128 Interview with Seymour Zeiberg, 27 June 1987.

8 The improved accuracy programme and Trident II

1 Memo for OP-21 (21 March 1974), quoted in 'Admirals' Admirable Quotes: An Incomplete Collection' (October 1981), typescript. My thanks to RADM Robert Wertheim for providing me with this – presumably an in-house SSPO production.

2 Thus Admiral Isaac C. Kidd Jr (former chief of Naval Material Command) would claim that: 'The missile sized the submarine.' M. Mintz, 'Depth Charge: Cost Overruns on New Trident Sub Leave a Muddied Wake', *Washington Post*, 4 October 1981, reprinted in Dina Rasor (ed.), *More Bucks, Less Bang: How The Pentagon Buys Ineffective Weapons* (Washington, DC: Fund for Constitutional Government, 1983), 211–23, at 213. However, in testimony on 22 May 1973 (following the Trident submarine design definition) Admiral Kaufman would 'emphasize that this missile [Trident II] has not been defined'. *SASC FY 1974 Part 5, Research and Development* (Washington, DC: US GPO, 1973), 3597.

3 Strategic Systems Program Office, *A Programmatic History of Trident II* (Washington, DC: SSPO, November 1982), 1.

4 Although in 1983 Richard DeLauer, Undersecretary of Defense for research and engineering, was still referring to Trident II having the same accuracy at 5500 miles that Trident I had at 4000. According to DeLauer: 'The big thing with D–5 is range, not accuracy.' See Robert C. Toth, 'U.S. Reliance on Nuclear Subs Being Debated', *Los Angeles Times*, 22 May 1984.

5 *SASC FY 1975* (Washington, DC: US GPO, 1974), 3298.

6 Letter from Vice Admiral Levering Smith, 27 August 1988.

7 *SASC FY 1975*, 3292.

8 See D. Ball, *Deja Vu: The Return to Counterforce in the Nixon Administration*

231

(Santa Monica, CA: Seminar on Arms Control and Foreign Policy, 1974); interview.

9 Interview by Donald MacKenzie with Vice Admiral Levering Smith, 23 February 1985.

10 Letter from Vice Admiral Levering Smith to Donald MacKenzie, 13 October 1986.

11 Interview by Donald MacKenzie with Vice Admiral Levering Smith, 23 February 1985.

12 *SASC FY 1975*, 3288.

13 *SASC FY 1976*, 5317.

14 *SASC FY 1975*, 3289–90.

15 *SASC FY 1977* (Washington, DC: GPO, 1976), 6640.

16 Captain Robert L. Topping, 'Submarine Launched Ballistic Missile Improved Accuracy', paper AIAA-81-0935 presented to American Institute of Aeronautics and Astronautics, Annual Meeting and Technical Display, 12–14 May 1981, Long Beach, California.

17 These DASO missile launches are a regular feature of setting off on a new patrol, providing both assurance that everything is working and 'hands on' experience for the crew.

18 See T. Thompson, 'Performance of the Satrack/Global Positioning System Trident I Missile Tracking System,' Proceedings of IEEE 1980, Position Location and Navigation Symposium, 445–49, at 445.

19 It is important to note that although accuracy understanding was greatly improved during the IAP there still remained much room for interpretation of the data. According to Captain Robert L. Topping, SPO guidance branch head during the IAP: 'the analyst interprets the results of these comparisons and draws conclusions about model validity, potential model improvements, and the causes of system inaccuracy. For this step, there are no well defined methodologies. The analyst must rely heavily on experience, insight, judgement, and good communications with experienced colleagues in the Fleet Ballistic Missile Weapon System community.' Topping, 'Improved Accuracy,' 5.

20 See the testimony of Rear Admiral Robert H. Wertheim, *SASC FY 1979, Part 9, Research and Development* (Washington, DC: US GPO, 1978), 6683.

21 Ibid., 6684.

22 *SASC FY 1979*, 6683.

23 *SASC FY 1978*, 6564.

24 Interview by Donald MacKenzie with Vice Admiral Glenwood Clark, 28 March 1985.

25 *SASC FY 1978*, 6544.

26 Interview with Ben Olson, 11 May 1987.

27 SSPO, *Programmatic History of Trident II*, 2–6.

28 *SASC FY 1978*, 6681–2; also SSPO, *Programmatic History of Trident II*, 3. Lockheed studies looked at designs known as C5B, C5C, and C5D. No-one wanted reminding about the C5A aircraft which was causing considerable trouble for another division of Lockheed.

29 Interview with Bob Dietz, 8 February 1989.

30 Physically the 'clear deck' had space for sixteen Mk. 4 reentry bodies, but

could not then achieve the desired range. Letter from Bob Dietz, 29 August 1991.

31 SSPO, *Programmatic History of Trident II*, 2.

32 Quoted in *SASC FY 1978*, 6570.

33 *SASC FY 1977*, 6532.

34 Quoted in D. A. Rosenberg, 'The Origins of Overkill: Nuclear Weapons and American Strategy, 1945–1960,' *International Security*, vol. 7, no. 4 (1983), 3–71, at 17.

35 Weapon System Evaluation Group Report no. 23, 'The Relative Military Advantages of Missiles and Manned Aircraft', (6 May 1957), 27 and 22.

36 See Desmond Ball, *Targeting for Strategic Deterrence* (London: International Institute for Strategic Studies, Adelphi Paper No. 185, 1983).

37 Paul Nitze, 'Deterring our Deterrent,' *Foreign Policy* (Winter 1976/77).

38 See, for example, Colin Gray, 'Nuclear Strategy: The Case for a Theory of Victory,' *International Security* (Summer 1979).

39 See Thomas Powers, 'Choosing a Strategy for World War III,' *Atlantic* (November 1982).

40 One such advocate was long-time stellar-inertial guidance proponent Marvin Stern who early in the Carter administration ran a study out of the Office of Net Assessment which argued for the war-fighting utility of having a FBM force with accuracy greater than Trident I. Interview with Marvin Stern, 13 July 1987.

41 Ball, 'Targeting.'

42 J. Edwards, *Superweapon: The Making of MX* (New York: Norton, 1982); H. Scoville, Jr, MX: *Prescription for Disaster* (Cambridge, MA: MIT Press, 1981).

43 Quoted in J. S. Wit, 'American SLBM: Counterforce Options and Strategic Implications,' *Survival*, vol. 24 (1982), 163–74 at 168.

44 Interview with Seymour Zeiberg, 27 June 1987.

45 Although many interviewees recalled their impressions that Admiral Smith was opposed to a hard-target FBM, he himself has denied this to be the case, except insomuch as he resisted accepting requirements that he was unsure could be met.

46 J. P. McManus, *A History of the FBM System* (Lockheed Missiles and Space Company, 1988), E-4.

47 Quoted in W. M. Arkin, 'Sleight of Hand with Trident II,' *Bulletin of the Atomic Scientists*, vol. 40 (December 1984), 5.

48 McManus, *A History of the FBM System*, E-4.

49 A typical modern thermonuclear weapon consists of a primary, which is essentially a fission bomb boosted by the addition of small amounts of thermonuclear fuel, and a secondary, which consists of thermonuclear fuel usually surrounded by uranium. Thus there is a complex mixture of fission and fusion which proceeds in the following manner. A high explosive compresses the fissile material in the primary to a critical state and the energy release burns the thermonuclear fuel which then in turn boosts the fission through the release of high energy neutrons. Roughly speaking these form the energy output of the primary which compresses the secondary thermonuclear fuel, and its neutron output then causes further fission

in the uranium casing. This extra fission can be obtained cheaply by using unenriched uranium for this stage, but is more efficient if enriched uranium (oralloy) is used. Apparently the more difficult part to design, and particularly to predict with any confidence, is the primary, because boosting is still not well understood. Secondary performance, on the other hand, can be predicted with much more confidence so long as the energy supplied by the primary falls within a certain band. Thus it is possible to test devices with the secondaries 'doctored' so as to give yields below the Threshold Test Ban Treaty limit, but still have confidence of the yield that they would produce at full strength. One obvious way of testing at below full strength would be to leave off the final uranium casing.

50 According to Donald Kerr, then Los Alamos Director, 'the nuclear designs for MX, Trident II (D–5), and Minuteman III (MK12A) were developed and tested at their full yield prior to the imposition of the 150 KT TTBT [Threshold Test Ban Treaty which stopped tests over 150 kiloton after March 1976] limitation. Their stockpile certification is, or will be, based on that testing'. Answer to questions submitted by Senator Kennedy, Senate Armed Services Committee, Hearings on Nuclear Testing, 29–30 April 1986.

51 Interviews with Thurman Talley, 12 April 1989, and John Harvey, 3 April 1990. Other recent warhead designs, including that for the MX, use insensitive high explosive which reduces the risk of accidental (almost certainly non-nuclear) explosions at some cost in extra weight. The decision by Los Alamos not to use insensitive high explosive was, not surprisingly, strongly and repeatedly contested by Livermore on safety grounds.

52 Interview with Ted Postol, 7 November 1988.

53 Interview with Bob Dietz, 8 February 1989.

54 'Administration official' quoted in Clarence A. Robinson, Jr, 'Congress Questioning Viability of MX ICBM,' Aviation Week and Space Technology (22 March 1982), 18–20 at 19. Highly enriched uranium (at least 93.5 per cent U-235) acquired the codename Oak Ridge alloy or oralloy during the Manhattan Project. The stockpile of oralloy has remained roughly constant since the early 1960s when production was stopped as more efficient weapons design and smaller warheads reduced demand. The recent trend to larger warheads and the large numbers of planned cruise missile warheads has again led to a perceived scarcity.

55 Anon., 'Navy to Develop New Trident Warhead,' Aviation Week and Space Technology (17 January 1983), 26.

56 Ibid.

57 Interview with Dave Montague, 8 May 1987.

58 General Electric Company manufactured the Mk. 12A for Minuteman III and had hoped this would be chosen for MX. When instead Avco were chosen to develop the Advanced Ballistic reentry Vehicle (ABRV), it looked like General Electric Company might be squeezed out of reentry vehicle work. This may be what Richard DeLauer, Under Secretary of Defense for Research and Engineering, meant when he referred to 'a problem with the industrial base' with respect to reentry vehicles. Aerospace Daily (18 June 1982), 268. Apparently the solution was to give General Electric Company the Trident II Mk. 5 heatshield production.

59 Philip J. Klass, 'Pentagon Seeks Penetration Aids Action,' *Aviation Week and Space Technology* (3 September 1984), 45.

60 McManus, *A History of the FBM System*, E-9 10.

61 Interview by Donald MacKenzie with Vice Admiral Glenwood Clark, 28 March 1985.

62 Interview with Captain Steven R. Cohen, 9 July 1987.

63 Interview with Paul C. Dow, 15 May 1987.

64 Interview by Donald MacKenzie with Draper Lab engineer, see Donald MacKenzie, *Inventing Accuracy: A Historical Sociology of Nuclear Missile Guidance* (Cambridge, MA: MIT Press, 1990), 290.

65 On the Mk. 6 accelerometer decision, see Anon., 'Trident Missile Capabilities Advance,' *Aviation Week and Space Technology* (16 June 1980), 91–100, at 99.

66 Interview with Paul C. Dow, 15 May 1987.

67 MacKenzie, *Inventing Accuracy*, 290.

68 Interview with Captain Steven R. Cohen, 9 July 1987.

69 Letter from Paul C. Dow, January 2. 1992.

70 Graydon M. Wheaton, 'Electronics Manufacturing for Inertial Guidance Systems' (May 1986), typescript, 5, 15.

71 Thus, although able to be fired over surface-to-surface trajectories, the reliance on a spherical earth model would not allow use of an unmodified Trident II missile in, say, an ABM mission or as a satellite booster.

72 Test and tactical missiles differ in what are considered ways necessary for safety in that test missiles do not carry nuclear warheads and have a destruct mechanism.

73 Letter from Captain Steven R. Cohen, 3 December 1991.

74 Early FBM guidance systems were simply calibrated at the factory, whereas later generations like Trident can be calibrated at dockside. The scheme for calibration at sea would have used all the missile guidance systems in conjunction to calibrate each one individually. It would have required 'a massive calculation', would not have taken advantage of the navigation system ('the guidance community would not want to use Navigation data as it would introduce another interface and would violate cultural independence'), and was killed by then Technical Director Admiral Clark in 1981, and 'about three more times after that'. Interview with Captain Steven R. Cohen, 9 July 1987 and letter, 3 December 1991.

75 T. A. King and H. Strell, 'Underwater Navigation' entry in *McGraw-Hill Encyclopedia of Science and Technology* (New York: McGraw-Hill Publishing Company, 1982), 399–402, at 401. A key role in developing the gradiometer as an adjunct to inertial navigation was played by Milton Trageser at the Instrumentation Laboratory. From 1966 onwards work at the laboratory was funded first by the Air Force, and then from about 1977 by SSPO. However, the gradiometer actually selected for Trident is not Trageser's spherical floated design. That was perceived as a 'gold plated' device – literally as well as metaphorically, in this case, since it incorporated silver-filled proof masses, gold electrodes, and 'gold plating is used extensively to minimize radiant heat transfer.' See M. B. Trageser, 'Floated Gravity Gradiometer,' *IEEE Transactions on Aerospace and Electronic Systems*, vol. 20

(1984), 417–19, at 419. Instead a completely different design built by Bell Aerospace Textron in Buffalo was chosen, basically because it was cheaper and easier to produce.

76 General Accounting Office, *Trident II Acquisition*, GAO/NSLAD–89–40 (Washington, DC: General Accounting Office, 1988), 20.

77 Anon., 'Geosat Data to Aid Trident 2 Accuracy,' *Aviation Week and Space Technology* (19 July 1982), 26.

78 Interview with Seymour Zeiberg, 27 June 1987: 'That was a deal I struck with them on accuracy. When I got them to agree with a CEP I kept trying to extract from them to do that at five or six thousand miles. They wouldn't agree and so we compromised at four thousand miles'.

79 Anon., 'Navstar offers "little improvement" in SLBM accuracy,' *Aerospace Daily*, vol. 123, no. 33 (19 October 1983), 257.

80 Interview with Derald Stuart, 6, 8 May 1987.

81 Ibid. The third stage was originally to have stayed with Kevlar, but was changed to graphite epoxy midway through development in 1988. McManus, *A History of the FBM System*, E-9.

82 Ibid., E-9.

83 Interview with Derald Stuart, 6, 8 May 1987.

84 Interview with Phil Faurot, 12 June 1987. The potential problem that caused concern with shallow launching was cavitation around the missile nose, that is, the formation of air bubbles which on breaking down could impose excessive stress on the missile at the launch velocities inevitable with a fixed energy system.

85 *SASC FY 1985* (Washington, DC: GPO, 1984), 3426.

86 Michael Mecham, 'Congress Favours Conventional Defense, Production Efficiency,' *Aviation Week and Space Technology* (23 November 1987), 23.

87 Anon., 'Seven Arrested at Trident Protest,' *Aviation Week and Space Technology* (2 November 1987), 27.

88 An important campaigner against Trident II was the former Lockheed FBM engineer Robert C. Aldridge, author of *First Strike! The Pentagon's Strategy for Nuclear War* (London: Pluto Press, 1983). The organization which campaigned most actively against Trident II was the Washington based Coalition For a New Foreign and Military Policy.

89 See Philip M. Boffey, 'Trident's Technology May Make It a Potent Rival to Land-Based Missiles,' *New York Times* (13 July 1982), C-1. Senator William Proxmire had the article reprinted in the Congressional Record on the same day.

90 *Congressional Record* (11 July 1985), Extension of Remarks, E 3227–28. In the event Markey was unable to offer the amendment 'due to the press for adjournment for the 4th of July recess'. In following years a similar amendment was defeated.

91 See Theodore A. Postol, 'The Trident and Strategic Stability', *Oceanus* (Summer 1985), 45–53.

92 Interview with Captain Steven R. Cohen, 9 July 1987.

93 Quoted in Edgar Ulsamer, 'Toward a New World Strategy', *Air Force Magazine* (January 1979), 60–65, at 61.

94 See the account of a report suggesting the US target 'every reasonable

adversary'. R. Jeffrey Smith, 'US urged to aim nuclear arms wider', originally printed in the *Washington Post*, reprinted in *The Guardian* (7 January 1992).

95 Of the nineteen carried out from 1987 January two were considered failures, and one as a 'non-test' because it was accidentally blown up by a range safety officer.

96 I am very grateful to Bob Dietz for keeping me up to date with these developments.

97 Another problem for the W-88 warhead was the re-emergence of the debate over safety and concern with its non-use of insensitive high explosive. This was highlighted in the 'Drell report' of December 1990. *Report of the Panel on Nuclear Weapons Safety of the Committee on Armed Services, House of Representatives* (Washington, DC: U.S. GPO, 1990).

98 This means a range potential of some 6500 nautical miles, but this is not generally considered to be of any particular utility.

9 Understanding technical change in weaponry

1 Some of the problems with maximizing the public good – in the context of science policy – are discussed in B. Barnes, *About Science* (Oxford: Basil Blackwell, 1985), 124–32.

2 Ralph E. Lapp, *Arms Beyond Doubt: The Tyranny of Weapons Technology* (New York: Cowles Book Co., 1970), 178.

3 United Nations, Report of the Secretary General, *Comprehensive Study on Nuclear Weapons* (New York: United Nations, 1981), para 67, cited in Marek Thee, *Military Technology, Military Strategy and the Arms Race* (London: Croom Helm, 1986), 47; emphasis added.

4 John Garnett, 'Technology and Strategy', in John Baylis, Ken Booth, John Garnett, and Phil Williams, *Contemporary Strategy* (New York: Holmes and Meier, 1987) vol. 1: *Theories and Concepts*, 92.

5 Interview with Carl Haussmann, 5 May 1987.

6 Interview by Donald MacKenzie with Thomas A. J. King, 2 April 1985.

7 On tacit knowledge see H. M. Collins, 'The TEA Set: Tacit Knowledge and Scientific Networks', *Science Studies*, vol. 4 (1974), 165–86.

8 Typically full-scale development has also been accompanied by production in the FBM programme, and concurrency between the two has been seen as an essential part of the programme's success. This was initially important in the rapid deployment of Polaris, but was defended throughout later FBM developments – in the face of increasing Congressional pressure for 'fly before buy' procurement – because of limitations on testing of the technology. Because a solid-fuel missile cannot be fully tested non-destructively it is seen as essential that test missiles and production missiles be the same, and this means that the same production processes should ideally be used. According to then SSPO Director, RADM Wertheim: 'It must be appreciated that the nature of the major end items of the FBM system is a complex, costly item of expendable ordnance which cannot be fully tested without destroying the missile tested. Much of what we think we know about the ballistic missiles that are operationally deployed is based upon extrapo-

lations from those we have destructively tested, and the validity of that extrapolation depends upon our ability to assure that no change has taken place in the materials, tools, processes or personnel used in their manufacture.' 'Presentation to the National Security Industrial Association', 11 April 1980 reprinted in 'Admirals' Admirable Quotes: An Incomplete Collection' (October 1981), typescript. For this reason Admiral Wertheim argued that 'it be recognized that because of the extensive concurrency required the Fleet Ballistic Missile Weapon Systems are a class of programs for which the decision to enter full scale development is tantamount to a decision to produce and deploy'. 'Memo to CNM: Revised Approval for Service Use (ASU) Instruction – Proposed NAVMATINST 4720.1A', 20 March 1978.

9 On the social construction of scientific knowledge, see Steven Shapin, 'History of Science and its Sociological Reconstructions', *History of Science*, vol. 20 (September 1982), 157–211.

10 B. Barnes, 'The Science–Technology Relationship: A Model and a Query', *Social Studies of Science*, vol. 12 (1982), 166–73.

11 As suggested, for example, by Richard R. Nelson and Sidney G. Winter in *An Evolutionary Theory of Economic Change* (Cambridge, MA: Harvard University Press, 1982), 258.

12 R. L. Tammen, *MIRV and the Arms Race: An Interpretation of Defense Strategy* (New York: Praeger, 1973), 126.

13 See D. MacKenzie, W. Rüdig, and G. Spinardi, 'Social Research on Technology and the Policy Agenda: An Example from the Strategic Arms Race', in Brian Elliott (ed.), *Technology and Social Process* (Edinburgh: Edinburgh University Press, 1988), 152–80.

14 Though it seems likely that this report was written by people concerned to play down the utility of ballistic missiles for counterforce missions.

15 See Donald MacKenzie, *Inventing Accuracy: A Historical Sociology of Nuclear Missile Guidance* (Cambridge, MA: MIT Press, 1990), 196–214 for an account of the Air Force move to counterforce and its effect on the design of their early ICBMs.

16 The argument that early FBMs – especially Poseidon – were capable of high counterforce capability is made explicitly in Albert Langer, 'Accurate Submarine-launched Ballistic Missiles and Nuclear Strategy', *Journal of Peace Research*, vol. 14, no. 1 (1977), 41–58.

17 Thus surfacing to allow a wider range of navigation fix techniques would still hardly have made the FBM submarine any more vulnerable than ICBM silos.

18 Ted Greenwood, *Making the MIRV: A Study of Defense Decision Making* (Cambridge, MA: Ballinger, 1975), 55. Also interview with Marvin Stern, 13 July 1987.

19 See T. J. Pinch and W. E. Bijker, 'The Social Construction of Facts and Artefacts: or How the Sociology of Science and the Sociology of Technology might Benefit Each Other', *Social Studies of Science*, vol. 14 (1984), 399–441; S. Russell, 'The Social Construction of Artefacts: A Response to Pinch and Bijker', *Social Studies of Science*, vol. 16 (1986), 331–46; T. Pinch and W. Bijker, 'Science, Relativism and the New Sociology of Technology', *Social Studies of Science*, vol. 16 (1986), 347–60.

20 Dietrich Schroeer, 'Quantifying Technological Imperatives in the Arms Race', in D. Carlton and C. Schaerf, *Reassessing Arms Control* (London: Macmillan, 1985), 60–71.

21 D. Shapley, 'Technology Creep and the Arms Race: ICBM Problem a Sleeper', *Science*, vol. 201 (22 September 1978), 1102–5.

22 See MacKenzie, Rüdig, and Spinardi, 'Social Research', 168–69.

23 Interview with Phil Faurot, 12 June 1987.

24 It is usually possible to restart production of a technology that is considered obsolescent if one is prepared to pay enough, as indeed the UK did when its Polaris A3 required the renovation of its solid-fuel motors.

25 'Navy Shifts Trident Management Focus', *Aviation Week and Space Technology* (16 June 1980), 111–13.

26 See L. Smith, R. H. Wertheim and R. A. Duffy, 'Innovative Engineering in the Trident Missile Development', *The Bridge* (National Academy of Engineering), vol. 10, no. 2 (Summer 1980), 10–19.

27 E.g. Lord Zuckerman, 'Science Advisers and Scientific Advisers', *Proceedings of the American Philosophical Society*, vol. 124 (1980), 124–55. For a view which focuses on the role of 'scientists', rather than 'technologists', see Bruno Vitale, 'Scientists as Military Hustlers', *Issues in Radical Science*, no. 17 (London: Free Association Books, 1985), 73–87.

28 Quoted in MacKenzie, *Inventing Accuracy*, 389.

29 See p. 71.

30 Livermore's vigorous 'selling' of warhead designs, and its close liaison with the services, helped to establish Livermore in the late 1950s when the leadership of Los Alamos was less aggressive.

31 See Matthew Evangelista, *Innovation and the Arms Race: How the United States and the Soviet Union Develop New Military Technologies* (Ithaca, NY: Cornell University Press, 1988).

32 See John Law, 'Technology and Heterogeneous Engineering: The Case of Portuguese Expansion', in W. Bijker, T. P. Hughes, and T. Pinch (eds.), *The Social Construction of Technological Systems* (Cambridge, MA: MIT Press, 1987), 111–34.

33 Interview with Vice Admiral Glenwood Clark, 21 May 1987.

34 Kenneth Waltz, *Theory of International Politics* (Reading, MA: Addison-Wesley, 1979), 127.

35 Evangelista, *Innovation and the Arms Race*, 233–34.

36 For example, a case has been made for the broad effect of Democrat politicians boosting military spending because of over-reaction to 'hawkish' criticism. See Alan Wolfe, *The Rise and Fall of the Soviet Threat: Domestic Sources of the Cold War Consensus* (Boston: South End Press, 1984). Thus President Kennedy, having 'milked' full electoral value out of the 'missile gap', sought a quick acceleration of the Polaris programme. Similarly (but with a Republican), on taking office Nixon instructed Defense Secretary Laird to bolster the defence posture in a visible, but cheap way – one result being the acceleration of the stellar-inertial option for Poseidon.

37 Barry R. Posen, *Sources of Military Doctrine: France, Britain, and Germany between the World Wars* (Ithaca, NY: Cornell University Press, 1984), 167–69.

38 Ibid., 169.

39 Interview with Captain Steven R. Cohen, 9 July 1987.
40 See, for examples in the case of the B1 bomber, Nick Kotz, *Wild Blue Yonder: Money, Politics, and the B-1 Bomber* (New York: Pantheon, 1988).
41 See T. Powers, 'Choosing a Strategy for World War III', *The Atlantic Monthly* (November 1982).
42 A classic account is G. T. Allison, *Essence of Decision: Explaining the Cuban Missile Crisis* (Boston: Little, Brown and Co., 1971). For its application to weapons development, see G. T. Allison and F. A. Morris, 'Armaments and Arms Control: Exploring the Determinants of Military Weapons', *Daedalus*, vol. 104 (Summer 1975), 99–129.
43 Elmo R. Zumwalt, Jr, *On Watch* (New York: Quadrangle, 1976), 490.
44 Ibid., 154.
45 John Newhouse, *Cold Dawn: The Story of SALT* (New York: Holt, Rinehart and Winston, 1973), 246.
46 See pp. 120–121.
47 See M. R. Sidrow, 'Politics and Military Weapons Acquisition: The Limits of Bureaucratic Political Theory' (PhD Thesis, University of California, Riverside, 1983).
48 D. J. Ball, 'The Blind Men and the Elephant: A Critique of Bureaucratic Politics Theory', *Australian Outlook*, vol. 28 (1974), 71–92: S. D. Krasner, 'Are Bureaucracies Important? (Or Allison Wonderland)', *Foreign Policy* (Summer 1972), 159–79.
49 Allison discusses these separately as two different models to contrast with the rational actor one, but clearly they can be combined as in G. T. Allison and M. H. Halperin, 'Bureaucratic Politics: A Paradigm and Some Policy Implication', *World Politics*, vol. 24 (Spring 1972), 40–79.
50 M. H. Halperin, 'The Decision to Deploy the ABM: Bureaucratic and Domestic Politics in the Johnson Administration', *World Politics*, vol. 25 (October 1972), 62–95.
51 See Ball, 'Critique of Bureaucratic Politics', 77, 83.
52 For a useful collection of essays, see Steven Rosen (ed.), *Testing the Theory of the Military-Industrial Complex* (Lexington, MA: Lexington Books, 1973).
53 For examples of this in the B1 bomber programme, see Kotz, *Wild Blue Yonder*.
54 A prime example, perhaps, of what Langdon Winner sees as the corporate basis of technological momentum, see Winner, *Autonomous Technology: Technics-out-of-control as a Theme in Political Thought* (Cambridge, MA: MIT Press, 1977).
55 Dwight D. Eisenhower, 'Farewell Radio and Television Address to the American People, 17 January 1961', in *Public Papers of the President of the United States, Dwight D. Eisenhower 1960–61* (Washington, DC: United States Government Printing Office, 1961), 1035–40.
56 Charles C. Moskos, Jr, 'The Military-Industrial Complex: Theoretical Antecedents and Conceptual Contradictions', in Sam C. Sarkesian (ed.), *The Military-Industrial Complex: A Reassessment* (Beverly Hills, CA: Sage, 1972), 3–23.
57 Robert Heilbroner, 'Military America', *New York Review of Books*, vol. 15, no. 2 (23 July 1970), 6, quoted in Moskos, 'Military-Industrial Complex', 10–11.

58 E.g. Seymour Melman, *Pentagon Capitalism: The Political Economy of War* (New York: McGraw-Hill Book Company, 1970) and *The Permanent War Economy* (New York: Simon and Schuster, 1974).

59 The year when Maxwell Taylor retired as Chairman of the Joint Chiefs of Staff and Curtis LeMay 'was pushed out' as Air Force Chief of Staff. Taylor was considered to be too much an administration man, whereas LeMay was uncompromising in his advocacy of air power. Lawrence J. Korb, 'The Secretary of Defense and the Joint Chiefs of Staff: The Budgetary Process', in Sarkesian, *The Military-Industrial Complex*, 317–18.

60 See James R. Kurth, 'American Production Lines and American Defense Spending', in Rosen (ed.), *Testing the Theory*, 135–56.

61 See, for a good example of this argument, Sidney Lens, *The Military-Industrial Complex* (Philadelphia: Pilgrim Press, 1970), Chapter 2.

62 Mike Davis, 'Nuclear Imperialism and Extended Deterrence', in *New Left Review, Exterminism and Cold War* (London: Verso, 1982), 35–64. I am grateful to Donald MacKenzie for raising this point, see also his 'Nuclear War Planning and Strategies of Coercion', *New Left Review* no. 148 (November–December 1984), 31–56.

63 John Edwards, *Superweapon: The Making of MX* (New York: Norton, 1982), 199.

64 Which in the case of the nuclear weapons laboratories has, for example, led to very active lobbying against nuclear test ban treaties.

65 Mary Kaldor, 'Military R&D: Cause or Consequence of the Arms Race?', *International Social Science Journal*, vol. 35, no. 1 (1983), 25–45.

66 Mary Kaldor, *The Baroque Arsenal* (London: Andre Deutsch, 1982), 5.

67 Jacques S. Gansler, *The Defense Industry* (Cambridge, MA: MIT Press, 1980), 101.

68 Kaldor, 'Military R&D', 42.

69 See Donald MacKenzie, 'Missile Accuracy: A Case Study in the Social Processes of Technological Change', in Wiebe E. Bijker, Thomas P. Hughes and Trevor Pinch, *The Social Construction of Technological Systems* (Cambridge, MA: MIT Press, 1987), 208–9.

70 Ernest J. Yanarella, 'The 'Technological Imperative' and the Strategic Arms Race', *Peace and Change*, vol. 3, no. 1 (Spring 1975), 3–16.

71 Ibid., 6.

72 Notably, the (admittedly somewhat arbitrary) quantification of 'assured destruction' and of the counterforce and 'damage-limiting' functions of strategic nuclear forces. See Alain C. Enthoven and K. Wayne Smith. *How Much Is Enough? Shaping the Defense Program, 1961–1969* (New York: Harper and Row, 1971), esp. Chapter 5.

73 Yanarella, 'Technological Imperative', 9.

74 Interview with Rear Admiral Robert Wertheim, 3 April 1987.

75 Yanarella, 'Technological Imperative', 9.

76 Enthoven and Smith, *How Much Is Enough?*, 171.

77 D. A. Rosenberg, 'The Origins of Overkill: Nuclear Weapons and American Strategy, 1945–1960', *International Security*, vol. 7, no. 4 (1983), 50.

78 Herbert York, *Race to Oblivion: A Participant's View of the Arms Race* (New York: Simon and Schuster, 1970), Chapter 4.

79 *Aviation Week* (1 December 1958), 28.
80 See Enthoven and Smith, *How Much Is Enough?*
81 See pp. 31–34.
82 Winner, *Autonomous Technology*.
83 Harvey Sapolsky, *The Polaris System Development: Bureaucratic and Programmic Success in Government* (Cambridge, MA: Harvard University Press, 1972).
84 Posen, *Sources of Military Doctrine*, 241.
85 On tacit knowledge see H. M. Collins, 'The TEA Set; Tacit Knowledge and Scientific Networks', *Science Studies*, vol. 4 (1974). 165–86.
86 A recent exposition of such an argument, with only slight deference to domestic factors, can be found in Ted Greenwood, 'Why Military Technology is difficult to Restrain', *Science, Technology, and Human Values*, vol. 15, no. 4 (Autumn 1990), 412–29.
87 On the creation of the division between what is 'technical' and what is 'political' see MacKenzie, *Inventing Accuracy*, 413–17.

INDEX

Note: Departments, forces, etc., refer to the USA unless otherwise indicated.

245

Norway, 50
Norwegian Sea, 58
Nova satellites, 102
NSDM, *see* National Security Decision
  Memorandum
nuclear arms race, *see* arms race
nuclear policy, *see* nuclear strategy
nuclear power/propulsion, 36, 37–8, 39,
  56, 189
  see also submarines, nuclear reactors
Nuclear Propulsion Directorate, 56, 78–9
nuclear strategy, 4–6, 31–4, 99–100,
  148–53, 150, 162, 187
  accuracy and, *see under* accuracy
  assured destruction (counter-city
    targeting), 4, 5, 6, 31–4, 59, 86,
    125–6, 149, 177–8
    Polaris and, 60
    Strat-X and, 113–14
  communications systems and, 82–3,
    161–2
  counter-city targeting, *see* assured
    destruction *in this entry*
  counterforce, 4–5, 6, 34, 86, 90, 125–6,
    139, 140, 167–8, 172; Air Force and,
    60, 147–8, 150; second-strike, 149;
    Trident and, 147–51
  deterrence, 34, 86
  extended deterrence, 184–5
  forces, differences, 60, 61, 89, 167–8
  hard target kill capability, 91, 112, 113,
    148, 150, 153, 162
  hidden agendas in, 178
  'internal arms race' theory and, 190
  limited nuclear options, 142
  National Security Decision
    Memorandum No. 242, 142, 147,
    149
  Polaris A1 and A2 compared, 65
  Polaris A3 and, 70–1
  political aspects, 191–3
  preemptive attack, 4, 5–6, 61, 161–2
  public opinion and, 149–51
  Single Integrated Operational Plan, 61,
    111, 142, 149
  targeting, 4–6, 33, 60, 67: MIRVs and,
    90–1; Polaris B3 and, 87, 88, 89;
    Poseidon and, 99
  technology and, 167–8
  Trident I and, 138–40
  and breakup of USSR, 162, 193
nuclear testing, 54, 55, 62–3, 66
  limitations on, 63, 65, 66, 152, 167
  see also testing
nuclear weapons, 3–6, 17–18, 54, 164
  testing, *see* nuclear testing
  warheads, 29–30; development,
    priorities in, 166–7; and hard targets,

152–3; numbers of, political context,
  168; preemptive design of, 173;
  safety, 55; size of, politics and, 167,
  168; yield, 54–5
  *see also individual warheads and under
    individual missiles*
  see also fleet ballistic missiles; nuclear
    strategy; weapons technology

Observation Island, 39
obsolescence, 170–1
Office of Naval Research, Underseas
  Warfare Branch, 48
Office of Strategic Offensive and
  Defensive Systems, 91
Ohio, 123–5
Operation Frigate Bird, 62–3
Operation Hot Foot, 57
Operation Phoenix, 57
organizational interaction, 15, 44, 180–1,
  187–93
Oscar satellites, 76, 102
over-design, 41, 69, 77, 88

Pacific, 62, 73, 145, 163
Pacific islanders, 169
Packard, David, 116, 118–21, 123, 179
PACs (penetration aid carriers), 73
PALs, 2
Partial Test Ban Treaty, 63
Patrick Henry, 58
pen-aids (penetration aids) *see under*
  reentry bodies
permissive action links, 2
Perry, William, 149, 184–5
Pershing, 84
PERT (programme evaluation review
  technique), 36
Phoenix, Operation, 57
PIGAs, *see under* accelerometers
PIPAs, *see under* accelerometers
Polaris, 6, 36–56
  accuracy, 34
  Air Force criticism of, 60–3
  background to, 19–36
  communications system, 80–4
  development, 36–56, 76–7
  fire control system, 38–9, 45–6, 56
  funding, 26, 35–6, 43, 56
  guidance system, 38–9, 42–5, 52, 57
  launcher system, 38, 39–42: changes in,
    84–5; launch tube design, 41;
    over-design, 41, 69; testing, 41–2
  comparison with Minuteman, 61–2
  missiles, 30–1, 35–6, 39, 50–5, 62–3, 84,
    85
  navigation system, 39, 46–50
  perceived need for, 79, 112

CAMBRIDGE STUDIES IN INTERNATIONAL RELATIONS